Complete Scottish Lowlands

RED GUIDE

Complete
Scottish Lowlands

Edinburgh and Glasgow
to the Border
The Scott Country,
Burns Country and
other places of interest

Edited by Reginald J. W. Hammond F.R.G.S.

WARD LOCK LIMITED

116 Baker Street, London W1M 2BB

© 1974 Ward Lock Limited

ISBN 0 7063 1529 4

Drawings by Colin Gibson

Photographs by Peter Baker, Tony Kersting, Geoffrey Wright
and K M Andrew.

Text filmset in Times Roman by
V Siviter Smith & Co Ltd, Birmingham, Warwickshire.

Printed and bound by Editorial Fher SA, Bilbao, Spain.

Contents

	Page
Introduction	11
A Historical Note	13
Berwick-upon-Tweed to Edinburgh	27
Dunbar to Edinburgh direct	32
Dunbar to Edinburgh by the coast	35
Dunbar to Edinburgh via Gifford	39
Berwick to Kelso	40
Berwick to Lauder via Duns	45
Carter Bar to Edinburgh	47
Melrose to Abbotsford	57
Melrose to Edinburgh via Lauder	60
Melrose to Edinburgh via Galashiels	62
Galashiels to Edinburgh via Peebles	65
Carlisle to Edinburgh:	
Tje Route via Hawick	69
Hawick to Selkirk	74
Selkirk to Galashiels	75
Selkirk to Moffat	77
Carlisle to Edinburgh (or Glasgow) via Beattock	79
Moffat to Edinburgh	84
Carlisle to Edinburgh via Biggar	87
Edinburgh: General Information	91
The Castle and Lawnmarket	101
The High Street – St Giles to the Tron	111
Lower High Street – Canongate and Holyrood	118
Grassmarket. Cowgate. Holyrood Park and Calton Hill	128
The University and Around	136
The New Town	144

CONTENTS

	Page
Bruntsfield – Braids – Blackford – Craigmillar	153
Portobella, Joppa and Musselburgh	159
Port of Leith, Newhaven and Granton	161
West from Edinburgh	166
Short Excursions from Edinburgh	172
Calisle to Glasgow:	
Via Beattock, Abington and Hamilton	177
From Abington via Lanark	178
Via Dumfries and Kilmarnock	179
Carlisle to Stranraer and Glasgow by the coast	186
Stranraer to Girvan by the coast	195
Castle Douglas to Ayr (direct)	196
Glasgow: General Information	199
Cathedral – Provand's Lordship – University – West End – The South Side – Cathcart	203
Glasgow to Edinburgh	215
The Upper Clyde	216
Bothwell and Hamilton	216
Lanark and Douglasdale	221
Glasgow to Ardrossan by the coast	226
Ardrossan to Ayr	235
Ayr	241
Aur to Maybole and Girvan	246
Index	249

Maps and Plans

Southern Scotland	*Pages* 24–25
Dryburgh Abbey	*Page* 51
Melrose Abbey	*Page* 54
Central Edinburgh	*Pages* 88–89
Edinburgh Castle	*Page* 104
St Giles' Cathedral	*Page* 113
Palace of Holyroodhouse	*Page* 125
Dumfries	*Page* 180
Central Glasgow	*Pages* 200–201
Ayr	*Page* 242

Illustrations

	Page
Water of Minnoch, Glen Trool	10
The Ayrshire Coast at Lendalfoot	26
Salmon Fishing on the Tweed	28
Dunbar Castle	31
Hailes Castle	32
Nungate Bridge, Haddington	33
Tantallon Castle	34
Bass Rock	35
Lennoxlove	39
Kelso Abbey	43
By Whitadder Water	44
Jedburgh Abbey	46
Jedburgh Abbey from south-west	48
The 'auld brig' Jedburgh	49
Dryburgh Abbey	50
Melrose Abbey	53
Abbotsford	56
Thirlestane Castle	61
Traquair House	66
Peebles, across the Tweed	67
Hermitage Castle	70
Langholm on the Esk	71
The Esk near Langholm	73
Selkirk	75
Near the Grey Mare's Tail	76
Park and Boat Pond, Moffat	80
Hart Fell	82
Covenanters' Memorial and Devil's Beef Tub	85
Looking towards Tinto Hill	86
Princes Street, Edinburgh	90
Scott Memorial	97
The Castle and Princes Street Gardens	102
The View from Castle Hill	107
Lady Stair's House	108
St Giles' Cathedral, Edinburgh	112
John Knox's House	119

	Page
The Royal Mile from Holyroodhouse	123
Holyroodhouse from Arthur's Seat	126
Usher Hall, Edinburgh	129
Princes Street and Calton Hill beyond	132
Floodlit National Memorial and Nelson Monument	134
The University, Edinburgh	137
An Edinburgh sunset from Calton Hill	141
Heriot Row	148
Dean Village, Edinburgh	151
Portobello from Joppa	158
Lamb's House, Leith	163
Lauriston Castle	167
At Corstorphine	169
The Forth Road Bridge	173
A View near Crawford	177
The Midsteeple, Dumfries	182
The Mennoch Pass	184
Sweetheart Abbey	187
Dundrennan Abbey	189
At Gatehouse of Fleet	190
View over Ballantrae to Ailsa Craig	195
The Kelvin and Glasgow University	198
George Square, Glasgow	204
Provand's Lordship	206
Bothwell Castle	217
Livingstone Memorial, Blantyre	218
County Buildings, Hamilton	220
Paisley Abbey	227
Gourock	230
Cloch Lighthouse	231
Ardrossan Castle	234
Rough Sea at Troon	236
Prestwick Cross	238
The Ayrshire Coast	240
View over Ayr and the river	244
Burns' Birthplace, Alloway	245

THE RED GUIDES

Edited by Reginald J. W. Hammond

Barmouth and District
Bournemouth, New Forest
Channel Islands
Cornwall : North
Cornwall : South
Cornwall : West
Cotswolds
Dorset Coast
Isle of Man
Isle of Wight
Lake District

Llandudno, Colwyn Bay
London
Norfolk and the Broads
Peak District
St. Ives and W. Cornwall
Tenby and South Wales
Wales N. (Northn. Section)
Wales N. (Southn. Section)
Yorkshire Dales
Northern Ireland

SCOTLAND

Aberdeen, Deeside, etc.
Edinburgh and District
Highlands

Northern Scotland
Western Scotland

RED TOURIST GUIDES

Complete England
Complete Scotland
Complete Ireland
Complete Wales
Lake District (Baddeley)

Complete Devon
Complete West Country
Complete South-East Coast
Complete Yorkshire
Complete Scottish Lowlands

Britain
Portugal (Sarah Bradford)
Japan (William Duncan)

WARD LOCK LIMITED

Water of Minnoch, Glen Trool

Introduction

This Guide describes the area between the Border and the great cities of Edinburgh and Glasgow. It thus covers the Burns' Country, the Ayr and Galloway area as important to Burns lovers as is Warwickshire to Shakespearians, and the Scott Country of Abbotsford, Melrose and the Eildons made famous by the romantic writings of Sir Walter Scott. Both Edinburgh, Auld Reekie, and Glasgow are described in detail.

The term Lowlands is something of a misnomer and does not really refer to height, or the lack of it. More correctly, in geographical parlance, the region is known as the Southern Uplands, for indeed parts of it have no mean altitude.

A marked difference between this region and the wilder Highlands is in the geological composition of the rocks, a cause of many other distinctive features. Whereas the Highlands consist of various igneous rocks, such as granite, and of slate, greywacke and mica schist, the Lowlands comprise chiefly of sandstones and conglomerates. So not only does the vegetation differ, but also, where locally quarried material has been used, the appearance of the villages and towns. The scenery might not have the grand natural wildness of the Highlands, but it is nevertheless of considerable beauty and appeal. Historically, the region is second to none in interest and abounds in castles, palaces, abbeys and battlefields. Even the briefest study of these will give a thrilling insight into the romances and tragedies, the cruelties and compassions of a truly tortuous Scottish history.

Motoring

For the most part we have followed the roads in our itineraries. There are few motorway miles as yet, except the M8 giving a fast link between Edinburgh and Glasgow and its remote kin at Renfrew, and the M74 running along the valley of the Clyde to act as both a feeder and a bypass of the latter city. Scottish roads, however, have a first-rate reputation and everywhere in the region good, safe and pleasant motoring is to be enjoyed.

Public Road Transport

Most towns and villages have their bus or coach services connecting with the surrounding neighbourhood and nearby centres. In more remote places where a scheduled service is not advertised, it is often possible to make use of local carriers, particulars of which are best obtained by local enquiry. Long distance coach services operate from Edinburgh and Glasgow to places of major interest. There are also numerous tours available, some extending over two or more days. The chief companies are Scottish Omnibuses Ltd in the south-east, and Western S.M.T. in the south-west.

Rail Services

British Rail have two entry points from England to Scotland—at Berwick-upon-Tweed and from Carlisle. The line through Berwick is the East Coast Route from London (King's Cross) and runs through Dunbar, Drem and Prestonpans to Edinburgh and the north. Through Carlisle, the Midland and West Coast routes, are services from London (Euston and St Pancras) the line dividing shortly after crossing the Border, one main branch heading for Lockerbie and Carstairs, from whence there are connections with both Edinburgh and Glasgow, and the other main line running via Dumfries and Kilmarnock to Glasgow. From Glasgow and Kilmarnock there are connections with Ardrossan for the boat services to Belfast, and there is also a line running down the west coast through Troon and Ayr to Stranraer for the boat connection with Larne in Northern Ireland.

Circular tour tickets are issued at special rates as also weekly 'runabout' tickets. It should be remembered that certain services are restricted or do not run on Sundays.

Hotels and Accommodation

Most towns have a good choice of accommodation ranging from large, often palatial, hotels to modest boarding houses and even private houses offering bed and breakfast. Except in the main holiday seasons, visitors should have little difficulty in obtaining accommodation. Throughout this Guide we have listed in each centre a representative selection of establishments of various grades known to give good service. More detailed particulars are available on application from local authorities and from the Scottish Tourist Board, 2 Rutland Place, Edinburgh.

Sport

Golf, fishing, bowls, tennis and pony-trekking are the major summer pursuits for which there are first-rate facilities available. Almost every hamlet and town in Scotland has, or is within easy reach of, a golfcourse and the visiting golfer will have no difficulty in getting a game. For the fisherman too there is sport in plenty for every burn, river and loch yields trout, whilst the salmon fishing is famous. Many hotels hold fishing rights where stretches of river or stream are reserved to residents, but there are still very many waters where fishing is entirely free. For the sea-fisherman, both coasts offer good sport.

A Historical Note

Though brief historical notes appear throughout this Guide it is thought that a more general account of the history of Scotland as a whole would be of help to the visitor. We feel we can do little better than reprint Professor J. D. Mackie's excellent article which appears in our Complete Scotland Guide.

Scotland in many ways is very like England. Both countries are contained, for the most part, in the same island. They use, for the most part, the same speech. They are far more akin in race than is usually recognised, for although the Anglo-Saxon stock predominates in England, both countries share in common a Norse strain, a 'Celtic strain', and a well-marked strain which was in these islands before ever the Celtic speakers came. And both countries have had very much the same political development; in both there arose, out of contending tribes, a monarchy, whose growth was conditioned by the influence of successive waves of culture from the south—Christianity, Feudalism, the Renaissance, for example.

But, despite all this, Scotland and England are two quite distinct countries. Alongside the similarities, differences are to be noted, and these differences, operating down the ages, have meant that the collective experience of the people to the north of 'The Border' has been different from that of the people to the south. Scottish nationality has developed as a thing apart from English nationality.

How has this come about? What are these differences which have made the collective experience, the nationality, of Scotland distinct from that of England?

Many explanations might with justice be given. The factors of race, of speech and of geography admittedly entered, though none of them would in itself account for the existing 'Border'. Geographically, the southern boundary of Scotland might have been the 'Highland Line', the line of the 'Firths' or even the Humber.

Yet a consideration of geography will go far to solve the problem. Scotland was more remote from the great world than was England, and the waves of culture which rolled in from the Continent reached the north of Britain only after long delay, and with diminished force. The early drifts of population, Roman imperialism, Anglo-Saxon invasion, feudalism—it was the same with them all. Each of these great movements had exhausted much of its power before it came to the land which is now called Scotland, and each met, as it moved north, an increasing resistance from the elements already in possession. Long before one wave had over-run the whole of Scotland, its successor was already pouring into England, and some of the waves never reached the north of Scotland at all.

What was the result?

One might say that Scotland lagged behind England in her political development, that she became the home of lost causes. It would be fair to add that she retained much of value, and that the old causes, defended with virility, were not utterly lost. Defending them, Scottish nationality was born.

The spirit of nationality was emerging before Scotland was called to encounter the full force of the English attack. Already it had taken political expression in the form of a monarchy. This monarchy, strengthened by borrowings from the south, proved to be strong enough, if only just strong enough, to survive repeated assaults from the south, and by the very fact of survival was itself consolidated. Often defeated, the Scots managed to hold their own until accident of dynasty produced the Union of the Crowns in 1603. A Scottish king ascended the English throne, and Scotland, feeling that she entered the partnership, not as a bondswoman but as a sister, moved reluctantly, but inevitably, towards the Parliamentary Union of 1707. Of that union, the outstanding merit was that Scotland, the smaller and the poorer of the contracting parties, was able to preserve her nationality; and in spite of two centuries of union with England, Scotland maintains her nationality intact at the present day.

This is the history of Scotland in a nutshell. To give the details of the long development is impossible, but at least the various stages can be made clear.

The Beginnings

Scotland has always been proud of her antiquity. When England alleged a descent from Brut, the mythical grandson of Aeneas, Scotland replied by deriving the names 'Gael' and 'Scot', from the marriage between a Greek prince Gaythelos, and Scota, daughter to that Pharaoh who was drowned in the Red Sea. Save that they may enshrine some vague recollection of an old connection with the Mediterranean, these stories mean nothing.

The discoveries made in the cave of Inchnadamph in Sutherland show that man was in Scotland towards the close of the Ice Age. From the shell-mounds of Oronsay and the Oban caves it can be proved that Scotland was still inhabited during the long centuries during which the primitive 'old-stone' (Paleolithic) culture gave place to the 'new-stone' (Neolithic). In the Neolithic Age Scotland carried a fairly big population, as the numerous traces of settlements show. Part of this population, at least, had drifted in from the south—a short, dark, long-headed folk, who brought with them the habit of erecting great stone monuments which they had first practised in their Mediterranean home.

The Circles of Callernish in the Lewis, and the Ring of Brogar in the Orkneys, are not unworthy of comparison with Stonehenge itself.

Soon after the arrival of this Mediterranean race, another stream came in, this time from the Rhineland–a taller, broad-headed people who probably introduced the use of bronze. Much later the use of iron came in, perhaps with a people speaking some form of Celtic. Certainly about the year A.D. 100 there were in the south of Scotland people who spoke a langauge akin to modern Welsh. There is no need to assume that each wave of invaders exterminated the peoples whom it found. The evidence of archaeology is that it did not. In the north we find the 'dun', which in its latest development became the majestic 'broch', a great stone tower; in the east-central area the 'earth-house'; in the south and south-west the 'hill-fort' and the 'crannog', or artificial island. And all four types seem to have been occupied at the time when the Romans came to Scotland.

Certainly the people of the south-west Strathclyde were Britons. The names of the other peoples are variously given. The term 'Pict', which has given rise to such controversies, was not used till A.D. 297, and then by an ill-informed Latin author. It is no more than a label on a closed box, and is best defined as a name given by foreigners to some of the inhabitants of Scotland between the third and the ninth centuries A.D.

The Visit of the Romans

To the Romans Scotland was never more than a troublesome border state, part of which was sometimes held for the purpose of defending the province of Britain to the south. In A.D. 80 Agricola entered Scotland, and in 84 he routed the inhabitants at Mons Graupius, probably in the south of Perthshire or in Angus. Some of the forts he built were long maintained, and about the year 142 a wall of turf, on a stone foundation, was carried from the Firth of Forth to the Firth of Clyde. Garnished with 19 forts, this rampart was 39 miles long. It was built by legionaries, whose 'distance-slabs'–records of the lengths of wall built by the various units–may be seen in the Hunterian Museum at Glasgow, but it was held by auxiliaries who came from many lands–Gauls, Belgians, Rhinelanders, Syrians and Thracians, whose business was rather to police the frontier than to wage aggressive war. But the Roman hold was weak. The wall was abandoned about 185 and thereafter Roman interference in Scotland was limited to punitive expeditions such as those of Severus (c. 210). Doubtless the contact with the great empire left some faint trace upon Scottish history, but it is essential to notice that Scotland, unlike England, felt hardly at all the shaping hand of Rome.

The Four Peoples

With the departure of the Romans a curtain drops upon the history of Scotland, and when, about the middle of the sixth century, the scene reappears, four peoples may be distinguished.

The **Picts**, perhaps not even a single race, were as yet hardly a single nation. Apart from tribal distinctions there was a well-marked division into North Picts and South Picts.

The **Scots**, a Gaelic-speaking people who had been associated with the Picts in the attack on the waning power of Rome, had drifted across from

Ireland in small numbers, and about 500 a definite colony was founded by Fergus Mac Erc and his brothers. The struggling kingdom of Dalriada which emerged was in constant danger from the Picts, and in 559 it was almost destroyed by Brude Mac Maelchon. In Strathclyde the **Britons** maintained their kingdom, in close relation with their kinsfolk in Cumbria and Wales, and with the Anglo-Saxon invasions a fourth element appeared when the **Angle** kingdom of Northumbria stretched north and embraced part of the Lothian, especially Berwickshire.

A United Scotland

Out of these four discordant elements, two of them parts of groups which lay mainly outside the limits of modern Scotland, a united monarchy emerged. This was due to the co-operation of three factors—the common acceptance of Christianity, the Norse attacks, and the rise of the Scoto-Pictish monarchy to a position of dominance.

Ever since, about A.D. 400, Ninian founded his *Candida Casa* at Whithorn, Strathclyde, and possibly other parts of what is now 'Scotland', had had a tincture of Christianity. About the middle of the sixth century St Mungo or Kentigern was settled at Glasgow, and the victory of the Christian forces at the battle of Arthuret (573) made the position safe for the new religion. The Scots in Ireland had nominally been Christians ever since the day of St Patrick, but Christianity took a firm hold in Dalriada only with the arrival of Columba (563). Of princely birth, eloquent and enthusiastic, Columba founded a community at Iona, and from this centre started a missionary enterprise which restored the waning fortunes of Dalriada and 'converted' Pictland. His successors carried their banners into Northumbria, but there the Irish form of Christianity was met and routed by the Roman form at the Synod of Whitby (664). The victorious Church advanced into Scotland, and about 710 the Pictish king himself gave his adhesion.

What a common faith began, a common peril expedited. The Norse attacks were dangerous to Scotland, for they established in the Islands a power which was sometimes as great as that of the Scottish king. But on the other hand they furthered the process of union in two ways. They drove Scotland in upon herself and hammered the reduced area into one. They also disintegrated the kingdom of Northumbria, and removed, for centuries, the danger of an English conquest. The union of Scotland and Pictland under Kenneth Mac Alpin (843) provided a strong nucleus round which a vague national sentiment could rally. In 1018 Malcolm II beat the Northumbrians at Carham, and annexed Lothian; and the death of the last King of Strathclyde in the same year gave that country to his heir Duncan, who was Malcolm's grandson. When Malcolm died in 1034 he handed a united Scotland to his successor. He was the first king to bear the title of King of Scotland; his successors were generally known as Kings of Scots.

The Development of the Monarchy

The monarchy was at first very weak—the machinery was primitive, and the very rule of succession uncertain. For some time the throne had been held alternately by the Atholl and the Moray lines of the House of Alpin, and Malcolm had secured his grandson's succession only by violence. The slaying of Duncan by Macbeth (1040) was a vindication of the rights of Moray, and although Atholl recovered the crown with Malcolm Canmore's victory in 1057, Moray rebellions occurred sporadically until 1230. The great earls, it must be added, were also prone to rebel. The Norse, too, were a constant danger, and it was not until 1266, after the attack of the Norwegian King Haakon had been repulsed at Largs (1263), that Scotland secured the Hebrides in return for an annual tribute. The Orkneys and Shetlands remained Norse till 1472.

That the monarchy triumphed over all these difficulties was due in part to the help it obtained from England both directly and indirectly. There was much inter-marriage between the royal houses; the Scottish kings came to hold land in England, and many English families were established in Scotland to become supporters of the Crown against uncertain 'Celts'.

From England also came the organisation of the Anglo-Norman monarchy. The King's household was used for administrative work, and in the twelfth and thirteenth centuries, the land was divided into sheriff-doms, each with a royal castle (of a very simple kind) in its midst. The close relationship with England, however, inevitably led the stronger country to claim suzerainty over her weaker sister, and between the years 1174 and 1189, Scotland, owing to the capture of her king William the Lion (1165–1214) by the English, was compelled to acknowledge herself a vassal state. In 1189 Richard I sold Scotland her independence in order to get money for his crusade, but later English kings showed themselves very overbearing. Alexander II and Alexander III were married to English princesses as a matter of course, but a plain English nobleman was considered good enough for a Scots princess. Scotland saw the danger, and both Alexander II and Alexander III married French brides *en secondes noces*.

The Struggle for Independence

The death of Alexander III, thrown from his horse over the cliff near Kinghorn, gave to Edward I of England an opportunity after his own heart. He at once betrothed his son to the baby 'Maid of Norway', the dead king's grand-daughter and heiress; and when that project was ruined by the death of the little girl in the Orkneys on her way from Norway to Scotland (1290), he found a fresh means to his end in the quarrels of the thirteen 'Competitors' who sought the Scottish crown. Appointed arbitrator, he coerced the claimants into acknowledging his suzerainty and, in 1292, selected as king John Balliol, whose claims were certainly the best according to feudal ideas. But he treated Balliol with a deliberate arrogance which drove the vassal king into revolt. In 1296 Edward suppressed the revolt and took the administration of Scotland into his own hands. He met, however, with a general resistance, in which plain William Wallace of Elderslie in Renfrewshire played a leading part. In 1297 Wallace and Andrew de Moray defeated the English at Stirling Bridge with great slaughter, but next year Edward himself came up and routed Wallace at Falkirk. In the next few years the English king steadily warred down the Scots who opposed him, and in 1305 Wallace was executed as a traitor, though he had never given allegiance to the oppressor.

Scotland, however, quickly found a new champion in Robert Bruce, grandson of one of the 'Competitors'. Bruce had met another hero of Scottish liberty, John Comyn, at Dumfries, possibly to concert rebellion, and, old hate having flared up, had slain him in the precincts of the church of the Grey Friars. Driven to desperation by this deed of blood, Bruce boldly assumed the crown, or rather the plain circlet of gold which alone was available, and after many defeats and escapes, gradually began to make headway. Whether or no he saw the celebrated spider, he certainly displayed a noble resolution, and he was fortunate in that the slack Edward II succeeded his father in 1307. The castles were steadily recovered–Edinburgh itself by a marvellous escalade in 1314–and in 1314 an English expedition to relieve the last stronghold of Stirling ended in the great Scottish victory of Bannockburn. By the Treaty of Northampton in 1328, Scotland gained formal recognition of her independence, and to her independence she clung, though David II (1329–71) came near to losing by folly all that his father had won by wisdom and manhood.

The Stewart Monarchy

David II left no heirs, and the crown passed to his nephew Robert Stewart, son of Marjorie Bruce and Walter, sixth hereditary High Steward of Scotland. The House of Stewart held the throne until the death of Anne in 1714, but the reigns of the earlier kings were filled by an unceasing struggle against a baronage which has grown too strong in the English wars and which regarded the Stewart as little more than one of themselves. The quarrels of the nobles, and the efforts of the Crown to assert itself, provided some of the most dramatic incidents in Scottish history. The Battle of the Clans, thirty against thirty, at Perth (1396); the mysterious death of Rothesay in prison at Falkland (1402); the kidnapping of James I at sea by the English (1406); the murder of James I at Perth (1437); the death of James II, killed by a bursting gun at Roxburgh (1460); the hanging of James III's favourites at Lauder Bridge in the face of an English attack (1482), and that monarch's tragic end in the rout of Sauchieburn (1488)–all these things tell the same tale.

Conspicuous amongst the rivals to the royal power were two great houses, each able to count on English support–the 'Black' Douglases of the Border, and the Macdonald chiefs who bore between 1350 and 1493 the proud title of 'Lord of the Isles'. Heroes of Otterburn (1388) and of many another struggle with the English, the Douglases became very arrogant, and only by brutal and dishonourable action were they suppressed. In 1440 the sixth earl was murdered in Edinburgh Castle by the regents of James II, and in 1452 the eighth earl was slain by the King's own hand in Stirling Castle, whither he had come under safe-conduct. Three years later the King made a grand attack upon the Douglas strongholds, which ended in the forfeiture and exile of the proud men of the 'Bleeding Heart'.

The attempt of the second Lord of the Isles to gain the earldom of Ross led to the battle of Harlaw in 1411, which saved Aberdeen from the sack;

but it was not until 1476 that the Lords were compelled to surrender Ross, and not till 1493 was the Crown able to abolish the haughty title. This is significant. It was in the reign of James IV (1488–1513) that the Crown gained undisputed supremacy.

England versus France

United by the strong hand of James IV, Scotland entered the arena of European politics. Ever since the day of John Balliol (1295) Scotland had maintained an 'auld alliance' with France, and at the beginning of the sixteenth century France was encircled by a ring of enemies which included England. Almost inevitably therefore Scotland tended to become a battlefield where French and English influences contended. Cautious Henry VII married his daughter Margaret to the Scottish king, but Henry VIII displayed the old Plantagenet ambition, and James, somewhat against his own will, was led by French pressure into the disastrous adventure of Flodden (1513), where he was killed and most of the Scots nobles with him. During the minority of James V the balance swung this way and that between the French and English parties, but the Anglophil 'Red' Douglases behaved so arrogantly that James, when he grew up, was entirely French in sympathies. He married Madeleine of France, and on her death Mary of Lorraine, and with them he espoused the cause of Rome as well as the cause of France; for by this time Henry VIII had achieved his remarkable Reformation, and the duel between England and France was merging into a war between the new and the old faiths.

Slain by the shame of the defeat at Solway Moss, James handed on to his baby daughter a most unhappy realm (1542). The long struggle went wearily on. In 1546 Cardinal Beaton, a courageous persecutor, was murdered by a handful of adventurers, who held the castle of St Andrews against all Scotland until July 1547, when the walls were beaten down by French guns, and the garrison, which by this time included John Knox, was taken off to row in the French galleys. A few weeks later the Scots were routed by Somerset at Pinkie, but the result of the English success was to drive Scotland entirely into the arms of France. Mary was sent to France for safety, and in 1558 she married the Dauphin; Scotland was governed almost as a French province between 1550 and 1560, Mary of Lorraine assuming the regency in 1554.

The Scottish Reformation

February 29, 1528, is reckoned the birthday of the Scottish Reformation, for on that day the learned and well-born Patrick Hamilton was burned at St Andrews; but the movement was really the outcome of deep spiritual, social and economic causes. Its actual course was shaped by two political forces already noted–the quarrel of England with France and the quarrel between the nobles and the King. The nobles made common cause with the third estate against the King and the Church, and success came to them in 1560, when England sent effective aid and France did not. By the Treaty of Leith French troops evacuated Scotland, and the title of Elizabeth to the

English throne was recognised. Immediately afterwards a hastily summoned Parliament abolished Roman Catholicism as the religion of Scotland.

The Title to the English Throne

To most Catholics, the legitimate heir to the English throne was not Elizabeth, daughter of Anne Boleyn, but Mary Stewart, grand-daughter of Margaret Tudor; and Mary herself, repudiating the arrangement made at Leith, spent her life in trying to make good her title. She had two alternative policies. She might come to terms with Elizabeth, abandoning her present claim in return for formal recognition of her right to succeed if Elizabeth left no heir; or she might make herself champion of the Counter-Reformation which had already begun in Europe. She tried both courses.

Returned to Scotland as a fascinating widow of eighteen in 1561, her first thought was to placate her jealous cousin. She let the Protestant settlement stand, tolerated the admonitions of Knox, and endeavoured to marry to Elizabeth's pleasure. Elizabeth replied by delays and covert insolence. In 1565 Mary lost patience, married her Catholic cousin Darnley, himself possessed of a claim to the crown of England, and made overtures to Spain and other Catholic powers. Tragedies followed in quick succession—the murder of Secretary Rizzio almost in Mary's sight, by assassins introduced through her husband's bedroom; the murder of Darnley at Kirk o' Field; the hasty marriage with Bothwell, commonly regarded as the 'first murderer'; the collapse, imprisonment at Lochleven and forced abdication; the escape and failure at Langside; the flight to England. And in captivity in England Mary remained till in 1587 she was executed for complicity, probable but not proved, in the Babington plot.

Her son James VI, whose long minority was vexed by the bitter wars between 'King's Men' and 'Queen's Men', showed himself, when he grew up, equally resolute to obtain the English throne. Like Mary he bargained with both Catholics and Protestants, but in 1586 he came to terms with England at Berwick, and thereafter, despite much intrigue with Elizabeth's enemies, his policy was really fixed. He tolerated his mother's death (which he could not have prevented); he married a Protestant bride, Anne of Denmark; he endured the rebukes of the ministers, until, with English support, he succeeded in breaking the power of the Kirk, even though Andrew Melville was its leader. In 1603 he had his reward. Elizabeth died at last, and he became, 'King of Great Britain, France and Ireland'.

Crown and Covenant

The removal of the monarchy to England damaged the prestige of Scotland, but it increased the power of the Crown. Far in the south country, beyond the reach of kidnapping nobles and rebuking ministers, James was able to rule Scotland, as he boasted, with his pen. He used his new authority to complete the overthrow of the Kirk, making its government episcopal, and effecting some alterations in its ritual, though he was wise enough not to push things too far. His son, Charles I, himself tactless and advised by tactless Laud, soon succeeded in uniting all parties in the Church against his policy, and the **National Covenant** of 1638 was the expression of a universal opposition. Its signatories bound themselves to defend both King and Kirk, but the Kirk was to be Presbyterian. The 'Bishops' Wars' which resulted (1639–40) ended in the defeat of the King, and proved the prelude of the Great Civil War in England between Charles and the Parliament. The opinion of Scotland was divided. The Covenanters sided with the Parliament, but they forced their allies to accept the **Solemn League and Covenant** (1643), enforcing upon all the British Isles a religious settlement which could only be Presbyterian. Montrose, on the other hand, abandoning the Covenant, rose for the King, and in 1644–5 won some astonishing victories before he was defeated at Philiphaugh. Charles was utterly beaten by 1646. But the Scots had no desire to get rid of their king; they only wanted him to be a Presbyterian, and at the end of 1647 made the compromise known as 'The Engagement'. This led only to the utter defeat of the Scots army by Cromwell and to the execution of the King. The Scottish reply was at once to acknowledge Charles II as King, and as the ruling party still adhered to the Covenant, the accommodating Charles came to Scotland as a 'Covenanted King' in 1650. Cromwell's practical sword put a bloody end to that evil pretence in the battles of Dunbar and Worcester, and his gay majesty, after astounding escapes, went 'on his travels again'. Scotland, for her part, enjoyed eight years of humiliation and good government at the hands of the triumphant Cromwell, who forced a complete parliamentary union, and sweetened the bitter pill by a grant of free trade between the two countries. When, in 1660, the King came back to enjoy his own again, he remembered nothing of the Covenant save the coercion he had had to endure. Episcopacy was established by force, and the Covenanters, goaded into rebellion in 1666, became ever more bitter in their opposition. In 1679 Archbishop Sharp was brutally murdered at Magnus Muir near St Andrews. The rebellion which followed was promptly suppressed at Bothwell Bridge, and the Covenanters suffered a persecution which became worse than ever when James II succeeded his brother in 1685.

The Union of the Parliaments

This 'Killing Time' produced an effect on Scotland which may be seen today, and in 1688 the resentment against James was so fierce that hardly a hand was raised to defend him when the English rejected him in favour of William of Orange. Gallant and ambitious John Graham of Claverhouse, 'Bluidy Clavers', was true to his salt, and won a dashing victory at Killiecrankie in 1689, but he fell on the field, and the King's cause fell with him. But though Scotland followed England in accepting William, the son of one Stewart princess and the husband of another, she did so without undue enthusiasm, and she took the opportunity not only to restore Presbyterianism, but to establish for the first time Parliamentary government. This achieved, it became plain that a mere personal union of the crowns would no longer suffice. William's policy of constant enmity to France meant that some Scots money and much Scots blood was spent in a quarrel against Scotland's oldest ally, and while Scottish trade suffered in consequence, the

English were careful to exclude Scotsmen from any share in their own Colonial commerce. Worse still, William as King of England helped to suppress the 'Company trading to Africa and the Indies' whose best-known venture was the 'Darien Scheme', which as King of Scotland he had actually legalised (1695), and the venture ended in utter ruin (1698–1700). Public opinion, already aroused by the 'Massacre of Glencoe' (1692), was thoroughly inflamed. There was nothing for it but a more complete union or a complete severance. Chance provided the solution.

William and Mary left no heir, and it was clear that Anne would leave none either. Scotland made it plain that she would not accept the Hanoverian succession already adopted by England unless the conditions of Union were revised. The result was the Act of Union of 1707, whereby Scotland, accepting a somewhat inadequate representation in a British Parliament to sit at Westminster, kept her Church and her legal system, and was given a share in the splendid commerce of England and her colonial empire. 'There's ane end o' ane auld sang,' said Chancellor Seafield when the 'Honours of Scotland'–the crown, sceptre and sword–were borne for the last time from the Parliament House in Edinburgh.

The Jacobite Risings

Economic prosperity did not at once follow the grant of free trade with England, and the obvious disregard of Scottish affairs by English statesmen was another cause of discontent. This discontent showed itself in the 'Malt Riots' in Glasgow in 1725, and in the Porteous affair in 1736, but its main expression may be seen in the Jacobite risings. 'The 'Fifteen' promised well, but it came to nothing because Louis XIV, dying in bankruptcy, could send no real aid, and because the 'Old Pretender' was an uninspiring leader. The one action of importance was at Sheriffmuir, and that was indecisive. A landing of Spanish troops near Glenshiel in 1719 did not accomplish anything, and did not deserve success, being only a sidewind of ambitious Spanish policy. 'The 'Forty-Five', on the other hand, had more success than it deserved, since the Young Pretender, 'Prince Charlie', produced it by his own rashness and personal charm in the face of the universal opposition of his supporters. France could send no troops for the moment; the Highland chiefs were most reluctant to call out their men; the Lowland Jacobites were most unwilling to rise. The action was dramatic; victory at Preston-pans, occupation of Edinburgh, advance to Derby, retreat, success at Falkirk and ruin at Culloden. The Prince, after desperate adventures in the Highlands and Islands, at length escaped to France, and later to other adventures less reputable (d. at Rome 1788). Scotland remained to pay the penalty. The nobles lost their hereditary jurisdictions; the Highlands were ruthlessly policed; the wearing of the kilt was forbidden (till 1782). The hanging of James of the Glens (*see* R. L. Stevenson's *Catriona*) is a commentary on the justice of the government. It seemed as if even the echo of the 'auld sang' was dead. This was not so.

Modern Scotland

After the failure of the Jacobite attempts, the development of Scotland was more in line with that of England. Economic prosperity came with the increase of the American trade, and with the so-called Industrial Revolution. With England, Scotland advanced along the path of political reform, and the ardent spirit of her people expressed itself in ecclesiastical controversies – neither dull nor foolish – and in military service under the Hanoverian king. The Lowland regiments were already old in the British service, and the Black Watch had fought at Fontenoy before the outbreak of 'The 'Forty-Five'. But it is worth noting that when Wolfe took Quebec in 1759, one third of the British casualties were borne by Fraser's Highlanders, a regiment recruited from an old Jacobite stronghold. During the Napoleonic wars, fresh Highland regiments were created, and in the wars and the adventures which created the British Empire Scotsmen have played no mean part.

Though now a part of the United Kingdom, Scotland is still keenly conscious of her own individuality, hopeful of her future and proud of her past. The National War Memorial in Edinburgh Castle is not only a monument to the brave dead; it is the expression of a living spirit.

SOUTHERN SCOTLAND

SCALE OF MILES

0   5   10   15

WARD LOCK LIMITED. LONDON.

© – John Bartholomew & Son Ltd. Edinburgh

The Ayrshire Coast at Lendalfoot

Berwick-upon-Tweed to Edinburgh

Throughout this, the final stage of the East Coast Route to Edinburgh, the railway keeps the road close company, throwing out a branch to North Berwick from Drem.

Berwick-upon-Tweed

Distances—Edinburgh, 58 m; Dunbar, 30 m; Newcastle, 63 m; London, 336 m; Kelso, 24 m.
Car Parking Places—Castlegate, Parade, Bridge Street and Walkergate.
Early Closing—Thursday.

Hotels—*King's Arms, Castle, Old Hen and Chickens, Salmon, Waterloo, Turret, Villa, Tweed View,* etc.
Sports—Bowls, tennis, bathing, boating, golf. Good fishing for brown and sea trout in Tweed and Whiteadder.

Geographically speaking, the crossing of the Tweed at Berwick should take one from England into Scotland or vice versa. Actually, although it stands on the north side of the Tweed, Berwick is accounted part of England (itself a county, it is included for administrative purposes in Northumberland), and at one time it held an even more anomalous position, since it claimed to be neither in Scotland nor in England.

The town is spread over the western flank of the tongue of hilly land which turns the Tweed south in the last mile of its course to the sea. On the seaward side of the promontory are golf links, sands and bathing pool; the town itself looks down upon the river and bridges, and the military strength of its position in olden times, when it hung like a portcullis over the Great North Road, led to incessant sieges and changes of ownership. Of those days the principal memorials are the relics of the walls built by Edward I and those built to enclose a smaller area in Elizabeth I's time: the narrow Scotsgate which so sorely hampers traffic in mid-season is part of the Elizabethan defences. The most historic spot in Berwick—the Castle—was demolished to make way for the railway station, and in view of the Castle's bitter story one is inclined to wonder whether Stephenson had only the building of the railway in mind when he caused the words 'The final act of union' to be inscribed over the station.

Certainly the history of the Castle tells of deeds best forgotten. With the town, the stronghold was burnt by the English during William the Lion's invasion of

27

Salmon Fishing on the Tweed

England in 1174, and subsequently formed part of his ransom. Henry II rebuilt the Castle; Richard Coeur de Lion sold it back to William the Lion and a few years later Richard's son John captured it anew, the town being burnt in the process. In 1292 Edward I from the Castle hall gave his decision concerning the rival claims of Bruce and Balliol to the Scottish throne, and four years later Balliol rebelled and held the Castle against the English. When Edward took and sacked Berwick, the Castle surrendered, though the garrison marched out with military honours, and there in 1306 he imprisoned the Countess of Buchan, for her offence in crowning Robert Bruce. Tradition asserts that the lady was hung in a cage outside the wall, but Edward's instructions make it plain that the cage was a device for solitary confinement inside a turret. The Castle was recaptured by Bruce in 1318, after the town had been taken in a brilliant night-attack by Douglas and Randolph. In 1333 Edward III, in a vain attempt to induce the governor, Sir Alexander Seton, to surrender, hanged his son Thomas, whom he held as hostage, within sight of the walls. The town and Castle were surrendered to him after the Scottish defeat at Halidon Hill. In 1461 Henry VI, a refugee in Scotland, gave up town and Castle to the Scots, but in 1482 they were regained, for Edward IV, by his brother Richard 'Crookback,' later Richard III. And Berwick remained a pillar of the English defences against Scotland till the Union of 1603, when these defences became unnecessary. Berwick later obtained a peculiar status as an independent town, belonging to neither country. This was its condition until the Reform Act of 1885, and until that time all Acts of Parliament, etc., contained the special allusion 'and to our town of Berwick-upon-Tweed.'

The Bridges of Berwick are interesting sentimentally and historically. The river-crossing here was responsible for the rise of the town and has been the cause of the greater part of its history down to the present day, when motors and vehicles of all kinds pour continuously across the two road bridges–the many-arched seventeenth-century bridge and the severely practical structure of reinforced concrete built in 1928–and trains rumble over the lofty viaduct.

The walk along the Elizabethan walls is most pleasant, and more or less extensive fragments of the earlier Edwardian fortifications also remain, but the glamour of Berwick the Border town is to be recaptured rather from a perusal of its history than by walking its streets. Of these the principal is the broad street known as Marygate, extending from the Scotsgate to the Town Hall. Eastward of Marygate lie the Parish Church, the Barracks and bastions; on the other side various streets lead down to the riverside, whence one can walk round to the Pier.

Across the wide mouth of the river Tweed is **Spittal,** the borough's seaside suburb; at the western end of the bridges is the more industrial suburb of **Tweedmouth.**

The salmon of Tweed are famous, and Berwick is a good centre both for the angler and for those interested in watching the proceedings of the net fishers.

Although Berwick has been deprived of its state of splendid isolation between England and Scotland, the County of the Borough and Town of Berwick-upon-Tweed is still an entity, and its landward boundary, running from sea to Tweed some 3 or 4 miles north and west of the centre of the town, still serves as the Anglo-Scottish border.

The coast-road and the railway cross the Border by **Lamberton**, which once had a reputation among runaway couples akin to that of Gretna (*see* p. 79).

In a narrow valley running steeply to the sea a mile or so from Lamberton is the primitive fishing village of **Burnmouth**. Like the railway, the main road (A1) to Edinburgh keeps inland (by Ayton, Reston and Grantshouse) as far as Cockburnspath, missing a picturesque stretch of coast.

A bus service from Burnmouth runs three miles north to–

Eyemouth

Early Closing Day–Thursday.
Fishing–Boats available for sea fishing.
  Angling in Eye and Ale.
Golf–9-hole course at Sunscreen.

Hotels–*Home Arms, Whale, Ship, Northumbria.*
Population–2,250.
Sports–Golf, tennis, boating and yachting.

Eyemouth though still a small but prosperous fishing port is one of the larger centres of population in Berwickshire. It is also a highly popular resort and offers bathing, boating, fishing, golf, tennis among its holiday attractions. The harbour has been rebuilt and is the base for a considerable seine net fishing fleet. A Herring Queen Week is a feature of the season in July each year. At one time the local alternative to herring-fishing was smuggling, and it has been said that the secret cellars and subterranean passages were so numerous that only a half of the town appeared above the surface, the other half being underground. North and south along the coast is rocky and picturesque with numerous caves which no doubt proved useful in those smuggling days.

On again is **Coldingham** (*Anchor ; St Veda's* (pte); *St Abb's Haven* (pte)), a quiet village famed for the remains of a Norman Priory and frequented in summer on account of the allurements of Coldingham Sands.

Coldingham Priory was founded in 1098 as a Benedictine establishment on the site, it is said, of a nunnery founded some centuries earlier by that St Ebba whose name is commemorated in that of the neighbouring St Abb's Head. The site is a little east of the village cross. There is an isolated archway, but the most noteworthy remnants of this once extensive establishment are what now form the north and east walls of the parish church. The tragic episode concluding the second Canto of *Marmion* was suggested to Scott by the discovery, at Coldingham, of a female skeleton standing upright built into the wall. In bygone days apostate nuns were buried alive in this position.

St Abb's Head is the most striking promontory on this coast, rising more than 300 feet above the sea. The Lighthouse, 224 feet above the waves, flashes every ten seconds and is visible 20 miles. Hardly less striking than this headland is the spot known as **Fast Castle**, 4 miles westward. Little remains of the Castle, which was built on a precipitous crag connected with the mainland by a narrow ridge. It must have been wellnigh impregnable: a miniature Dunnottar or Tintagel.

The road from Coldingham to **Cockburnspath** (colloquially 'Co'path') rejoins the main road shortly after passing above the charmingly wooded *Pease Dean* by a lofty bridge from which the stream can be heard but not seen as it rushes through the woods below. The main road winding across this eastern end of the Lammermuirs suggests the origin of the name Cockburnspath. A nearby ruined Tower is supposed to be all that is left of 'Ravenswood Castle' in the *Bride of Lammermuir*, Fast Castle being the original of 'Wolf's Crag'.

Siccar Point, near Cockburnspath, is of interest to geologists as the site of Hutton's famous unconformity, where gently inclined Old Red Sandstone beds rest on the upturned edges of the Silurian.

From Cockburnspath to Dunbar the coast is seldom out of sight. The tall white lighthouse at Barns Ness is away on the right; then on the left is the field where Leslie's men found themselves on the morning of September 3, 1650, a sight which, according to Bishop Burnet, moved Cromwell to cry, 'The Lord hath delivered them into our hands!'. The main road now bypasses Dunbar.

Dunbar

Amusements–Cinema, dancing, motor tours, pony trekking, etc.
Caravan Sites–Kirk Park; Winterfield.
Distances–Berwick-on-Tweed, 30 m; North Berwick, 10½ m; Edinburgh, 28 m.
Early Closing–Wednesday (except from May 16–September 15).

Hotels–*Bellevue* (43 rooms); *Roxburghe* (37 rooms); *Royal Mackintosh* (15 rooms); *Craig-en-Gelt* (23 rooms); *Bayswell* (15 rooms); *Golden Stones* (13 rooms); *St. George* (13 rooms); *Lothian* (16 rooms), etc.
Sports–Bathing, open-air pool, boating, bowls, golf, tennis, sea-fishing.

Famed for centuries on account of its almost impregnable Castle, and afterwards as an agricultural and fishing centre, Dunbar is today highly regarded as a holiday resort. There are golf (two first-class courses), tennis, bathing, fishing, etc, and the inexhaustible attractions of the harbour. The chief feature of the long, wide street around which the town groups itself is the old Town House with its tower. The large building at the end of the street was originally a seat of the Lauderdale family; but is now used for civic and cultural purposes. From this wide street one turns off for the Harbour and the Castle ruins or for the modern promenade overlooking Bayswell Beach, with its boating lake and swimming pool.

Of the Castle–'built upon a chain of rocks stretching into the sea and having only one passage to the mainland, which was well fortified'–there are sufficient remains to kindle the imagination of those who know their Scottish history. Here Edward II, fleeing from Bannockburn, sheltered until a boat took him on to Berwick; here, in 1338, in the absence of her husband, the Earl of Dunbar, 'Black Agnes' defied the Earl of Salisbury for nineteen weeks, until the siege was raised on the arrival of supplies by sea; here, too, Mary Queen of Scots sought sanctuary after the murder of Rizzio in 1565. Two years later she was brought there, willing or unwilling, by her abductor, Bothwell; a third time she returned, this time to prepare for the disastrous encounter on Carberry Hill. Not without reason, the Regent Moray ordered the dismantling of such a favourite refuge, and today only the crumbling red sandstone walls remain to tell of one of the most formidable strongholds in Scotland.

Dunbar Castle

31

Hailes Castle

Dunbar to Edinburgh direct

The direct road from Dunbar to Edinburgh runs via East Linton and Haddington. In the vicinity of **East Linton** (Sir John Rennie was born at Phantassie House, near the east end of the by-pass, in 1761) are **Preston Mill**, a charming seventeenth-century meal-mill (National Trust for Scotland), and Hailes Castle.

Hailes Castle (*open summer 9.30–7, Sundays from 2; winter closes at 4.30, fee*) is a fortified manor house now ruined and standing in a lovely position on the bank of the River Tyne. It is of interest on account of its older portions which date from before the War of Independence. It belonged to the Gourlays, but later passed to the Hepburns, who built the huge square tower and high curtain walls. There is a fine sixteenth-century chapel. The castle was heavily engaged in the War of the Rough Wooing, and was dismantled by Cromwell in 1650.

On **Traprain Law**, a hill which assumes striking proportions when viewed from east or west, was discovered in 1919, along with other antiquities, a pit, 2 feet deep and 2 feet wide, filled with a rich collection of fourth-century silver plate, crushed and broken as if destined for the melting-pot. It is supposed that the plate (now restored and exhibited in the National Museum of Antiquities of Scotland, Edinburgh) was concealed by Angle or Saxon pirates in the early fifth century.

Seventeen miles from Edinburgh is—

Haddington

Early Closing Day – Thursday.
Golf – Municipal course.

Hotels – *George, Black Bull, Tyne House, Maitlandfield.*
Population – 6,750.

Haddington is the county headquarters town of East Lothian and has been a Royal Burgh since the time of David I. The main A1 road now by-passes the town and it has regained something of its earlier tranquility. It has associations with John Knox who is believed to have been born here in 1505, and Edward Irving. The fine church of St Mary, known as the 'Lamp of Lothian' is a cruciform structure of the fifteenth century, its choir and transepts in a ruined state. Here is the tomb of Jane Welsh, wife of Thomas Carlyle. Of older date is the ruined church of St Martin nearby—twelfth century. The two bridges over the Tyne, the sixteenth-century Nungate Bridge and the Abbey Bridge a mile to the east, a few years older, are attractive. The Town House was built in 1748 by William Adam, father of Robert Adam. On the wall is a useful map outlining a suggested walk round the town.

Five miles west of Haddington is **Trent** (*Crown, Tranmere*) an old mining town with a pre-Reformation church in the churchyard of which are several interesting monuments.

For Edinburgh, the road continues westward through Musselburgh (*see* p. 160).

Nungate Bridge, Haddington

Tantallon Castle

Dunbar to Edinburgh by the Coast

The road for Tantallon and North Berwick turns northward from the main highway about 4 miles west of Dunbar, running across the woods and rich pastoral lands of Tynninghame to **Whitekirk**, with its interesting Parish Church, burned by suffragettes in 1914, but since restored.

The place was the scene of the labours of the eighth-century St Baldred, but owed its early importance to a well credited with miraculous powers of healing. The Countess of March, fleeing in 1294 from Edward I at Dunbar, drank of its waters and was cured of a wound, and in gratitude built a chapel in honour of Our Lady. So famous did the well become that upwards of 15,000 pilgrims came to it in 1413; while in 1435 the future Pope Pius II walked barefoot from Dunbar, a feat which so convinced James I of the worth of the well that he took the place under his care, added to the buildings and changed the name from Fairknowe to White Chapel.

About 2 miles north of Whitekirk and 3 miles east of North Berwick are the magnificent ruins of—

Tantallon Castle (*daily, fee*). Tantallon was a stronghold of the Douglases, and dates back to the latter part of the fourteenth-century. The Castle occupies a striking position on a rocky promontory overlooking the North Sea. Readers of Scott will recall the well-known lines in *Marmion:*

34

'Tantallon's dizzy steep
Hung o'er the margin of the deep.'

Hugh Miller's description is also worth quoting: 'Tantallon has three sides of wall-like rock and one side of rock-like wall.'

The impregnable character of the stronghold gave rise to a local legend: 'Ding doon Tantallon! Mak' a brig to the Bass' – feats considered equally impossible of achievement. In 1528 the Earl of Angus successfully defied James V and even captured the King's artillery. But in 1639 the Covenanters compelled the small garrison of the 11th Earl (1st Marquess of Douglas) to surrender; in 1651 the Castle was captured from the Scots by General Monk, after a heavy bombardment, and never again did it rank as a fortress, though it has since been in some parts restored.

Bass Rock. This rock lies 1¼ miles offshore opposite the castle. It measures about a mile in circumference, its sides in many places rising perpendicular from the water for some 300 feet. In summer there is a frequent service of motor launches from North Berwick harbour, and the trip is certainly one that should not be

Bass Rock

missed. The island was a favourite haunt of St Baldred (*see* p. 35, under White-kirk), and those whose visits are made on days when the tide permits landing on the rock may search the vicinity for the saint's well, cradle and cobble—the last-named a great rock which 'at his nod' was transplanted from a position off the island where it was dangerous to shipping. In later times the island was used as a prison for the Covenanters. Nowadays the rock is the haunt of innumerable sea-birds, notably the gannet or solan goose, which line the cliffs in such numbers as to give them at a distance the appearance of chalk. It will be remembered that David Balfour's adventures on the island form an exciting episode in Stevenson's *Catriona*.

On the left along the road for North Berwick, the conical **North Berwick Law** (612 feet) is a prominent landmark.

North Berwick

Distances—Berwick-upon-Tweed, 40 m; Dunbar, 11 m; Edinburgh, 23 m.
Early Closing—Thursday.
Hotels—*Royal* (43 rooms), *Marine* (74 rooms), *Imperial* (24 rooms), *Dalrymple, Golf, Redan, Westerdunes,* etc., etc.
Motor Launch Trips—In season from harbour to Bass Rock and other islands off the coast.

Population—4,161.
Sports—Tennis, bowls, swimming pond, yachting, and golf on a dozen courses, including some of the best in Britain. Sunday play on both the West Links (18 holes) and the Burgh Course (18 holes). There are also excellent putting courses along the front.

In modern times the name and fame of North Berwick have been so linked with golf that one looks almost with surprise upon the ruins of a twelfth-century Church and of a nunnery of like antiquity. North Berwick is a prosperous little town with splendid sands and other natural facilities for holiday-making, to which have been added tennis courts, bowling greens, swimming pool and yacht pond—and the golf links. Golf was played at North Berwick in the early seventeenth century, and today there are two full-sized links and a shorter course, while within a few miles are a dozen or more courses of varying characteristics.

Dirleton is a pretty village with a population of about 400. The *Open Arms Hotel* offers accommodation. The parish church dates from the seventeenth century but it has been restored and modernised.

Dirleton Castle (*open daily, fee*) is a massive ruin, one of the most picturesque in Scotland. This ancient stronghold of the de Vaux family stands in a beautiful flower-garden in the centre of the village. The building was destroyed by Lambert in 1650. The oldest work remaining comprises the clustered donjon of thirteenth-century towers. Beneath the ruins are several dungeons hewn out of the rock. The garden surrounded by yew trees includes a seventeenth-century bowling green.

To the north-east lies important Muirfield, most famous of the surrounding golfing centres. Here is the fine Championship course and the head-quarters of the Hon Company of Edinburgh Golfers.

Gullane

Bathing–Splendid sandy beach backed by dunes.
Early Closing Day–Wednesday.
Golf–Five first-rate courses in the vicinity.

Hotels–*Bissets* (25 rooms), *Gables* (10 rooms), *Queen's* (26 rooms), *Mallard* (13 rooms), *Greywalls* (19 rooms).
Population–1,400.

Gullane is another golfing centre adjoining the Muirfield links. There are five courses available including a special children's course (*free*). The sandy shore here has long been subject to erosion, but in recent years successful rehabilitation has been carried out by the use of brushwood fences to contain the sand and marram grass. The church here is a ruin but shows some Norman work.

At **Kilspindle** is yet another course (Sunday play); in fact, the road from North Berwick towards Edinburgh is a veritable golfer's progress, so numerous are the links. Some miles away to the south the Hopetoun Monument on Garleton Hill is prominent; in the other direction are views across the Forth.

Aberlady (*Kilspindle House*) is a tiny village with a long main street and a fifteenth-century turreted church at one end. A rather plain market cross, restored, stands nearby.

Close at hand is the Aberlady Nature Reserve with a wealth of sea birds. Some 200 species of birds have been recorded in the Reserve.

Beyond **Aberlady** the road runs close to the coast–a favourite neighbourhood with picnic parties. **Longniddry** is known for its long golf course, and then comes Port Seton, in the vicinity of which are **Seton Chapel** and House, the latter erected in the eighteenth century on the site of Seton Palace, where dwelt the fifth Lord Seton, the staunch adherent of Queen Mary, who with Bothwell spent a week here after Darnley's murder. The Chapel, a sixteenth-century collegiate building, consisting of choir, transepts and tower, is of much archaeological interest.

In the village of **Preston**, a little inland, is a fine seventeenth-century Mercat Cross replete with a unicorn and a crier's platform. Notable buildings include Northfield House a late sixteenth-century tower house with turreted stairs, the fifteenth-century Preston Tower, and **Hamilton House** (NT, *open on application to tenant*) built in 1628 and said to have been occupied by Prince Charles Edward's troops after the Battle of Prestonpans.

Prestonpans

The final syllable of the word **Prestonpans** is a reminder of that local industry concerned with the abstraction of salt from seawater, but the name also introduces us to a small area which for various reasons became the site of three important battles.

Chronologically, the first of these was the **Battle of Pinkie**, fought a few miles south-west of Prestonpans in 1547, when the Protector Somerset, with 18,000 men, utterly routed a very much larger Scottish force, slaying at least 10,000, though the English losses were only about 200.

PRESTONPANS

The next affair in point of time hardly merits the name of battle in comparison with Pinkie, but its effects were at least as momentous, for it was at **Carberry Hill** in 1567 that Mary Queen of Scots, after leaving Bothwell, surrendered to the insurgent nobles, to enter upon that long term of imprisonment which began at Lochleven and was to last almost without interruption until her execution (1587).

The **Battle of Prestonpans** was probably one of the most heartening incidents of Prince Charlie's 1745 adventure. The English under Sir John Cope had failed to engage his ragged force in the Highlands, and had therefore been shipped from Aberdeen to Dunbar in order to encounter them from the south, and so the two forces met at Prestonpans on the afternoon of September 19, 1745. Each side prepared for battle on the morrow; but the English placed too much confidence in a morass between them and their foes, who found a way through it during the night and at break of day staged such a surprise that in the brief space of fifteen minutes Cope's army was utterly routed.

The village of Preston boasts a fine seventeenth-century Mercat Cross.

At **Musselburgh** (p. 160) the Esk is crossed by a venerable bridge generally alluded to (incorrectly) as 'Roman'. Across the river is **Fisherrow**, which as its name implies is absorbed in fishing. Then comes **Joppa** (p. 159) and **Portobello** (p. 159) very popular seaside resorts. Portobello beach–and the open-air swimming pool–on a fine day must be seen to be believed.

Beyond Portobello the rugged heights of Arthur's Seat are seen beyond the houses to the left as we run through Restalrig, and as the road climbs the shoulder of Calton Hill to enter Edinburgh a glimpse will be caught on the left of the Palace of Holyroodhouse.

For Edinburgh, *see* pages 91–151.

Lennoxlove

Dunbar to Edinburgh via Gifford

An alternative route from Dunbar skirts the northern slopes of the Lammermuirs. A road runs below Whittinghame (Earl Balfour's home now a school), and Traprain Law to Garvald. Nunrow monastery was of old a fortalice as well as a Cistercian nunnery. At **Gifford** are Yester House (Marquess of Tweeddale) and ruined Yester Castle, with Goblin Ha', a rock-hewn chamber of the thirteenth century. Between Gifford and Haddington lies Lennoxlove (*open in summer*) associated with Mary's adviser, Maitland of Lethington, and with Charles I's lady-love, La Belle Stuart.

For the route beyond Haddington, *see* page 33.

Berwick to Kelso

Between Paxton and Kelso, where the Liberties of the Borough and Town of Berwick come down to the river, the Tweed forms the Anglo-Scottish boundary for the greater part of the distance. There are good roads on each side of the river; that on the south side being the shorter.

Some 5 miles from Berwick, and on the Scottish bank, is the village of **Paxton**, supposed to have suggested the song of 'Robin Adair'. The neighbouring suspension bridge is of interest as the first of its kind to be built in Britain.

Further up river and reached by turning off the main Kelso road through Horndean is **Ladykirk**, owing its name to a vow of James IV, who when in danger while fording the river promised to build a church to the Virgin Mary if he came safely to land. *Upsettlington*, on the outskirts of Ladykirk, is historically important as the place where Edward I extracted from the candidates for the Scottish throne the promise of vassalship–a promise which was fraught with such momentous results for Scotland and hardly less for England.

Across the river, in England, is **Norham**, with the remains of a twelfth-century castle celebrated as the opening scene of *Marmion*. (*The ruins are open daily, fee.*)

From its bold position, the Castle must have appeared as hardly less a fortress than a challenge, and it is not surprising that it changed hands incessantly. King John here concluded a treaty (1209) with William of Scotland which was so ambiguously worded that a year or so later Alexander of Scotland, the Papal legate and a representative of the English sovereign met at Berwick to define its meaning. Edward I was here during the Scottish interregnum, 1290–2, and here presided over the preliminaries for the Bruce-Balliol debates. In 1497 the celebrated Mons Meg was brought from Edinburgh Castle to assist in the unsuccessful assault and in 1513 James IV captured and partially wrecked the Castle on his way to Flodden.

Norham Church is interesting as a Norman building which has also seen warlike days, for in 1318 the Scots made it a strong-point during a siege of the Castle, and one of the numerous Anglo-Scottish treaties was signed within its walls.

A few miles above Norham the Tweed is joined by the Till, and finely placed in the angle formed by the two streams are the ruins of **Twizel Castle**, which, for all its Norman architecture, dates only from the eighteenth century. Near by are remnants of a small chapel in which the remains of St Cuthbert rested when, tiring of Melrose Abbey–let us quote Scott:

'In his stone coffin forth he rides,
A ponderous bark for river tides;
Yet, light as gossamer it glides
    Downward to Tillmouth cell.'

Scott's footnote is also interesting: 'This boat is finely shaped, 10 feet long, $3\frac{1}{2}$ feet in diameter and only 4 inches thick, so that with very little assistance it might certainly have swum. It lies, or at least did so a few years ago, beside the ruined chapel of Tillmouth.' Twizel might have been a greater name in history had James IV been wise enough to prevent, or to try to prevent, the English from crossing the Till in 1513. As it was, they crossed unchallenged and so followed the **Battle of Flodden Field**, one of the most tragic of the many tragic encounters on the Border. The site of the Battle is $3\frac{1}{2}$ miles south-east of Coldstream.

The object of James IV in crossing the Border was to cause Henry VIII to recall the forces with which he was warring against Louis XII in Flanders, and Pitscottie adds the information that the French Queen urged him to the invasion by sending him the ring from off her finger, fourteen thousand crowns to pay his expenses and inviting him to 'come three feet on English ground for her sake'. On the morning after the battle the chivalry of Scotland was no more, the King, his natural son, an archbishop, a bishop, two abbots, twelve earls, fourteen lords, many knights and gentlemen and about nine thousand men were slain; on the English side few men of title were slain. A monument near Branxton Church is said to mark the spot where James IV fell.

Coldstream

Caravans–Municipal Site.
Early Closing Day–Thursday.
Golf–9-hole course on Kelso Road.

Hotels–*Newcastle Arms, Crown*.
Population–1,250.
Sports–Tennis, bowls, fishing.

Coldstream is famous the world over by reason of the regiment of guards founded here in 1660 by General Monck. Overlooking the site of a ford (replaced by a picturesque bridge designed by Smeaton in 1763), Coldstream has always been of considerable importance, but most of the military crossings of the Border at this point seem to have been undisturbed, and the more exciting happenings in the history of the town have been provided by the runaway couples who came to be married at the bridge toll-house or elsewhere in this, the first burgh over the Border (see also Gretna Green). It is a remarkable fact that no fewer than three Lord Chancellors of England were married thus–Lords Eldon, Erskine and Brougham.

Two miles north-west of the town is **The Hirsel** the seat of Sir Alec Douglas Home, situated in splendid grounds and incorporating the beautiful woods of Dundock with their fine rhododendrons and azaleas.

Coldstream is the point at which the Border is crossed by motorists using the Morpeth-Wooler-Lauder-Edinburgh road, and as such is a very busy place in the season. For those going north the road leaves the Kelso road about 2 miles from Coldstream, almost opposite Wark Castle. Greenlaw is 10 miles and Lauder 22 miles from Coldstream.

West from Coldstream a mile or so, and on the English bank, is the site of **Wark Castle**, the traditional scene of the ball at which Edward III, retrieving the Countess of Salisbury's garter, uttered the words 'Honi soit qui mal y pense', which became the motto of the most Noble Order of the Garter. Here as elsewhere, however, tradition and historical truth do not march side by side, and the whole episode is regarded as fiction.

Carham has little to show of historic interest, but it was the scene of a great battle in 1018. Here the Tweed ceases to mark the Border, which now runs south towards the Cheviot (2,676 ft in Northumberland), the highest point in the range, which separates the two countries for the next 30 to 40 miles.

Kelso

Angling—Tickets for trout fishing in the Tweed and Teviot from Kelso Angling Association and tackle shops.

Bowls—Green in Victoria Street.

Caravans—Springwood Caravan Park.

Curling and Skating—Ice Rink.

Distances—Berwick 23 m; Edinburgh 45 m; Hawick 21 m; Newcastle 68 m; London 341 m.

Early Closing Day—Wednesday.

Golf—9-hole course at Berrymoss, near racecourse.

Hotels—*Ednam House* (31 rooms), *Queen's Head* (10 rooms), *Border* (10 rooms), *Black Swan* (7 rooms), *Cross Keys* (20 rooms), *Spread Eagle* (8 rooms).

Population—4,400.

Racing—Meetings in March, April, May, October and December.

Finely placed in a bend of the Tweed, where that river is joined by the Teviot about 25 miles above Berwick, Kelso is one of the most attractive of the Border towns, having a fine Rennie bridge, a wide picturesque market square, good shops and romantic surroundings.

Kelso Abbey. The chief monument of the town is the remains of Kelso Abbey (*daily, free*)—little more than the tower of the building founded by David I in the twelfth century. Standing so near the Border, the Abbey had a chequered history, and was finally besieged by the Earl of Hertford in 1545. Subsequently it was 'restored' but happily the signs of restoration have been removed. The building is almost wholly Norman and Transitional work and is unusual in that it had western as well as eastern transepts with the tower over both the crossings. The north transept was beautifully designed.

The bridge over the Tweed, a picturesque 5-arched structure was built by Rennie in 1803 and replaces one destroyed by floods in 1797.

Kelso has claims to a place in the history of literature, for it was at the local Grammar School that Scott received part of his education and made friends with the then youthful Ballantynes, who later became his publishers.

On the western outskirts of Kelso are the grounds of **Floors Castle** (*see notices*) enclosed in a formidable wall pierced, at the point nearest the town, by good modern iron gates. A holly tree in Floors Park marks the spot where James II was killed by the bursting of a cannon during the siege of

Kelso Abbey

Roxburgh Castle in 1460. Pinnacle Hill is a good viewpoint in the vicinity. **Roxburgh**, now a mere village, was formerly more important than Kelso.

For St Boswells and Dryburgh, *see* p. 50.

Kirk Yetholm (*Youth Hostel*) lies some 8 miles south-east of Kelso. The place was long the headquarters of the Scottish gypsies, the *Faas*, and the 'Palace' still stands. A little westward is the quiet village of **Morebattle** at the foot of the Cheviots and north of it **Linton** where the church has a unique carved stone panel above its door. At **Cessford**, south-west of Morebattle, are the ruins of Cessford Castle long a stronghold of the Kers.

North of Kelso, on the Eccles road, with a bridge over the Eden Water is the village of **Ednam**, the birthplace of James Thomson and Henry Francis Lyte. Thomson (*b.* 1700) wrote the words of *Rule Britannia* and Lyte (1793) authored the hymns 'Abide with Me' and 'Praise my Soul, the King of Heaven'.

By Whitadder Water

Berwick to Lauder via Duns

Although not much used as a through route, this road is a very pleasant introduction to the southern slopes of the Lammermuirs, especially for those with time to explore some of the roads running up into the hills. The route leaves Berwick by the Scots Gate. Keep to the left after crossing the railway, soon passing on the right **Halidon Hill**, the site of a memorable battle in 1333, when the Scots endeavouring to relieve Berwick Castle were themselves severely beaten.

Chirnside (*Countryhouse, Waterloo Arms*) is a pleasant village mostly of two long streets on a hill-top and from which there are wide-spreading views. Anglers particularly are attracted here for the fishing in the nearby Whiteadder Water. The parish church has a Norman doorway incorporated in the tower. In the churchyard is the grave of James Clark, the world-champion racing driver killed whilst racing in Germany.

Duns

Caravan Park – Bridgend (Municipal).
Early Closing Day – Wednesday.
Golf – 9-hole course.

Hotels – *Barniken House* (6 rooms), *Black Bull, Waverley, White Swan* (7 rooms).
Population – 1,900.

Duns is a pleasant little market town near the slopes of the Lammermuir Hills. It is the county headquarters town of Berwickshire. Formerly known as Dunse, its present name is derived from the Celtic word *Dun* meaning hill or fort, obviously from Duns Law (714 feet) a rounded hill to the north from which there is a wide view over Lower Tweeddale. On this hill in 1639 General Leslie's army set up their standard. A Covenanters' stone marks the spot. The church dates from 1880. In the modern Council Building is a James Clark Memorial Room; the racing driver was an Honorary Burgess of the town. In the Park is the old Mercat Cross and a bust of John Duns Scotus, the thirteenth-century philosopher and divine.

Duns Castle to the north-west is modern but retains an ancient tower and has a castellated gatehouse. A long avenue of limes is a feature of the grounds.

From Duns a wildly beautiful road runs across the hills to Haddington, following the Whiteadder almost to its source.

Polwarth lies a few miles west of Duns on the Greenlaw road. Its church, in the grounds of Marchmount House and rebuilt in 1703, has several interesting features. The major road westward leads by Westruther to **Lauder** (p. 60) 18 miles from Duns and 33 miles from Berwick.

Jedburgh Abbey

Carter Bar to Edinburgh

Jedburgh, Melrose, Galashiels, Peebles

Of the half-dozen points at which the Border is generally crossed, this is easily the most romantic. The road comes up from Corbridge or Newcastle and for many miles runs across fine but in no way remarkable moorland. Then, almost imperceptibly, one begins to climb the Cheviots. Signboards announce 'the last hotel in England', Catcleugh reservoir is skirted—and suddenly at the top of a rise the whole landscape in front falls away to reveal a scene of great beauty, hills and valleys and woods, castles, churches, towns and villages innumerable being spread before one, and beside the road a simple board with dramatic touch reminds us that this is The Border (Carter Bar, 1,371 feet). As the road winds down the farther side there are further views of the wooded hills, and so to—

Jedburgh

Bowls and Tennis.
Caravans–Annan Caravan Site and Mossburnford (4 miles).
Distances–Edinburgh 48 m; Galashiels 16 m; Glasgow 85 m; Hawick 11 m; Kelso 11 m; London 325 m; Melrose 14 m; Newcastle 58 m.
Early Closing Day–Thursday.

Golf–9-hole Dunion Course.
Hotels–*Spread Eagle* (11 rooms), *Jedforest* (9 rooms), *Royal* (7 rooms).
Museums–Mary Queen of Scots House; The Abbey.
Population–3,850.
Swimming Pool–Laidlaw Baths.

Though there is less suggestion of the Border town in Jedburgh than in, say, Hawick, yet few places have had a closer acquaintance with the perils which beset the nearest town to a disputed frontier, particularly when that town boasts a very fine abbey. The chief town in the middle marches, its castle (now no more) was alternately held by English and Scots and the place was almost from its foundation in the ninth century a scene of constant strife and bloodshed. Not only the town acquired fame in warlike circles: Jedburgh men were to be found on many a battlefield wielding the 'Jeddart axe and staff' to such purpose that their war-cry 'Jeddart's here' struck terror into many a heart—

> Then rose the slogan, with a shout—
> 'To it, Tynedale, Jethart's here!'

Jedburgh Abbey from south-west

There was also 'Jeddart justice', that useful way of dealing with robbers and others which, like 'Lydford law', consisted in hanging a man first and trying him afterwards.

The Act of Union deprived Jedburgh of much of its importance as a Border town, and it is now occupied with the manufacture of woollen goods and precision tools.

Jedburgh Abbey (*open daily, fee*). The remains, still the most distinguished among the Border abbeys, are well seen from the road into the town from the south, though the best view is from the banks of the river to the left of the road. Founded by David I in the year 1118 for Canons Regular from Beauvais, the Abbey had a stormy history, being frequently involved in the incessant border frays. It was destroyed at Henry VIII's instigation when the Scots refused to betroth Mary Queen of Scots with Edward VI. A reformed church was built in the shell and used until 1875. (*Open 9.30–7, 2–7 Sundays; winter, 10–4, 2–4. Fee.*)

Only the Church of the Abbey remains, although in recent years excavations on the south side have disclosed remains of the cloistral buildings. The Church was a large cruciform building comprising nave, with side aisles, transepts and a choir with chapels. With the exception of the eastern end of the choir, the walls are fairly complete, and it is obvious that the building in its hey-day was of considerable beauty. The architectural styles range from the Norman piers in the choir to the Early English superstructure of the nave, but the architectural pride of the Abbey are the two late Norman doorways–that at the west end and that which led from the naive aisle to the cloisters. Unfortunately time has erased much of the finer detail work, but also in the south wall of the church a facsimile of the cloister doorway has been built. The cloister affords a splendid view of the south side of

48

the church, with its fine unbroken ranges of windows. Note also the excellent tracery in the window in the north transept. Attached to the building is a small *Museum* with an important collection of early sculptured stones.

Mary Queen of Scots House (*open daily, charge*) is reached by a lane leading off the main street. It is a substantial building and houses an interesting collection of the Queen's relics. It was while Mary Queen of Scots was here, holding assizes, that news was brought to her of Bothwell, lying wounded in Hermitage Castle, 25 miles distant. Characteristically she went to visit him, but the effort of riding there and back in a day brought on a fever to which she nearly succumbed.

Of the former Castle nothing now remains and the site is now occupied by a building erected in 1823 to serve as the county jail.

The old medieval bridge over the Jed with its three ribbed arches is most picturesque.

To the south-west of the town, and easily reached by the Hawick road, *Dunion Hill* rises 1,092 feet and affords splendid views. The walk could be continued over *Black Law* (1,110 feet) and Watch Knowe. The Waterloo Monument, $3\frac{1}{2}$ miles north at Penielheugh, is another good view-point. Those with time should explore the Jed valley for at least 3 miles up: that is to say, as far as **Ferniehirst Castle,** which as a stronghold of the Kerr family bore its share of border warfare. It is now a Youth Hostel. The

The 'auld brig', Jedburgh

original site of Jedburgh is at **Old Jedward,** some 3 miles farther up the valley.

Two miles north of Jedburgh the road forks: one branch running with the Teviot down to Kelso (p. 42), the other bearing westward for Hawick.

The Lauder-Edinburgh road turns out of the Hawick road in about a mile and crosses the river close to the hill crowned by the Waterloo Monument. This road follows the line of the Roman Dere Street and passes the battlefield of *Ancrum Moor* (1545), where the Scots defeated the English invaders. A few miles farther is **St Boswells Green** (*Buccleuch Arms*), on the banks of the Tweed at the point where it bends to enclose the remains of Dryburgh Abbey. A wide common links with St Boswells village.

Dryburgh Abbey

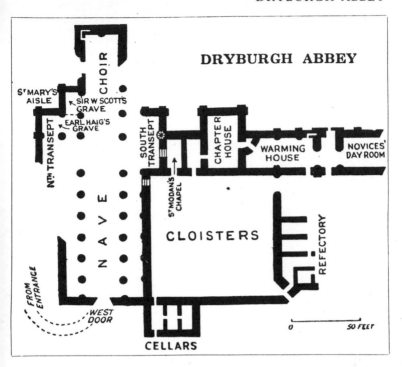

DRYBURGH ABBEY

St MARY'S AISLE

CHOIR

SIR W SCOTT'S GRAVE

EARL HAIG'S GRAVE

Nth TRANSEPT

SOUTH TRANSEPT

St MODAN'S CHAPEL

CHAPTER HOUSE

WARMING HOUSE

NOVICES' DAY ROOM

N A V E

CLOISTERS

REFECTORY

FROM ENTRANCE

WEST DOOR

0   50 FEET

CELLARS

Dryburgh Abbey

Access–A footbridge crosses the river to the Abbey from near St Boswells Green. The nearest road bridge is a mile or so downstream. Leave the main road at St Boswells Green, cross river to Clint Mains, where turn left, turning left at each subsequent choice of road. There is another road bridge at **Leaderfoot**, about 3 miles upstream, just below the lofty railway viaduct. After crossing this bridge turn immediately to the right, and to the right at each subsequent choice of road. This road gives good views across the river to the Eildon Hills, with the Bemersyde estate in the foreground.

Admission–Daily all the year round. In summer 10 am to 7 pm and 2–7 on Sundays; in winter the grounds are closed at 4 pm. Admission, *fee*.

Hotels–*Dryburgh Abbey* (licensed) at entrance to Abbey (34 rooms); *Buccleuch Arms*, St. Boswells Green; *Station*, *Dryburgh Arms* at Newton St Boswells.

This is surely the most beautiful of Scotland's many lovely ruins. The remains comprise portions of the Abbey church, to the south of which lie the cloisters, refectory, chapter house, and other buildings, but the chief delight of the place is its lovely situation in a bend of the river, surrounded by the greenest of lawns from which rise gracious trees of all kinds. The ruins themselves can be quickly seen, but Dryburgh is a place in which to linger.

The Abbey was founded about 1150 for Praemonstratensian canons from Alnwick. In course of time the community became very rich and powerful, but the proximity of Dryburgh to the Border brought it to the attention of successive invading armies and it was burnt and plundered four times in as many centuries. In 1919 Lord Glenconner presented the ruins to the nation, and the Department of the Environment now maintain it.

The remains need little description, though attention must be called to the richly-moulded west doorway of the church; the rose window at the west end of the refectory; the Chapter House, adjoining which are the vault of the Biber Erskines and St Modan's Chapel. St Modan is said to have been abbot of a monastery which stood here in the sixth century. A peculiarity of the buildings on this side of the cloister is that they are on different levels. Outside the Chapter House, and supported on props, is a very old juniper tree; on the other side, at the boundary wall, is a yew said to be coeval with the Abbey.

For many the most important part of the Abbey is on the north side of the Church, where are the graves of Sir Walter Scott (d. September 21, 1832) and of Earl Haig (d. January 29, 1928), the latter generally strewn with Flanders poppies.

On the hillside behind the Abbey is a colossal statue of Wallace.

The road from Dryburgh to Leaderfoot passes the **Bemersyde** estate, the residence of the Haig family since the days of Thomas the Rhymer, who uttered the prophecy:

> 'Tyde what may, whate'er betide,
> Haig shall be Haig of Bemersyde.'

An ancient Border tower forms part of the mansion, which with the adjoining lands was presented after the 1914–18 War, by his friends and admirers, to Earl Haig of Bemersyde.

From Bemersyde, Melrose can be reached by Newstead (p. 55) or alternatively by returning to St Boswell's for Newtown St Boswells and skirting the Eildon Hills. The kennels of the Buccleuch Hunt are located at Newtown St Boswells.

Melrose

Angling–In River Tweed for trout. Melrose Angling Association.

Bowls–Bowling club at Weirhill.

Caravans–Gibson Park.

Car Parks–Close to Abbey. Cars may also be left in the Market Square, a short distance to the south.

Distances–Edinburgh 37 m; Jedburgh 13 m; Dryburgh 4 m; Galashiels 4 m; Glasgow 73 m; London 337 m; Kelso 14 m; Selkirk 8 m.

Early Closing Day–Thursday.

Golf–9-hole course on Dingleton Common.

Hotels–*Burt's* (17 rooms), *King's Arms* (11 rooms), *Waverley Castle* (80 rooms), *George and Abbotsford* (20 rooms), *Bon Accord* (10 rooms), *Station* (3 rooms).

Population–2,200.

Tennis–Gibson Park (hard courts).

Melrose is a quiet little town on the southern bank of the Tweed which is much visited by those exploring the Scott Country. There are golf links

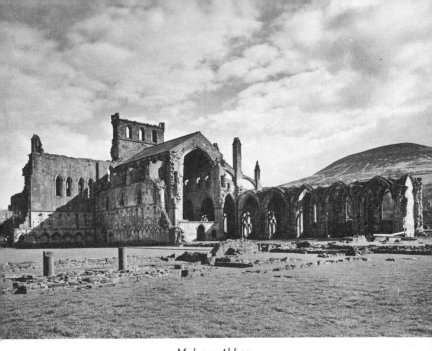

Melrose Abbey

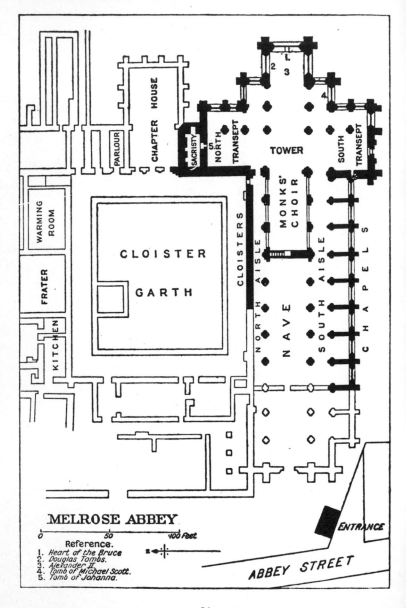

MELROSE ABBEY

Reference.
1. Heart of the Bruce.
2. Douglas Tombs.
3. Alexander II.
4. Tomb of Michael Scott.
5. Tomb of Johanna.

0   50   100 Feet

ABBEY STREET

ENTRANCE

and other amenities; to rugby enthusiasts it is the birthplace of the 'seven-a-side' form of the game; but it is, of course, on account of its **Abbey** that the place is best known.

Melrose Abbey (*open daily, fee*) was founded, like so many others, by David I early in the twelfth century and was occupied by Cistercians from Rievaulx Abbey in Yorkshire. Destroyed by Edward II, it was rebuilt from a grant made for the purpose by the Bruce and despite the hindrances caused by attacks from Richard II. A considerable part of the fabric belongs to the fifteenth–sixteenth-centuries. From 1545 it was subjected to the tender mercies of Reformers, Covenanters and natives who regarded it as a very convenient quarry whenever building-stone was required. The remains are now under the protection of the Department of the Environment, and much has been done to rid the grounds of unsightly encumbrances and generally to enhance and preserve this beautiful ruin.

The entrance lodge stands at the west end of the nave, the northern and western walls of which were long ago razed to the ground, though most of the south wall remains, with its series of chapels. Walking eastward we are confronted by the remains of the rood loft, passing which we are among high walls and can appreciate the former grandeur of the building. The Abbey is remarkable for the beauty and variety of its carved capitals: notice that over the clustered shaft adjoining the south-west pier of the tower. Notice, too, the splendid windows of the transepts and the great east window. In the vicinity of the High Altar, the heart of the Bruce was believed buried; a few yards westward lie the remains of Alexander II; to the north of them are tombs of the Douglases, and on the south, at the entrance to the sanctuary, is the tomb of Michael Scott, the Eildon wizard (*see* p. 59). North of the north transept was the sacristy, and in the doorway was buried Johanna, wife of Alexander II. From this point the extreme narrowness of the north aisle is well seen.

In recent years the Commendator's House and additional ground have been acquired and it has been possible to expose the foundations of an extensive range of domestic buildings to the north of the cloisters. The former magnificence of the place must be apparent even to the most hurried visitor; nevertheless, it is only to the leisurely examiner of its walls that the greatness of the Abbey is fully apparent.

In the churchyard are the graves of many of Scott's friends and retainers.

Newstead lies a mile east of Melrose on the south bank of the Tweed (*see* p. 52).

Melrose to **Dryburgh**–Follow Abbey Street, past the entrance to the ruins, northward, shortly swinging to the right. Through Newstead to the bridge at Leaderfoot, where cross the river and turn immediately to the right, taking the right-hand road at each subsequent choice. For Dryburgh *see* page 51.

Abbotsford

Melrose to Abbotsford

Take the main road westward out of the town. In about a mile this crosses the river by a picturesque bridge; for Abbotsford do not cross the bridge, but keep to the left, and in about a mile the house will be seen below the road on the right.

Abbotsford

Access – Abbotsford lies on the right bank of the Tweed about 3 miles to the west of Melrose from whence a good road runs as above. Cars can be hired at Melrose. On the other side of the river Galashiels is but 2 miles distant in a direct line, but vehicles must go upstream to Lindean or down towards Melrose in order to cross the river. About 4 miles south of Abbotsford is Selkirk, also with motor connections. Pedestrians can use the Galashiels–Melrose bus service to Abbotsford Toll, from whence it is a walk of 1½ miles. Various motor firms, notably in Edinburgh, organize 'Scott Country' tours, including Abbotsford.
Admission – Weekdays, 10–5. Admission charge. Open from April to end of October. Also Sunday afternoons 2–5.
Car Parking – Cars, etc., are left beside the road at the entrance to the path leading down to the house.

Strikingly beautiful in its situation, Abbotsford is of greater interest as the creation of Sir Walter Scott, and of hardly less interest as a veritable museum of authentic relics of the Scotland which Scott loved, wrote about and, in fact, made known to the world at large, for until the publication of the Waverley novels the Highlands were generally regarded as far beyond the pale of civilization. Scott acquired the estate in 1811, and at first contented himself with enlarging the then existing Newharthaugh Farm (Clarty Hole). Subsequently, however, he built the present mansion, and planted many of the trees which now lend such charm to the countryside around, and at Abbotsford he died in 1832.

Abbotsford is distinguished among a host of houses associated with famous figures in that almost every yard of it bears the impress of its creator; here is no collection of 'relics' scraped together with but little justification after Scott's death, but a wonderful assembly of arms, armour and the like, collected by himself during his lifetime and of which many pieces live eternally in his pages.

Attention will be attracted by the stone, half-way up the wall near the front door, inscribed:

> 'The Lord of armies is my Protector
> Blessit ar thay that trust in the Lord.   1575.'

This stone was the lintel of the old Edinburgh Tolbooth, the Heart of Midlothian, and is but one example of the manner in which historic relics have been incorporated into the house. The rooms shown include the Armoury and Entrance

ABBOTSFORD

Hall, crammed with weapons and armour, and with some pictures which we leave the guides to describe; Scott's Study, with its little 'speak-a-bit' closet containing the 'death mask'; the Drawing-room, with its century-old Chinese wall-paper and furniture, perhaps the least picturesque of the Abbotsford apartments; the Library, with Chantrey's bust of Scott, a case containing relics of Prince Charlie, Flora Macdonald, Rob Roy, etc.; and dining-room with lovely views of the river recalling Lockhart's picture of the scene in this room in September, 1832: 'A beautiful day; so warm that every window was wide open, and so perfectly still that the sound of all others most delicious to his ear, the gentle ripple of the Tweed over its pebbles, was distinctly audible as we knelt around the bed, and his eldest son kissed and closed his eyes.'

Sir Walter Scott belongs to the numerous company of great Scotsmen whose careers ended in tragedy. Born in Edinburgh on August 15, 1771, he developed in infancy an incurable lameness; and although this did not at any time daunt his spirit–his physical energy, for example, was prodigious, enabling him even in later life to walk 30 miles in a day or to ride a hundred without resting–the infirmity did undoubtedly help to intensify a natural love of reading. He would read everything that came his way, and in his early teens had probably read more (and, what is of greater importance, remembered more) than most men of three times his age.

In 1786 he was apprenticed to his father, a Writer to the Signet (a position more or less equivalent to that of an English attorney), but he seems never to have applied himself with much enthusiasm to the Law, although he was called to the Bar in 1792. In 1799 he became Sheriff-Deputy of Selkirkshire and in 1806 a Clerk of the Court of Session, both fairly lucrative posts, the latter especially making small claim upon his time. He wrote, but from the first he resolved to use literature 'as a staff and not a crutch'. His first publication, in 1799, was a translation of Goethe's *Götz von Berlichingen*; in 1802 the *Border Minstrelsy* was printed and published by his old school friend Ballantyne, whom he had met at Kelso–where also he had come across the copy of Percy's *Reliques* which made such a profound impression upon his youthful imagination. The *Border Minstrelsy* made Scott famous so that publication of *The Lay of the Last Minstrel* created something of a sensation. His fame rose higher with *Marmion* and *The Lady of the Lake*, of which 20,000 copies sold in a few months. The *Lady*, however, marked the zenith of Scott's popularity as a poet, and the publication of several other poems confirmed the fact that his popularity as a poet was actually waning. Scott had, however, already issued *Waverley*, and its success (notwithstanding the anonymity of the author) encouraged him to confine his attentions to novels. In that vein he had no rival, and for years the novels poured from his pen with wonderful regularity and, all things considered, equally wonderful maintenance of standard.

In 1797 he had married Charlotte Margaret Carpenter. Their first home was at Lasswade; subsequently they moved to Ashiestiel, on the Tweed. With his rising success in the literary world Scott bought the farm of Clarty Hole, between Melrose and Galashiels, changed the name to the far more appropriate (since it referred to the home of the author of *Waverley*) Abbotsford and proceeded to rebuild the place in accordance with the same feudal spirit. Few men of the time could have conceived and carried out such a plan. He bought many historical relics, but a greater number were showered upon him by admiring readers, and when in 1820 he was knighted his future must have seemed assured.

But tragedy was impending. Scott had not only made the reputation of Ballantyne's and Constable's, the printers and publishers; he had also accepted partnerships in both the publishing and the printing businesses of these firms; and when in 1826 these firms became bankrupt Scott found himself liable, through no fault of his own except an excess of generosity towards those he regarded as his friends, for debts amounting to something like £117,000.

With a brave boast to his creditors ('Time and I against any two') he turned his pen and his intellect to the production of works which would not only pay the debts of his partners, but would enable him to regain all that he had lost. In six years he had repaid £70,000, but the task was greater than even his physique and will-power could perform. In February, 1830, symptoms of paralysis appeared. He continued his writing and in 1831 was induced to go abroad in the hope of restoring his health, but the hope was vain, and from Rome he made his way back to Scotland in the knowledge that the end was near. A tablet beside the road near Galashiels records his delight at again setting eyes on the country he loved so well. A few hours later he was back at Abbotsford and there it was that he died on September 21, 1832.

The **Eildon Hills,** to the south of Melrose, are best appreciated at a little distance – they are very well seen from the Bemersyde road to Dryburgh. Although there is but one hill, there are three peaks (of which the highest rises 1,400 feet above the sea), a subdivision popularly attributed (*vide The Lay of the Last Minstrel*) to that Michael Scott who lies buried at Melrose and who, as a wizard, was condemned to find constant employment for a troublesome spirit. But alas! the partition of the Eildons was accomplished in a night, so that to find occupation for the spirit, Scott was forced to fall back on the manufacture of ropes from sand.

Roman remains have been found on the hills, which are commonly identified with the great legionary station of *Trimontium*. Each peak (the middle one has an indicator on its summit) is an excellent view-point, and it was Sir Walter Scott's boast that they commanded more than forty places 'famous in war and verse'. The ascent is quite easy: pass under the bridge beside the old Melrose station and climb the road to the golf links, beyond which are the three peaks. As for *Trimontium*, the site is marked with a large stone in the form of a Roman altar half a mile east of the village of Newstead, near Melrose. This was the largest Roman camp in the South of Scotland and several relics now in the National Museum of Antiquities, Edinburgh, were excavated there in 1908.

Melrose to Edinburgh, via Lauder

This is a distance of some 40 miles. The town is left by Abbey Street, shortly turning to the right for Newstead and the bridge at Leaderfoot, on the far side of which take the middle road (the road to the right leads to Dryburgh) and keep up the course of the Leader Water. Near **Earlston** are the remains of a residence of Sir Thomas Learmount, the prophetic poet of the thirteenth century, who is better known as Thomas the Rhymer, or Thomas of Ercildoune. Under the Eildon Tree (it was sited east of Melrose) he was wont to meet the Fairy Queen.

To Mellerstain House. From Earlston the A6105 road runs off north-eastward for **Gordon** and **Greenlaw**. In a little over a mile a right fork turns away eastward and then south-eastward for Kelso. A little way off this road is **Mellerstain House** (*open May-September, daily except Saturdays, fee*) the seat of Lord Binning. The mansion dates from 1725 and was begun by William Adam who was responsible for the two wings. Some 40 years later his famous son Robert Adam built the main block who was also responsible for most of the interior decoration seen today. There is a splendid library and a fine collection of paintings and antique furniture. From the grounds there is a wonderful view across the lake to the distant Cheviot Hills.

By our main route from Earleston it is 7 miles to—

Lauder

Angling—In the Leader and its small streams.
Bowls and Tennis.
Distances—Berwick-upon-Tweed 32 m; Coldstream 22 m; Edinburgh 27 m; Glasgow 71 m; Jedburgh 21 m; Kelso 17 m; London 346 m; Melrose 12 m.

Early Closing Day—Thursday.
Golf—9-hole course.
Hotels—*Lauderdale* (8 rooms), *Eagle* (6 rooms), *Loanside* (*guest*) (13 rooms), *Black Bull* (19 rooms).
Population—570.

Lauder is a small Royal Burgh situated in Lauderdale and dating from the days of William the Lion. It is in fact the only Royal Burgh in the county. A portion of the old town walls existed until 1911. An interesting survival is the system of old burgess rights and customs still maintained in the ancient burgh, and a Border Riding ceremony is still held annually. It was here that Archibald, 5th Earl of Angus, earned his title of 'Bell-the-Cat' by declaring his readiness to carry out the sentence of his fellow conspirators against Cochrane and others of James III's favourites who were hanged, it is said, from Lauder Bridge in 1482.

The unusual parish church is built on the plan of a Greek cross, has an octagonal steeple, and is thought to have been designed by Sir William Bruce. The old Tolbooth has a small flight of steps and a tower with a bell which is used to summon councillors to meetings.

Thirlestane Castle (*open May–September by prior arrangement*) is situated just outside the burgh. The seat of the Earls of Lauderdale, it is one of Scotland's oldest castles having been rebuilt from the late sixteenth century with additions by Sir William Bruce. It is now a splendid manor house, turreted and towered. There are fine gardens.

Westward from Lauder is a fine drive by a road which climbs to 1100 feet above sea level before descending to **Stow** on the Gala Water and the Galashiels–Edinburgh road.

From Lauder our road northward continues to climb over the Lammermuirs, the highest point (1,192 feet) being gained a mile or so short of **Soutra** (Soutra 'aisle', to the left of the road, is the remnant of a hospice which formerly stood here). From the hill there are grand views. As the road descends the northern flank of the range there is a fine prospect ahead, on a clear day, across the Forth to Fifeshire, the Forth Bridges showing up through the haze of 'auld Reekie' and Inchkeith keeping its lonely watch more to the right.

Thirlestane Castle

Melrose to Edinburgh, via Galashiels

The distance along this route from Melrose is 37 miles. Leave the town as for Abbotsford, but cross the river by the old bridge beyond **Darnick,** with its old peel tower built in 1425 and one of the few still in good preservation. The road now runs beside the Tweed, and then above the Gala Water.

On the outskirts of Galashiels a wall-tablet records that 'At this spot, on his pathetic journey from Italy home to Abbotsford and his beloved Borderland, Sir Walter Scott, gazing on this scene for the last time, "sprang up with a cry of delight", 11th July, 1832—Lockhart, chapter xxxviii'.

Galashiels

Angling—Long reaches of the Tweed and free fishing for trout in the Gala Water.
Bowls—Several greens, at Tweed Road, Scott Crescent and Kirkbrae.
Distances—Berwick-upon-Tweed 39 m; Edinburgh 33 m; Glasgow 69 m; Hawick 18 m; Jedburgh 16 m; Kelso 18 m; London 341 m; Peebles 19 m; Selkirk 6 m.
Early Closing Day—Wednesday.

Golf—18-hole course at Ladhope Recreation Ground.
Hotels—*Douglas* (26 rooms), *Maxwell* (17 rooms), *Abbotsford Arms* (7 rooms), *King's* (6 rooms), *Royal* (19 rooms), *Waverley* (9 rooms), *Kingsknowes* (12 rooms).
Population—12,500.
Tennis and Squash—Abbotsford Road.

Galashiels is a busy and prosperous industrial town on the Gala Water 4 miles north-west of Melrose. It is mainly concerned with the manufacture of tweed and woollen goods. There are a number of mills and some may be visited on prior application. The Scottish College of Textiles, the centre for higher education in textiles in Scotland, is situated in the town. The War Memorial is a clock-tower by Sir Robert Lorimer before which is a spirited piece of sculpture by T J Clapperton representing a Border 'Reiver', and which many will like to compare with the representations of the old reivers at Selkirk, Hawick and other places on the Border. The old Mercat Cross dates from 1695.

A Braw Lads' Gathering is a popular local festival held annually in the town in June. Galashiels is a very good centre for tours through the Scott Country and there are facilities for most sports.

From Galashiels the road traces the Gala Water towards its source in the hills, those on the east of the road being the Lammermuirs, the Moorfoots on the west. Pretty little Stow is passed, and still the road ascends, coming out finally on the high waste of Middleton Moor, from which it runs down to **Borthwick**, with a fine fifteenth-century Castle (*not open*). Mary Queen of Scots and Bothwell made this their retreat in 1567, and were here nearly captured by Morton, Mary having to escape in the disguise of a page.

Crichton Castle (*open daily except Fridays in winter, fee*) stands a mile to the north-east and is well-known to readers of *Marmion*. The grand ruin is one of the oldest and finest in Scotland. It overlooks the Tyne from a bare and lofty site. It comprises a fourteenth-century tower house to which were added several buildings in succeeding centuries to form a quadrangular mansion enclosing a courtyard. Of note is the arcaded range in Italianate style completed in 1591.

The parish church nearby dates from the fifteenth century.

West of the main road are the woods of Arniston Temple (the name recalling an early association with the Knights Templar) and the house from which Lord Rosebery takes his title.

Also to the west of the road is **Cockpen**, a district which yields at least a title to Lady Nairne's humorous song 'The Laird of Cockpen'; with Dalhousie Castle (now a school); **Lasswade**, where Sir Walter Scott lived for some years after his marriage and which is supposed to be the original of 'Gandercleuch' in the *Tales of my Landlord*; and **Hawthornden**, a modern residence on the site of an old one associated with William Drummond, the poet, who was here visited by Ben Jonson. (*No longer open to the public.*)

A mile or so south-west, and the goal of a delightful riverside walk from Lasswade or from Polton, is Roslin, with its fine chapel and castle ruin, (but see p. 175).

For Penicuik see p. 68.

Continuing from Borthwick towards Edinburgh the main road reaches Newbattle Abbey and Dalkeith both of which are described in the excursions section under Edinburgh (*see* Index). A more interesting way to Edinburgh passes Craigmillar Castle (*see* p. 157).

Ward Lock's
Red Guides

Edited by Reginald J. W. Hammond

Complete England

Complete Scotland

Complete Wales

Complete Ireland

Lake District (*Baddeley*)

Complete West Country

Complete Devon

Complete South-East Coast

Complete Yorkshire

Complete Scottish Lowlands

WARD LOCK LIMITED

Galashiels to Edinburgh
via Peebles

Along the breast of the hills westward of Galashiels runs the *Catrail*, a defensive work attributed to the Britons and originally consisting of a chain of forts connected by deep fosse and rampart. The terminal fort on Rink Hill commands lovely views over Tweeddale.

For the first few miles the road is occupied in swinging round the group of hills across which the Catrail runs. Then Tweeddale is entered at Caddonfoot, and across the valley is *Ashiestiel*, which was for some years the residence of Sir Walter Scott, prior to his removal to Abbotsford. It is charmingly situated against a background of hills–there are vivid descriptions of local scenery in the first four cantos of *Marmion*. The most interesting of the hills beyond Tweeddale is *Minchmoor* (1,856 feet): a short way north of the highest point is the Cheesewell, so called from the habit of travellers who dropped into its waters crumbs of cheese in order to propitiate the fairies reputed to haunt the spot.

By Walkerburn, busy with its woollen manufacture we come to–
Innerleithen (*Traquair Arms, St Ronans*) an attractive little place boasting medicinal springs which are claimed as the prototype of Scott's 'St Ronan's Well'. The town is a good centre for walks over the surrounding hills, and there is fishing in the Tweed and tributary streams. An excellent moorland road cuts through the Moorfoots by Glentress to join the Edinburgh–Galashiels road.

Across the Tweed from Innerleithen is–

Traquair House (*open afternoons except Fridays, July–September, Sundays from early May. Admission fee to house and/or grounds*) the oldest inhabited house in Scotland. Only the tower (reputed to be 1000 years old) dates from prior to Charles I's time. Either side of the main gateway are the carved bears mentioned in *Waverley* as the Bears of Bradwardine. The house is rich in fascinating souvenirs and romantic history, but perhaps the most interesting legends attach to the main gates, which were locked after the visit from Prince Charlie in 1745, never to be opened until a Stuart king comes to the throne.

Traquair House

Peebles

Bowls – Green near Drill Hall.

Distances – Edinburgh 23 m; Galashiels 19 m; Glasgow 50 m; Lanark 28 m; London 360 m; Moffat 33 m; Selkirk 21 m.

Early Closing Day – Wednesday.

Fishing – For trout and salmon in the Tweed and tributary streams, controlled by local angling associations.

Golf – 18-hole course. Clubhouse in Kirkland Street. Putting green at Tweed Green.

Hotels – *Hydro* (160 rooms), *Tontine* (30 rooms), *Cross Keys* (12 rooms), *Park* (24 rooms), *Venlaw Castle* (12 rooms), *County* (6 rooms), *Green Tree* (16 rooms), *Countryside* (10 rooms), *Cringletie House* (12 rooms) and others.

Market Day – Friday.

Population – 43,000.

Tennis – Peebles Lawn Tennis Club, Springhill Road.

A Royal Burgh since the fourteenth century, and the county town, Peebles is delightfully situated astride the Tweed. Screened on every side by hills, it has long enjoyed a reputation as a health and pleasure resort and is celebrated in the old Scots poem *Peblis to the Play*, ascribed to James I of Scotland. The *Cross Keys*, a quaint old hostelry, is the original of Cleikum Inn, and Miss Ritchie, who ran it in Scott's day, was the prototype of Meg Dods in *St Ronan's Well*. On the north side of the town are the ruins of the thirteenth-century **Cross Church**, all that is left of a monastic establishment which derived fame from possession of a fragment of the true Cross and the relics of St Nicholas of Peebles and to the patronage of James IV. The property is now under the care of the Department of the Environment (open).

Peebles was the birthplace (in 1800 and 1802) of William and Robert Chambers, the publishers, the former of whom presented to the town the Chambers Institution, a remarkable building once known as the Queensberry Lodging, where is said to have been born in 1725 the fourth Duke of Queensberry–'Old Q' of sporting fame–the 'degenerate Douglas' denounced by Wordsworth's sonnet for cutting down the fine woods around Neidpath Castle.

Neidpath Castle (*Easter to mid-October, daily, fee*) stands a mile westward of the town. It is finely situated at a bend in the Tweed and commands lovely views. Neidpath originally consisted of a plain peel tower. It belonged to the Frasers (cf. the carved strawberries over the courtyard gateway–French, *fraises*), who probably added the part which is now almost all that remains. In the eighteenth century the Castle was held by William Douglas, third Earl of March, who in 1778 succeeded as the Duke of Queensberry–'Old Q.'

A mile or so beyond the Castle a road crosses the Tweed and runs up to the village of Manor, whence it is less than a mile to the *Black Dwarf's Cottage*. David Ritchie, from whom Scott obtained his character, was a brush-maker whose misshapen figure was matched by an equally unfortu-

Peebles, across the Tweed

nate sourness of disposition, so that he was forced to become a recluse. As described by Scott, he built a cottage on this site, but his landlord rebuilt it a few years before his death (in 1811), since which the building has again been renewed. Ritchie was buried in Manor Churchyard. Strong walkers will find it a fine wild route up beside the Manor Water and over to St Mary's Loch, though the walk should not be attempted by solitary strangers when mist is about. (*See also* p. 85.)

Biggar (p. 87) can be reached from Peebles by taking the Neidpath road and branching off left just before Hallyne for Stobo. A little beyond this village are **Dawyck House Gardens** a beautiful woodland garden with rare trees and shrubs open to the public, *fee, daily during May and June*. Biggar is then reached by Broughton by the B7016.

The first few miles of the road from Peebles to Edinburgh are alongside the Eddleston water, past Eddleston village (*Black Barony*) to the moors about **Leadburn** (*Leadburn Hotel*), a haunt of anglers: in addition to various streams, there are the Gladhouse and other reservoirs (*apply Edinburgh Waterworks Department*).

From Leadburn the road runs down to **Penicuik** (Pen-y-cook: the hill of the cuckoo), a paper-making place on the North Esk a few miles below that part of the river known as *Habbie's Howe*:

> 'Gae far'er up the burn to Habbie's Howe,
> Where a' the sweets o' spring and summer grow.
> There, 'tween two birks out o'er a little linn,
> The water falls and makes a singing din;
> A pool breast-deep, beneath as clear as glass,
> Kisses wi' easy whirls the bord'ring grass.'

To reach Habbie's Howe and the neighbouring *Newhall House* (with its memories of Allan Ramsay's *Gentle Shepherd*) follow the Carlops road. For Habbie's Howe take the first opening on the left beyond Newhall gates.

Eastward from Penicuik is Roslin (p. 175). Hence to Edinburgh the road needs no description.

Carlisle to Edinburgh

The Route via Hawick

For the first few miles this route is identical with that *via* Beattock either to Edinburgh or Glasgow. At **Stanwix** (the Roman *Petriana*) the line of the Great Wall is crossed. Traces of the wall can be seen by digressing to the right, but the more impressive remains lie some way farther east, on the higher ground beyond Brampton and Castlesteads.

Two miles after crossing Carlisle's bridge over the Eden the Longtown and Hawick road keeps to the right at the fork. The Esk is crossed at Longtown, and beyond the railway level crossing go to the right. Ahead is seen the lofty Malcolm monument over Langholm; to the left is *Solway Moss* where in 1542 the Scots suffered a severe defeat. The news of the battle reached James V at Falkland at the same moment as tidings of the birth of Mary at Linlithgow, an ill-omened conjunction which the King summed up in the oft-quoted remark, 'It came wi' a lass, and it'll gang wi' a lass.'

The Border is crossed some 3 miles from Longtown at **Scotsdyke**: the point is marked by a small board bearing the word 'Scotland'–a welcome contrast to the long stream of advertisements along the Gretna road (*see* p. 79).

To **Hermitage Castle**. A little above Scotsdyke the Liddel Water joins the Esk, and for some miles marks the Border. Beyond Newcastleton, in Liddesdale, the valley of the Hermitage leads to **Hermitage Castle**, about 20 miles from Scotsdyke. The Castle (*weekdays,* 10–4 or 7; *Sundays,* 2–4 or 7; *fee.*) is one of the largest and best preserved in the Borders. Founded in the thirteenth century, it came into the hands of the Douglases, who exchanged it with the Earl of Bothwell for Bothwell Castle. It was Bothwell's illness here which brought Mary riding over from Jedburgh. From Hermitage a wild road across the Cheviots carries on to Hawick.

From Canonbie to Langholm the main road is at times very beautiful, running beside the tree-embowered Esk. In days past it was a favourite hunting-ground of Johnny Armstrong of Gilnockie, a notorious freebooter whose name was feared as far off as Newcastle, until James V took him at Carlenrig in Teviotdale and there hanged him and his company. The famous ballad suggests that the King acted dishonourably, but this is not so.

Hermitage Castle

Langholm

Distances – Carlise 21 m; Edinburgh 73 m; Glasgow 88 m; Hawick 23 m; Lockerbie 18 m; London 320 m; Longtown 12 m.
Early Closing Day – Wednesday.
Golf – 9-hole course.

Hotels – *Crown, Eskdale, Ashley Bank, Buck, Ardill House.*
Population – 2,400.
Tennis, etc.

Langholm is a pleasant town situated near the confluence of the Ewes and Wauchope Waters with the Esk. It is a good angling centre (Esk and Liddel Fisheries Association issues tickets) and there are some good walks over the neighbouring hills.

A Common Riding custom survives and is held towards the end of July whilst the September show is popular. The monument on Whita Hill, to the east of the town, commemorates General Sir J Malcolm (1769–1833), a governor of Bombay.

To **Eskdale.** The excursion from Langholm up Eskdale is especially pleasing. At Westerkirk in 1757 was born Thomas Telford, the engineer, and thence onward there are ample evidences of even greater engineers, for Roman camps and castles, or remains of them, are sprinkled to Eskdalemuir. (The Church is 600 feet above the sea.) Hence a wild road leads up the valley to Foulbog summit (1096 feet) and then down Ettrickdale to Tushielaw Inn (*see* p. 78). Walkers can continue along a rough track to Tibbie Shiel's, on St Mary's Loch (6 miles; *see* p. 77). Motorists reach St Mary's Loch *via* the *Gordon Arms Hotel* on the Selkirk–Moffat road.

Another good excursion from Langholm is beside the Wauchope Water and on into the vale of the Kirtle Water and so to Ecclefechan (*see* p. 79).

From Langholm to Hawick the main road at first follows the Ewes Water. Ewes hamlet is 4 miles out, and then the road begins the steep, relentless climb from pleasant Ewesdale to the grim uplands around **Mosspaul**, with *Wisp Hill* (1,950 feet) left of the summit. Beyond *Mosspaul Hotel* we cross the summit (853 feet) and enter Roxburghshire. Teviotdale is entered at the hamlet of **Teviothead**, with a pointed monument to Riddell, the poet (author of 'Scotland Yet'), and a churchyard wall bearing a tablet recording the burial of Johnny Armstrong of Gilnockie (*see* p. 69) and his 'galant companie'.

The rest of the way to Hawick by Teviotdale is pleasant going through the wooded vale.

Branxholm Tower, on the left as Hawick is approached, bravely bears the memory of the day when, as recorded in *The Lay of the Last Minstrel*—

> 'Nine and twenty knights of fame
> Hung their shields in Branksome Hall;
> Nine and twenty squires of name
> Brought their steeds to bower from stall.'

Langholm on the Esk

On the right is *Goldielands*, an old border peel; then on the left the Borthwick Water comes in, and so to—

Hawick

Angling – In River Teviot.

Distances – Carlisle 43 m; Edinburgh 51 m; Galashiels 18 m; Glasgow 83 m; Kelso 21 m; London 331 m; Newcastle-upon-Tyne 63 m; Selkirk 12 m.

Early Closing Day – Tuesday.

Golf – 18-hole course, Vertish Hill.

Hotels – *Buccleuch* (25 rooms), *Crown* (33 rooms), *Tower* (37 rooms), *Kirklands* (8 rooms).

Population – 16,280.

Swimming – Indoor pool.

Of all the Border towns Hawick seems best to have retained that air of aloofness so often found along debated frontiers. The main street is dominated by the fine tower of the town buildings, and at the far end is a stirring sculpture to the 'Callants' who in 1514 defeated an English force at Hornshole (*see below*) and captured their colours.

The Mote Hill, 450 feet high, is supposed to have been the meeting-place of the ancient Court of Justice. The *Tower Hotel* announces in its name that it incorporates a fragment of one of the fortified residences of Borderland. Hawick is a busy centre of mills for woollens, hosiery, etc, and is also a noted anglers' centre (Upper Teviotdale Fisheries Association). There are golf links and facilities for tennis, putting, etc, in the splendid Wilton Lodge Park. The annual Common Riding is held in June.

Hawick to Jedburgh (11 miles) – a charming road beside the Teviot. *Hornshole Bridge* ($2\frac{1}{2}$ miles) was the site of the 'Callants'' skirmish after Flodden; an encounter duly commemorated by a cross and the 'Common Riding'. **Denholm** was the birthplace of Leyden, the poet: a more celebrated 'son' was Sir John Murray, whose fame lives in the New English Dictionary. Across the river, *Minto House* (Earl of Minto) is backed by the Minto Crags, where are the ruins of Fatlips Castle. Southward rises the shapely *Rubers Law* (1,392 feet), on the east side of which is the valley of the Rule Water, up which a wild road (summit level 1,250 feet) leads over to Liddesdale and Newcastleton: an easterly branch runs off to Carter Bar (p. 47) and Catcleugh. Ahead as the main road approaches Jedburgh (*see* p. 47) is the Waterloo Monument above Jedfoot.

The Esk near Langholm

Hawick to Selkirk

The distance is 11 miles. The road calls for no special mention, being characterised by far-spreading views over mountain and moorland.

Selkirk

Distances– Edinburgh 39 m; Galashiels 6 m; Glasgow 71 m; Hawick 12 m; Jedburgh 17 m; Kelso 19 m; London 342 m; Moffat 34 m; Peebles 21 m.
Early Closing Day– Thursday.

Golf– 9-hole course.
Hotels– *County* (11 rooms), *Woodburn* (5 rooms), *Heatherlie Hill* (9 rooms), *Glen* (12 rooms), *Fleece* (10 rooms).
Population– 5,700.

Selkirk is well placed above the south bank of the Ettrick, and is a favourite resort of those walking or riding in the Border country.

There is golf and plenty of fishing and all around are places of interest and beauty. The Common Riding and races in June attract large crowds.

At the east end of the High Street is another of the inspiriting Border monuments of which Hawick and Galashiels provide examples. 'O Flodden Field' runs the inscription. It was erected in 1913 to mark the four-hundredth anniversary of the Battle of Flodden.

Selkirk is a very old town. It was incorporated as a Royal Burgh in 1535. A reminder of its antiquity is found on its coat-of-arms which portrays the Virgin and Child and the Royal Arms of Scotland with the Kirk of St Mary's in the background. In the early years of the twelfth century, King David, before ascending the throne, brought monks from France and founded a monastery in Selkirk, but after a stay of several years the monastery was removed to Kelso.

The souters (i.e. shoemakers) of Selkirk were famed for their single-soled shoes, a fact enshrined in the lines beginning:

'Up wi' the souters of Selkirk,'

but shoemaking has given place to tweed manufacture as the predominating local industry.

In the Market Place behind a statue of Sir Walter Scott stands the old Sheriff Courthouse (*apply Town Clerk*) used by Scott when Shirra of Ettrick Forest. In the High Street another statue portrays Mungo Park, the explorer, who was born at Foulshiels near the town in 1771 (*see below*). A tablet in the Public Library brings a timely reminder that Selkirk was also the birthplace of Andrew Lang (d. 1912), and there is a good memorial bust of Tom Scott, RSA, the artist. Selkirk no longer has a train service; it is linked with Galashiels by bus.

For the road through the Ettrick Forest to Moffat, see p. 77.

Selkirk

Selkirk to Galashiels

The Edinburgh road now runs along the eastern bank of the river for 2 miles. At **Lindean** it crosses the Ettrick Water (the road to the right at the entrance to the bridge leads prettily to Abbotsford in about 2 miles), and shortly after that it crosses the Tweed just above the point where that river joins the Ettrick Water. Near Abbotsford Ferry a glimpse will be caught of Abbotsford House, across the river, and then the road swings round Gala Hill to Galashiels.

For a description of Galashiels and the routes on to Edinburgh, *see* pp. 62–8.

Near the Grey Mare's Tail

76

Selkirk to Moffat

Selkirk is at the eastern edge of the **Ettrick Forest**—a grand region of mountain and moor, loch and burn, through which runs the road to Moffat (34 miles; *bus but no railway*). From Selkirk Market Place go down the suggestively-named West Port, where stood the old Forest Inn, visited by Burns. Cross the bridge and keep to the left. On the right is *Philiphaugh*, where Leslie defeated Montrose in 1645, and on the left is soon seen the gaunt ruin of **Newark**, 'renowned in Border story'. Between Selkirk and Newark is the Duke of Buccleuch's estate, Bowhill. A cottage at Foulshiels, almost opposite the remains of a bridge leading across the river to Newark Castle, was the birthplace of Mungo Park. On Broadmeadows (now a Youth Hostel) came down the old drove road over Minchmoor (*see* p. 65).

On by **Yarrowford** the scenery is very lovely. Yarrow Church is passed, and the Yarrow Feus (feu=rent or lease), and then comes the intersection with the roads from Innerleithen (to the north: *see* p. 65) and Tushielaw and Ettrick, 7 miles southward. This point is at the entrance to a neighbourhood celebrated in the history of Border minstrelsy. Mount Benger, half a mile north of the Gordon Arms, was for some time farmed by James Hogg, the 'Ettrick Shepherd' (*see below*). **Dryhope Tower**, above the road on the right near the foot of St Mary's Loch, was the home of Mary Scott, the 'Flower of Yarrow'. A little farther along is the ruin of 12th-century **St Mary's Kirk**, with a quietly beautiful burying-ground, well known to lovers of Border ballads; and on the narrow isthmus separating St Mary's Loch from the Loch of the Lowes is **'Tibbie Shiel's'**, which by the witchery of Scott, Christopher North (who made it the scene of so many *Noctes Ambrosianæ*), De Quincey, Aytoun, Lockhart, not forgetting James Hogg, arose from a humble cottage to a famous hostelry. 'Tibbie Shiel' (Mrs Richardson), the first hostess of the place, must be credited with at least as much of the transformation, for she was a 'character' capable of holding her own with the great ones. She died in 1878 and lies buried near Hogg in Ettrick Churchyard.

A hilly road goes up the Meggat Water and over to Tweedsmuir by Talla Reservoir (*see* p. 85).

St Mary's Loch is a beautiful sheet 3 miles long and about half a mile wide. In depth 80 to 90 feet it is 808 feet above sea-level, and is easily accessible by road. There is excellent fishing for trout, pike and perch (*Tibbie Shiel's*, the *Rodono* and *Gordon Arms Hotels* provide boats, etc).

On the hill-side just above the isthmus dividing the two lochs is a monument to James Hogg, the Ettrick Shepherd.

A track crossing the isthmus climbs to 1,405 feet and joins the road from the *Gordon Arms* down to Ettrick Dale at **Tushielaw**, whence it is 3 miles up the valley to **Ettrick Church**, beside which Hogg was born and in the churchyard of which he was buried. Tushielaw (*inn*) is 15 miles from Selkirk by Ettrickbridge (*hotel*).

James Hogg (1770–1835), the 'Ettrick Shepherd' of Wilson's *Noctes Ambrosianæ*, was the son of a farmer. His education appears to have been very slight, but at the age of about 25 he took to writing verse–'songs and ballads made up for the lassies to sing in chorus.' His first poems were published anonymously, but subsequently he made the acquaintance of Sir Walter Scott, and as the result of encouragement from that kindly quarter he gave up shepherding and moved to Edinburgh to embark on a literary career. Although he has been acclaimed as 'after Burns, the greatest poet that had ever sprung from the bosom of the common people', and the *Edinburgh Review* hailed him as 'a poet in the highest acceptance of the term', he seems to have been beset by constant financial difficulties. He died in 1835 at the farm of Altrive, a couple of miles up the road from the *Gordon Arms* to Tushielaw, and, as already stated, was buried in Ettrick churchyard.

Beyond Tibbie Shiel's the Moffat road passes **Loch of the Lowes** and runs between steep hill-sides for some 3 miles. Then, on the right, a glimpse is caught of the **Grey Mare's Tail**, a magnificent cascade, one of the highest and finest in Scotland–now in the care of the National Trust. Although it can be seen from the road, a closer view amply repays the stroll of a few hundred yards to the mouth of the little glen into which it tumbles. The water comes from wild **Loch Skeen**, between White Coomb (2,695 feet) and Lochcraig Head (2,625 feet): a path strikes up the steep hill-side to the loch from a point about a mile below the road bridge near the Grey Mare's Tail (*see also* p. 83).

For the remainder of this route *see under* Moffat.

Carlisle to Edinburgh (or Glasgow) via Beattock

Throughout most of this route the road and the railway keep close company. The road distances are: to Beattock, 40 miles, to Edinburgh 93 miles, and to Glasgow 96 miles.

This is the best known of the various routes over the Border, but in point of picturesqueness the first 20 miles north of Carlisle do not compare with similar stages on the Carter Bar or Coldstream crossings. Two miles beyond the bridge over the Eden, the road keeps to the left (that to the right leads to Longtown and Hawick, *see* p. 69). Four miles farther the Esk is crossed, and then the bridge over the little River Sark which here actually links the two countries. The road is devoid of romance today, if one may judge from appearances, but for centuries it has been famed as the way to **Gretna Green** (*Hall*), and many a fine race between runaway couples and thwarted parents has been decided along this straight and almost level stretch of road. Formerly hasty young couples could be married at a moment's notice by the smith at Gretna, since Scottish law recognised as man and wife a couple who had made a plain declaration before witnesses, but since 1940 it has been necessary for both parties to qualify by a residence of at least fifteen clear days in Scotland before giving notice of intention to marry. Marriages still take place at Gretna. Not only Gretna, but Coldstream and Lamberton also were noted for runaway marriages. Originally the Gretna 'ceremonies' took place in the village, but with the erection of a new toll bridge over the Sark, business was attracted to the toll-house, since it lay only a few yards over the Border and often only a few yards spelt the difference between victory and defeat. Both the old 'Smithies' are open to visitors at a fee and contain various relics of Gretna in its hey-day.

Disregarding the road westward to Annan and Dumfries (*see* p. 179) continue by Kirkpatrick and Kirtlebridge to **Ecclefechan** (*Ecclefechan*), where Thomas Carlyle was born in 1795 and in the churchyard of which he was buried. His birthplace, 'The Arched House', contains a number of relics and is open on weekdays from 10 to 6 (National Trust). Readers of *Sartor Resartus* will have small difficulty in recognising 'Entephul'.

LOCKERBIE

Hoddam Castle, a few miles south-west of Ecclefechan by a lovely avenue which Carlyle named 'the kindly beech rows', was the original castle of Scott's *Redgauntlet*. On the hills north-east of the village is *Burnswark*, worth visiting on account of the views over Solway and for its numerous remains of camps and forts indifferently ascribed to Hadrian and Agricola.

Six miles farther is –

Lockerbie

Distances – Abington 33 m; Annan 11 m; Carlisle 25 m; Dumfries 13 m; Edinburgh 68 m; Glasgow 70 m; Langholm 18 m; London 324 m.
Early Closing Day – Tuesday.
Golf – 9-hole course.
Hotels – *Somerton House* (11 rooms), *Blue Bell* (12 rooms), *Crown* (6 rooms), *Lockerbie House* (40 rooms), *Dryfasdale* (15 rooms), *Townhead* (10 rooms).
Population – 2,900.
Sports – Bowls, tennis, golf, ice rink for skating and curling, indoor bowls, hunting.

Lockerbie is a small market town in a prosperous agricultural area, its cattle market being one of the most important in the Border country. There are good facilities for various sports. The district is hunted by the Dumfriesshire Foxhounds and the county otterhounds.

Park and Boat Pond, Moffat

Lockerbie to Dumfries. A road runs off westward from Lockerbie for Dumfries crossing the Annan close to its junction with the Dryfe Water, and skirting Castle Loch. A little beyond is **Lochmaben** the scene in 1593 of the last great contest between feudal houses on the Border, the Johnstones defeating the Maxwells in a savage contest which is commemorated in the phrase 'a Lockerbie lick'.

The Castle of Lochmaben, now a shapeless ruin, claims to have been the birthplace of the Bruce (1278). The Castle loch is said to contain ten different kinds of fish, among them being the vendace, a small white fish somewhat resembling a dace (French: *vandoise*), which takes no bait and is only found in this and two adjacent lochs. The fish is netted in August.

Nearby is Hightae Loch also with good fishing. Both lochs provide good sailing opportunities.

From Lochmaben the road continues for 14 miles to Dumfries, passing **Torthorwald** where is a little Cottage Museum (*key at nearby cottage*) fronted by a period herb garden.

From Lockerbie our route skirts the eastern side of Annandale, pregnant with memories of Border frays. At Beattock the main road from Dumfries comes in on the left. That for Moffat goes off on the right.

Moffat

Distances–Abington 18 m; Carlisle 41 m; Dumfries 21 m; Edinburgh 52 m; Glasgow 54 m; Lockerbie 16 m; London 340 m; Peebles 33 m; Selkirk 34 m.
Early Closing Day–Wednesday.
Golf–18-hole course.
Hotels–*Buccleuch Arms* (17 rooms), *Annandale Arms* (24 rooms), *Moffat House* (14 rooms), *Balmoral* (18 rooms), *Star* (12 rooms), *Auchen Castle* (26 rooms).
Population–2,050.
Sports–Bowls, tennis, golf, fishing in numerous burns, in Loch Skene, St. Mary's Loch and the Loch of the Lowes.

Moffat is a very attractive little town near the head of Annandale and with good scenery on every hand. The discovery of mineral springs in the middle of the eighteenth century first attracted visitors, and although the place is now more generally known as a splendid centre for hill-walkers, anglers, golfers and motorists, it is still faintly reminiscent of Cheltenham in the gardened villas which augment the accommodation offered by the hotels.

At Moffat House, James Macpherson ('Ossian Macpherson') stayed during 1759, probably spending part of his time in working upon the poems which subsequently caused such controversy. Burns was also at Moffat, and is credited with writing on the window of the Black Bull Hotel the following comment aroused by the sight of two ladies who passed, the one small and dainty, the other more broadly built:

'Ask why God made the gem so small,
And why so huge the granite
Because God meant mankind should set
That higher value on it.'

Hart Fell

In the churchyard is the grave of J L McAdam, the roadmaker, whose name is perpetuated, though now only in abbreviated form, in the second syllable of the word 'tarmac'.

Two miles south of Moffat is *Three Waters Meet,* where the Evan and Moffat Waters contribute their stream to the Annan. On the way are passed the Standing Stones, of which little seems to be known, and just beyond is Loch House Tower, an old square fortress with an echo from the high-road.

Westward from the Crawford road at Beattock the Garpol Water makes a pretty little glen with waterfalls (the ruin is that of Auchencat Castle, once held for the Bruce), and on the other side of the Moffat Water, near the Three Waters Meet, is Bell Craig Linn, another pretty spot; farther south is Wamphray with its pretty glen. But the prettiest thing of the kind in the neighbourhood is **Raehills Glen**, about 8 miles from Moffat on the Dumfries road.

The tapering hill of **Queensberry** (2,285 feet), 8–9 miles south-west of Moffat, commands a wide view, but the ascent in itself is less interesting than that to White Coomb and Hart Fell (*see* p. 83). The route is by a side road from Beattock Bridge to Earshaig and Kinnelhead, where cross the stream, turn left, and pass in front of a cottage. The mountain shortly comes into full view and further directions are unnecessary.

The left-hand road at the foot of Moffat Market Place runs out into **Moffat Dale**, down which the Moffat Water rushes through scenery that in the lower parts of the glen is very pretty. The upper parts are somewhat bare; forming a fitting prelude to the beauties of Yarrow, beyond **St Mary's Loch** (*see* p. 77). Between 2 and 3 miles from Moffat the road crosses the picturesque *Craigie Burn* (*private*). Here lived Jean Lorimer, heroine of nearly a dozen of Burns's love songs. A house rather more than half a mile farther on occupies the site of an ale-house in which 'Willie brew'd a peck o' maut' is supposed to have been written. As the road proceeds Saddle Yoke (2,412 feet) presents on the left a peaked appearance that is unusual in these parts.

From Bodesbeck Farm a walking route strikes up the eastern side of the valley into Ettrick Dale (about 10 miles to Ettrick Church; another 6 over the hills down to Tibbie Shiel's; longer by the road past Tushielaw).

Just under 10 miles from Moffat is the **Grey Mare's Tail**, for which and the route on to St Mary's Loch and Selkirk *see* pages 77–8.

To **White Coomb and Hart Fell** – This is the best hill excursion in the immediate neighbourhood of Moffat. A whole day should be allowed unless a lift can be arranged as far as Birkhill, on the Selkirk road, at the top of the rise beyond the Grey Mare's Tail. The footpath which leaves the road here soon vanishes, and one takes a westerly direction to the ridge, keeping the burn that drops into Dobs Gill considerably below on the left. The ridge gained, White Coomb appears in front and soon afterwards **Loch Skeen** shows itself below, amid wild scenery with screes descending steeply to its upper end. At the southern end are ancient moraines through which the Tail Burn makes its way to form the **Grey Mare's Tail** (*see* p. 78). Make for this end of the loch and continue westward to a long green slope, beyond which is the almost level plateau of grass forming the top of **White Coomb** (2,695 feet). From White Coomb to Hart Fell is a walk of $1\frac{1}{2}$–2 hours along the northern edge of the coombes that furrow the range from Moffat Dale. The views are good: especially that down the valley of the Blackhope Burn. **Hart Fell** (2,651 feet) is even more of a plateau than White Coomb; its summit is distinguished by a cairn attached to which is a small stone enclosure. There is a fine prospect of the rich lowland country from this point. Westward the Devil's Beef Tub and the Edinburgh road are conspicuous, but those who descend that way will find a deep hollow to be crossed about half-way. The best way of prolonging the hill walk is to return to Moffat by a path (a couple of cairns mark the way) down the shoulder that has the Auchencat Burn on the left and passes above Hart Fell Spa.

Moffat to Edinburgh

At the northern end of Moffat the Edinburgh road diverges to the left, crosses the Annan and begins the steep climb which does not cease for 7 miles and which carries it to 1,348 feet above sea-level. On the way up there are charming views back over Moffat, and at *Holehouse Linn* (2½ miles) a road on the left strikes over the hills to the main Glasgow road through **Evandale** (*see* p. 87). Two miles farther we look down into the **Devil's Beef Tub**, a remarkable green basin, 500 or 600 feet deep, with abrupt sides broken only by an outlet on the south, through which the infant Annan finds a way. In origin it recalls the corries of the Highlands, a terminal valley widened and deepened by glacial action. The name is said to have been derived from the fact that the Johnstones used the place as a pound for stolen cattle. In *Redgauntlet* the place is described as a 'd . . ., deep, black, blackguard-looking abyss that goes straight down from the roadside as straight as it can do'; and pictures the Laird of Summertrees escaping from his captors by rolling from top to bottom 'like a barrel down Chalmers' Close in Auld Reekie'.

A mile beyond the Tub the road crosses the watershed at a height of 1,334 feet and shortly after passes to the left of *Tweed's Well*, the source of the Tweed. The road then follows the left bank of the Tweed and 15 miles from Moffat reaches **Tweedsmuir** (*Crook Inn*), south-east of which is the **Talla Reservoir** (Edinburgh water supply). At the head of the reservoir in 1682 took place the Covenanting conventicle at which Davie Deans was present, as described in *The Heart of Midlothian*. *Drumelzier*, to the right of the road, is often pointed out as the burial-place of Merlin, but the grave near the Kirk covers the remains of Merlin Caledonius and not Merlin Emrys, the great Welsh Bard.

The road through Drumelzier reaches Peebles (p. 66) in about a dozen miles, passing on the right the remains of Tennis Castle, the Church of Dawyck and on the left **Stobo**, with a church containing much Norman work. Then comes **Lyne**, with a tiny church containing some good Flemish woodwork and with some standing stones and the remains of a Roman Camp. On the hill south of the village over a footbridge across the Tweed is *Barns Tower*, a sixteenth-century stronghold now a youth hostel. The road from Barns to the south which joins the road along Manor Valley brings one in 2 miles to the Black Dwarf's Cottage (*see* p. 67) and provides a good walk over the hills to St Mary's Loch (*see* p. 77). For Peebles and the road on to Edinburgh, *see* pages 66–7.

The road beside the Lyne Water leads in about 3 miles to the ruins of *Drochil Castle*, a project of the Regent Morton's which was never completed owing to his death.

From Broughton the Edinburgh road strikes northward to Blyth Bridge (*Blyth Bridge Hotel*), on past the picturesque hamlet of Romanno Bridge, and so by Leadburn to Penicuik and Edinburgh as described on page 68.

Covenanters' Memorial and Devil's Beef Tub

Looking towards Tinto Hill

Carlisle to Edinburgh via Biggar

As far as Beattock, the route from Carlisle is as described on pages 79–80, but instead of turning off to the east for Moffat it follows the Evan Water through the narrow valley. (Motorists who wish to include the Devil's Beef Tub in this route may do so at the cost of only slight extra mileage by going through Moffat to the 'Tub' as described on page 83.) From the Tub retrace the route for a couple of miles to the road which turns off at Holehouse Linn and descends to the Evan valley about 5 miles short of the summit, which is 1,029 feet above the sea. Just beyond this point the infant Clyde is crossed, and a mile or so farther we definitely enter Clydesdale.

From Elvanfoot two fine mountain roads go westward to Nithsdale, the Clyde being crossed by a bridge about a mile below the village. That running south-west from the village goes through the Dalveen Pass (*see* p. 183) to Thornhill; the more westerly road, less suitable for motoring, goes to Sanquhar by Leadhills, Wanlockhead and the Mennock Pass (*see* p. 185).

Crawford (*Hillview*, *West End*) is a roadside village with numerous walks and excursions at hand.

Abington (*Hotels: Abington, Arbory*), 5 miles beyond Elvanfoot, is near an important parting of the ways: from the village a road on the left goes across to Hamilton (*see* p. 219) and about 2 miles beyond it the main road forks, the Biggar–Edinburgh road crossing the river, the Tinto–Lanark road keeping to the western bank.

(a) The road which crosses the Clyde about 2 miles north of Abington follows the river downstream and then by Culter reaches **Biggar** (*Elphinstone*, *Hartree*), a small town spread out along one wide street. It was the birthplace of Dr John Brown (1810–82), author of *Rab and His Friends* and other works popular reading in his time, and was also the home of early branches of the Gladstone family. Biggar is a clean, pleasant little place at which to stay, being a fair centre, among bracing surroundings, and with golf, fishing, bowling and other sports.

Half a mile beyond Biggar the road forks: that on the right goes by Skirling to Leadburn (*see* p. 68); straight ahead is the route by Dolphinton to West Linton and Carlops, on the eastern slopes of the Pentlands, and so to Edinburgh.

(b) The road which keeps to the west side of the Clyde below Abington and running round **Tinto**, 2,335 feet, leads to Lanark. But a little over 9 miles from Abington a sharp right turn is made into a minor road which runs by Wolfclyde to join the Biggar road a little way beyond Causewayend.

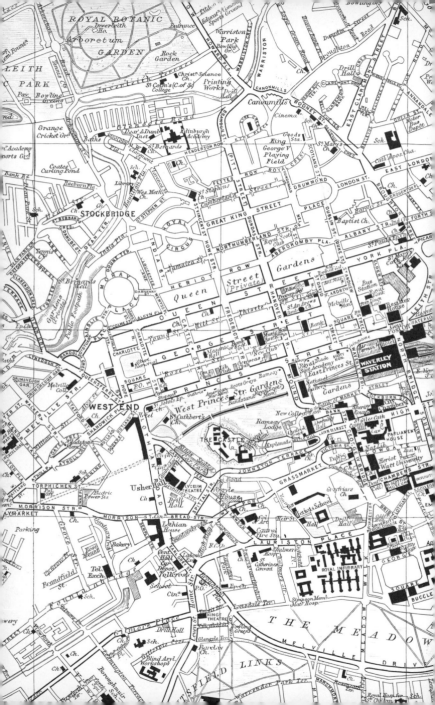

CENTRAL EDINBURGH
SCALE OF HALF A MILE
0   ¼   ½

WARD LOCK LIMITED. LONDON.
© – John Bartholomew & Son Ltd. Edinburgh

Princes Street, Edinburgh

Edinburgh

Airport – At Turnhouse (A9) about 6 miles west from Princes Street, reached by the Corstorphine road (A8) via Maybury.

Banks – *Bank of Scotland*, Bank Street (Head of Mound). *Royal Bank of Scotland*, 42 St Andrew Square. *British Linen Bank*, 38 St Andrew Square. *Clydesdale Bank*, chief Edinburgh Office, 29 George Street. *Edinburgh Savings Bank*, 28 Hanover Street.

Buses and Coaches – Routes traverse the City and connect the outlying parts with the centre. In the season Corporation and other coaches make circular tours of the City and its surroundings.

Throughout the year *Scottish Omnibuses Ltd*. (Eastern Scottish) run buses (green and cream) at short intervals to towns and villages in the Lothians, including Musselburgh, Loanhead, Lasswade, Roslin, Penicuik, Dalkeith, Eskbank, Gorebridge, Tranent, Haddington, North Berwick, Dunbar, Balerno, Midcalder, Bathgate, Linlithgow, and to South Queensferry (for the Forth Bridge). Regular bus services are also maintained to London; to Newcastle and Carlisle, Berwick, Kelso, Jedburgh, Hawick, Moffat and Dumfries; to Glasgow (including an express service); to Stirling, Callander and Crieff; to Perth, Dundee, Aberdeen and (in summer) Inverness and Oban. Long distance services are operated to London, Blackpool, Manchester, Liverpool, Bournemouth. Services are also operated over the Forth Bridge to Dunfermline, Kirkcaldy and Leven. Besides these services, coaches run daily (Sundays included) during the tourist season to Melrose, the Scott Country and St. Mary's Loch, the Trossachs, the Burns Country, etc. These all start from St Andrew Square. Booking and Enquiry Offices are located in the Square.

Cinemas – The principal cinemas in the centre of the city are the *ABC* (Lothian Road), *Playhouse* (Greenside Place), *Caley* (Lothian Road), *Odeon* (Clerk Street), *Cameo* (Tollcross), *Jacey's* (news) is in Princes Street.

Concert and Lecture Halls – *Usher Hall*, Lothian Road; *Music Hall*, 54 George Street; *McEwan Hall*, New University, Teviot Row; *Assembly Hall*, Mound; *Central Hall*, Tollcross; *Freemasons' Hall*, 96 George Street; *Leith Town Hall*, Ferry Road. The BBC Studio is at 5 Queen Street.

Early Closing – On *Monday*, fishmongers close at 1 o'clock; on *Tuesday*, drapers and jewellers; on *Wednesday*, bakers, butchers, grocers, chemists, hairdressers and stationers. Shops of the kind in Princes Street and other fashionable quarters usually close instead at 1 o'clock on *Saturday*. Many of the leading stores now open late on Thursday evenings.

Festival – During latter half of August and early September. Intending visitors should bear in mind that early booking, both for performances and for accommodation, is essential. A useful programme of events is issued about April and booking begins soon afterwards. Application should be made to the *Festival Office, 21 Market Street, Edinburgh, 1;* or to the usual tourist agencies.

Golf –

Public Courses

Braid Hills. Two 18-hole courses: No. 1 among the famous municipal courses in Britain. No Sunday play on Braids. Other municipal courses at Carrickknowe, Silverknowes, Craigentinny (Leith) and Portobello.

There are numerous putting-courses throughout the city, notably those on *Bruntsfield Links* (clubs and balls available), where too is a 36-hole pitching-course. This is one of the early homes of golf.

Private Courses in or near Edinburgh

On many of these visitors require an introduction. Green-fees vary. During the Festival a number of clubs extend the courtesy of the green to visitors; application should be made to the Festival Club Information Bureau. Sunday play is allowed on almost all private courses. Of over a dozen such courses within the city bounds the best-known are: **Barnton** (*Royal Burgess Golfing Society*), **Bruntsfield** (at Davidson's Mains: *Bruntsfield Links Golfing Society*), **Duddingston**, **Mortonhall** and **Murrayfield**.

EDINBURGH

Hotels–Few places in Britain can boast hotels more palatial and comfortable than those of Edinburgh. The largest are mostly located in or near Princes Street, but throughout the city there are establishments of every grade. We append a list of some of the principal.

CENTRAL DISTRICT

North British, Princes Street (East End). (204 rooms) Tel.: 031-556 2414.

Darling's Regent, Waterloo Place. (U) (50 rooms) Tel.: 031-556 4125.

Mount Royal, 53 Princes Street. (156 rooms) Tel.: 031-225 7161.

Royal Circus, Royal Circus. (42 rooms) Tel.: 031-225 4051.

Edward, 58 Great King Street. (U) (12 rooms) Tel.: 031-556 1154.

Royal British, 20 Princes Street. (47 rooms) Tel.: 031-556 4901.

Shelbourne, Hart Street. (U) (140 rooms) Tel.: 031-556 2345.

Adelphi, Cockburn Street. (60 rooms) Tel.: 031-225 1520.

Carlton, North Bridge. (89 rooms) Tel.: 031-556 7277.

Craigholme, 12 Royal Circus. (20 rooms) Tel.: 031-225 3788.

Maitland, Shandwick Place. (25 rooms) Tel.: 031-229 1467.

George, 19 George Street. (90 rooms) Tel.: 031-225 1251.

Gordon, 7 Royal Circus. (U) (29 rooms) Tel.: 031-225 3000.

Old Waverley, 43 Princes Street. (89 rooms) Tel.: 031-556 4648.

Gloucester, Gloucester Place. (11 rooms) Tel.: 031-225 2378.

Glencairn, Royal Circus. (27 rooms) Tel.: 031-225 7777.

Menzies, Royal Terrace. (10 rooms) Tel.: 031-556 6055.

Donmaree, 21 Mayfield Gardens, 9. (25 rooms) Tel.: 031-667 3641.

Park, Royal Terrace. (12 rooms) Tel.: 031-556 1156.

Arden, 18 Royal Terrace. (25 rooms) Tel.: 031-556 5879.

Raeburn, Royal Terrace. (12 rooms) Tel.: 031-556 4588.

Royal Abbey, Carlton Terrace. (27 rooms) Tel.: 031-556 1189.

County, 9 Abercromby Place. (55 rooms) Tel.: 031-556 2333.

Abercromby, 32–3 Abercromby Place. (34 rooms) Tel.: 031-556 1063.

Clifton Private, Clifton Terrace. (U) (10 rooms) Tel.: 031-337 1002.

Scotia, Great King Street. (50 rooms) Tel.: 031-556 3266.

Palace, 1 Castle Street (41 rooms) Tel.: 031-225 6222.

Minto, 18 Minto Street (32 rooms) Tel.: 031-667 1534.

Oratava, 41 Craigmillar Park. (20 rooms) Tel.: 031-667 1182.

Prestonfield House, Priestfield Road. Tel.: 031-667 3479.

WEST END

Angus House, Lynedoch Place. (U) (8 rooms) Tel.: 031-225 5251.

Buckingham, 7 Buckingham Terrace. (14 rooms) Tel.: 031-332 1436.

Caledonian, Princes Street. (174 rooms) Tel.: 031-225 2433.

Crown, Torphichen Street. (25 rooms) Tel.: 031-229 1144.

Dean, Clarendon Crescent. (12 rooms) Tel.: 031-332 1052.

Grosvenor, 19 Grosvenor Street. (160 rooms) Tel.: 031-225 5255.

Roxburghe, 38 Charlotte Square. (72 rooms) Tel.: 031-225 3921.

Douglas, Douglas Crescent. (U) (22 rooms) Tel.: 031-225 4931.

Dorchester, 18 Clarendon Crescent. (24 rooms) Tel.: 031-332 2256.

Learmouth, 18 Learmouth Terrace. (200 rooms) Tel.: 031-332 1795.

Pirie's, Coates Gardens. (19 rooms) Tel.: 031-337 1108.

Palmerston, 56 Palmerston Place. (15 rooms) Tel.: 031-225 3468.

Rutland, Rutland Street. (19 rooms) Tel.: 031-229 3402.

West End, Palmerston Place. (11 rooms) Tel.: 031-225 3656.

Yester, Coates Gardens. (U) (9 rooms) Tel.: 031-337 1029.

Forres, Forres Street. (U) (10 rooms) Tel.: 031-225 5066.

Saxe Coburg, Saxe Coburg Place. (5 rooms) Tel.: 031-332 1050.

Adam, Lansdowne Crescent. (12 rooms) Tel.: 031-337 1148.

Highfield, Magdala Crescent. (U) (9 rooms) Tel.: 031-337 1004.

Green's, 24 Eglinton Crescent. (U) (40 rooms) Tel.: 031-337 6311.

Barnton, Queensferry Road (30 rooms) Tel.: 031-336 2291.

Clarendon, Grosvenor Street. Tel.: 031-337 1154.

Murrayfield, Corstorphine Road (23 rooms) Tel.: 031-337 2207.

Queensway, 1 Queensferry Road. Tel.: 031-332 6492.

BRUNTSFIELD AREA

Bruntsfield, Bruntsfield Place. (59 rooms) Tel.: 031-229 1393.

Leamington, 75 Leamington Terrace. (17 rooms) Tel.: 031-229 2761.

Merchiston, 12 Merchiston Crescent. (U) (10 rooms) Tel.: 031-229 3086.

MORNINGSIDE AREA

Braid Hills, Braid Road. (70 rooms) Tel.: 031-447 6291.

Iona, 17 Strathearn Place. (9 rooms) Tel.: 031-447 6264.

Barra House, Greenhill Terrace. (U) (8 rooms) Tel.: 031-447 3197.

Information Centres, etc. – *Tourist Information and Accommodation Service*, 1 Cockburn Street, EH2 (031-226 6591). *City Transport Centre*, Waverley Bridge (031-556 5656). At the General Post Office and the Central Public Library also during the Festival season at the Festival offices, 21 Market Street (031-229 1432). The offices of the *Scottish Tourist Board* are in Rutland Place (031-229 1561) and *BEA* (Reservations) 135 Princes Street.

Other useful addresses are:

Automobile Association, 18-22 Melville Street (031-225 6591)

British Council (Scottish Office), 3 Bruntsfield Crescent

Citizens' Advice Bureau, 58 Dundas Street (031-556 6179)

English Speaking Union, 22 Atholl Crescent

French Institute, 13 Randolph Crescent

National Trust for Scotland, 5 Charlotte Square

Royal Automobile Club, 17 Rutland Square (031-229 3555)

Royal Overseas League and House, 100 Princes Street

YMCA, 14 South St Andrew Street

YWCA, 116 George Street.

Parking Places – There is normally limited accommodation on the south side of Princes Street. The principal parking places in the vicinity of Princes Street are: The Mound (weekdays only); Charlotte Square (parking meters); George Street (in centre: meters); St Andrew Square (meters); Rutland Square; St James's Square; Queen Street (between Hanover Street and Frederick Street); Abercromby Place, Heriot Row; Atholl Crescent; Coates Crescent; Castle Terrace; Lady Lawson Street; Johnston Terrace; King's Stables Road; Grassmarket; Blenheim Place; West Market Street; Chambers Street (centre).

Population – 453,400.

Post Office – General Post Office in Waterloo Place, at the east end of Princes Street. There are large sub-offices in Hope Street (West End), Frederick Street and Broughton Street.

Restaurants – The large hotels have restaurant service, as do the principal stores and bakery shops. The following offer good fare: *Albyn*, 77 Queen Street; *Apéritif*, 24 Frederick Street; *Beehive*, 18-20 Grassmarket; *Café Royal*, 17 West Register Street; *Epicure*, 19 Shandwick Place; *Handsel*, Stafford Street; *White Cockade*, 55 Rose Street.

Theatres – *Lyceum*, Grindlay Street; *King's*, Leven Street; *Adam House*, Chambers Street; *Church Hill*, Morningside Road; *Traverse*, Grassmarket.

Youth Hostels – The Scottish Youth Hostels Association, whose Edinburgh Office is at 7-8 Bruntsfield Crescent, has well-appointed hostels there and at Hailes House, Lanark Road, Kingsknowe (Corporation bus No. 44, also SO Ltd).

Principal places of interest

Botanic Garden and Arboretum, Inverleith Row. Free, from 9 am (Sunday, 11 am) till sundown. Hothouses, 10 am (Sunday, 11) till 5 pm.

Canongate Tolbooth. Weekdays, 10-5. Charge.

Castle. *Admission fee.* Open weekdays, 9.30-6 pm all apartments; 6-9 pm precincts only. These hours apply May to October inclusive – hours slightly shorter in winter and during Tattoo period. Sundays from 11 am.

City Museum, Huntly House, Canongate. Weekdays, 10-5; also (in summer Wednesdays, 6-9; closed Sundays except during Festival when it is open 2-5. *Admission fee.*

Holyroodhouse, Palace of, and Chapel Royal. *Historical and State Apartments:* Open daily. *Admission charge. Hours:* 9.30 (Sunday, 11) till 6; in winter, 9.30 (Sunday, 12.30) till 4.30. During Royal Visits and at General Assembly time (mid-May–mid-June) the Palace is closed to the public.

John Knox's House, High Street. Weekdays, 10–5, *admission fee.*

Lady Stair's House, Lawnmarket. Weekdays, 10–4; Saturday, 10–1; 10–5 daily during Festival; closed Sunday except during Festival when it is open 2–5. *Admission fee.*

Museum of Childhood, Hyndford's Close, High Street. Weekdays, 10–5 and Sundays during Festival, 2–5. *Admission fee.*

National Gallery, The Mound. Free. Weekdays, 10–5; Sunday, 2–5. During Festival, 10–8.

National Library of Scotland, George IV Bridge. Free. Reading Rooms for purposes of reference and research open daily, 9.30–8.30; Saturday, 9.30–1. Exhibition open daily, 9.30–5; Saturday, 9.30–1; Sunday, 2–5; and during the Festival in addition, every day (except Sunday) till 8.30.

National Museum of Antiquities of Scotland, Queen Street. Free. Weekdays, 10–5; Sunday, 2–5 (later during Festival). **Museum Gallery,** 18 Shandwick Place. Weekdays, 10–5.

Nelson Monument, Calton Hill. Open daily, 10–7: October–March, 10–3: closed Sundays. *Admission fee.*

Outlook Tower, Castle Hill. Open April–October, 10–6. Sunday, 12.30–6. *Admission fee.* Café.

Parliament House, Parliament Square. Daily (during the sitting of the Courts), 10–4.30; Saturdays, 10–12.30. Free.

Public Library, George IV Bridge. Reference, Fine Art, Music, and Edinburgh and Scottish departments. Open daily, except Sundays.

Register House. Daily, 9.30–4.30. Saturday, 9.30–12.30. Free.

Royal College of Surgeons Museum, Nicolson Street. Free. Open to the Medical Profession daily, 9–5, Saturday, 9–12. Public admitted by special permission only.

Royal Scottish Academy, Mound. Annual Exhibition held from late April until early August. Reopens later in August for special Festival Exhibition. Weekdays, 10 am–9 pm, Sundays, 2–5 pm. *Admission fee.*

Royal Scottish Museum, Chambers Street. Free. Daily, from 10 till 5; Sunday, 2–5 p.m. Tea room except Sundays.

St Giles Cathedral, High Street. Daily, 10–5. Free. Thistle Chapel, *admission fee.* Sunday services at 11 and 6.30.

Scottish National Gallery of Modern Art (Royal Botanic Gardens). Open 10–6, Sundays 2–5. Free.

Scottish National Portrait Gallery, Queen Street. Free. Open weekdays, 10–5; Sunday, 2–5.

Scottish National War Memorial. *See* under Castle.

Scott Monument, Princes Street. Open daily, April 1–September 30, from 10–7, Sunday, 1–7; October 1–March 31, from 10–3; closed Sundays. *Admission fee.*

Signet Library, Parliament Square. Open on weekdays from 10–4; Saturday, 10–12.

Sports Centres – Meadowbank Sports Centre, London Road, daily 9–11; Royal Commonwealth Pool, Dalkeith Road, daily; Hillend Ski Centre, daily.

University, South Bridge. Open free daily. *Library:* admission on written application.

Zoological Park, Corstorphine. Open 9–7 in season (Sunday, 12–7); other months 9 (Sunday, 12) till sundown. *Admission fee.* Aquarium, charge. Restaurants. Car park.

In and about Edinburgh

Edinburgh–'the grey metropolis of the North'–need fear no rival in its claim to be the most picturesque and beautiful city of the British Isles. Its site and its buildings combine to give it a visual appeal that is immediate and irresistible, at all hours of the day, at all seasons of the year.

But the city has other claims on our attention. No other place in Britain save London can boast of greater historical interest or more intimate association with important events and famous personages. It has been the scene of some of the most stirring episodes in the national life, and in our own day the annual *International Festival of Music and Drama* has added a new attraction to the city's proud record.

Edinburgh is essentially a city of impressions: splendid buildings, spacious streets, narrow closes, high tenements, restoration of old buildings, side by side. Washington Irving said of the view from Castle Hill: 'Nowhere else can you see so well the contrast between the character of the two towns–the Old and the New–the latter gay and glittering like a section of Paris as seen from Notre Dame, smiling as if there were no such things as death and change in the universe; the other with the shadows of a thousand sad memories mingling with the light of other days upon it, sombre, sublime, silent in its age.' Scott summed up the subtle witchery of the city in the memorable phrase, 'Mine own *romantic* town'.

The long, ridgy line of the Old Town ending with the lofty Castle Rock– to the geologist a classic example of 'crag and tail' formation; the towering tenements and spires; the Calton Hill, with its Nelson Tower and Parthenon-like 'National Monument'; the New Town's broad streets and squares, with churches, columns, statues and graceful domes; the lion-like outline of Arthur's Seat, with the natural embattlements of Salisbury Crags; the enframing Firth of Forth and Pentland Hills–all go to make up a picture of infinite variety and beauty.

Princes Street

This beautiful promenade, admitted to be unsurpassed in Europe, might more appropriately have been named 'Princes Terrace'; with the exception of a short section at its eastern end, it is certainly a terrace rather than a street. It is slightly under a mile in length–1,579 yards, to be exact–from its junction with Shandwick Place to the Register House. One side is occupied by shops, big and little, hotels, restaurants, dignified clubs, banks and offices; the other, almost entirely devoid of buildings, commands extensive and beautiful gardens, in which are statues and monuments to Edinburgh's 'mighty dead'. Beyond is an unbroken view of the towering Castle Rock – no less entrancing by floodlight – and the lofty ridge of the Old Town.

The eternal glory of Princes Street is its view, which is picturesque in the highest degree as we stand in front of the Register House and look westward.

The **General Post Office** occupies the site of Shakespeare Square, where stood the Theatre Royal in which Mrs Siddons performed.

The Register House (*Admission, see* p. 94). The Register House contains the principal records of Scottish law and government from earliest times to the present day. The famous Robert Adam (1728–92) was the architect and the Register House remains the finest of his public buildings and a model of functional architecture. It is also one of the first buildings in Europe to be erected as a self-contained archive repository.

The task of preserving the records and making them accessible to the public is that of a government department, known as the Scottish Record Office. There are two public search rooms for consultation of the records. Under the central dome, which has a fine Adam ceiling, lawyers and professional searchers consult modern legal records. In the Historical Search Room which is in the north range designed by Robert Reid in the 1820s, historical enquirers study records which stretch in date from the twelfth century to the twentieth.

Public exhibition facilities are provided at the new West Register House, a conversion of the former St George's Church, Charlotte Square.

Behind the General Register House is the **New Register House** (1859–63). It is used, among other purposes, for housing the registers of births, deaths and marriages. Here also is the Court of the Lord Lyon King of Arms, the Scottish Government department for armorial bearings and genealogies. In West Register Street the *Café Royal* maintains old traditions with its lobster bar. In attic lodgings in St James's Square, entered by East Register Street and now involved in 'redevelopment', Burns pined for his Clarinda in 1787–88.

In front of the Register House is an equestrian **Statue of the Duke of Wellington,** by Sir John Steell, R.S.A. Behind this statue of 'the Iron Duke in Bronze by Steell' is a clock, electrically controlled, giving exact Greenwich time. Here, too, is a helpful plan of Central Edinburgh – one of several displayed in the city. Opposite the Register House is the splendid *North British Hotel* (the 'NB'), erected (1902) by the North British Railway Company from plans by Hamilton Beattie. Its conspicuous clock tower is nearly 200 feet high.

For a note on the **North Bridge,** *see* p. 135.

To the west of the hotel are steps leading down to the **Waverley Station,** which ranks among the largest in the world, covering an area of $25\frac{3}{4}$ acres, of which 13 are under roof. The total length of the platforms is about $2\frac{3}{4}$ miles.

The top of the **Waverley Steps,** running down into the station, has the reputation of being one of the windiest corners in Britain, especially when the wind blows from the south-west quarter.

Scott Memorial

Immediately to the right of the steps is the **Waverley Market,** its roof laid out in *parterres* and clumps of shrubbery. The market (1872) serves on occasion as a hall for monster meetings, shows, carnivals and what not.

A little westward, the **Waverley Bridge** leads down to the station and up *via* Cockburn Street to the High Street. Built in 1872–73, the bridge was enlarged in 1894–95. It is the starting-point of the Corporation bus tours. At its southern end are the Festival Offices and Accommodation Bureau. The Corporation Enquiry Office is at the Princes Street end.

The **East Princes Street Gardens**–with an esplanade level with the street and about a hundred feet wide–extend from the Waverley Bridge to the Mound. At all seasons the flower-beds in these gardens are a beautiful sight and in spring the slopes are gay with crocuses or dancing daffodils. At their eastern end is a bronze *Statue of David Livingstone*, missionary and explorer of Central Africa. A few yards farther, facing St David Street, is–

The Scott Monument, an open Gothic cross or tower, 200 feet high. The central spire is supported by four arches which form a canopy, beneath which is a figure (floodlit at times) of Sir Walter Scott, in grey Carrara marble, by *Sir John Steell*. Scott (born in Edinburgh, August 15, 1771) is shown seated, wrapped in a shepherd's plaid, with his favourite hound, Maida, at his feet.

Above the centres of the first arches are niches filled by statuettes; on the north, Prince Charles Stewart; south, The Lady of the Lake; east, Meg Merrilees; west,

The Last Minstrel. All over the monument are represented the principal characters in Scott's poems and in the Waverley Novels. An interior staircase leads to a series of open galleries, encircling the spire, commanding a magnificent view of the city. (A certificate of attainment ($2\frac{1}{2}$p) is issued to any person who climbs the 287 steps – a feat which, while being perfectly safe, requires a good 'head'.) The architect was *George Meikle Kemp*, a young self-taught artist, who had travelled through Europe, studying Gothic architecture and supporting himself by working as an ordinary mason. He was accidentally drowned before the completion of the work in 1844. The monument, which cost only £16,154 7*s*. 11*d*., was inaugurated on August 15, 1846.

A little to the west of the Scott Monument is a *Statue of Adam Black,* founder of the publishing house of A & C Black, who for two terms (1843–48) was Lord Provost of the city and who also served as its representative in Parliament. Adjoining is a *Statue of Professor John Wilson* (1785–1854), the 'Christopher North' of *Blackwood's*. At its foot abound tame pigeons.

The **Mound,** a huge accumulation of earth, bisects the noble valley above which tower the Castle and the Old Town. Known in 1781 as 'Geordie Boyd's Mud Brig', it became the depository for the rubbish from the foundations of the streets laid down in the New Town, and by 1830 had grown into the mighty mass we see today. Underground electric heating safeguards traffic in winter.

On the lower part of the Mound (whence, incidentally, is a particularly fine view of the Castle) are two important public buildings, the old *Royal Institution*, Doric in style, with its façade (surmounted by a huge statue of Queen Victoria) on Princes Street, and behind it, Ionic in style, the National Gallery; both were designed by *W. H. Playfair* (1789–1857). In 1910, the interior of the Royal Institution, which till then had housed the Royal Society of Edinburgh, was entirely reconstructed and the building is now occupied by the **Royal Scottish Academy** (founded 1826). Periodical Exhibitions of the works of living artists and special Festival and Commemorative Exhibitions are held here. The permanent Diploma Collection of the Academicians is also housed in it.

Behind the Royal Scottish Academy is–

The National Gallery (*Admission, see* p. 94). The collection consists of European paintings from the fourteenth century to about 1900 and British paintings of the seventeenth to nineteenth centuries. There are several sculptures, including works by Degas, Rodin and Maillol.

Outstanding among the earlier works are the panels painted by Hugo van der Goes about 1478 for the Collegiate Church of the Holy Trinity, Edinburgh; these are lent by HM The Queen. Three scenes from the life of St Nicholas by Gerard David show the more intimate side of the early Flemish genius. From Florence there is Andrea del Sarto's appealing Self Portrait, and from Venice Bassano's large and glowing 'Adoration of the Kings' and Tiepolo's 'Finding of Moses', the finest work by this artist in Britain. The few Spanish pictures include two fine El Greco's, Velazquez' 'An Old Woman Cooking Eggs', and works by Zurbaran and Goya.

Notable seventeenth-century works from northern Europe include Rubens' 'The Feast of Herod', Rembrandt's 'A Woman in Bed', Vermeer's early 'Christ in the House of Martha and Mary' and Ruisdael's 'The Banks of a River'. Claude's largest surviving canvas, 'Landscape with Apollo and the Muses', was painted in Rome in the same century. Later French paintings include Watteau's exquisite 'Fêtes Vénitiennes' and works by Chardin, Lancret, Boucher, Greuze, Corot, Delacroix and Courbet. Impressionist and post-impressionist paintings include works by Monet, Sisley, Degas, Renoir, Cézanne, three fine Gauguins, van Gogh, Bonnard and Vuillard.

Since 1946, thirty of the finest paintings from the Bridgewater House collection have been kindly lent by the Duke of Sutherland. Among them are a group of Raphaels, four superb Titians, two Tintorettos, eight Poussins (including seven paintings of the Sacraments), and a group of Rembrandts.

English paintings include two landscapes by Gainsborough and his 'The Hon Mrs Graham', Reynolds' 'The Ladies Waldegrave', Constable's 'Dedham Vale' and Turner's 'Somer Hill'. Scottish painting is fairly fully represented: special mention may be made of Allan Ramsay's portraits of his second wife and Jean-Jacques Rousseau and of Raeburn's 'Sir John Sinclair', but there are other notable works by these artists and by Geddes, Wilkie, McTaggart and many others.

On the west side of Hanover Street, which meets Princes Street at the Mound, are the Merchants' Hall and Offices of the Merchant Company (founded in 1681), and the headquarters of the Edinburgh Savings Bank (1940: founded 1836).

Beyond the Mound are the **West Princes Street Gardens,** another picturesque expanse, embracing the Castle Hill (northern and eastern slopes) and the valley at the foot of the rock. They occupy what was formerly the bed of the *Nor' Loch*, an item in the scheme of defence formulated by James II in 1450. In 1816 a statute was passed for the beautification of the 'North Loch Valley'. The Gardens were laid out under the direction of Sir Walter Scott's friend, James Skene of Rubislaw.

The gardens contain a *Fountain* (1869) and the *Ross Bandstand* (1935). In summer, concerts, games, dancing, etc., attract large gatherings to the Bandstand. Close to the Mound is a *Statue of Allan Ramsay* (1686–1758), the poet of 'The Gentle Shepherd', and father of the portrait-painter. Below it, in the holiday season, is a large *Floral Clock* of ingenious design. Electrically driven, it incorporates some 20,000 plants and has a diverting cuckoo. Towards the railway is the *Royal Scots Monument* (unveiled in 1952). Designed by Sir Frank Mears, it consists of a series of monoliths arranged in a curve and bearing the proud record of the First Regiment of the Line, and a telling excerpt from the Declaration of Arbroath. Opposite Frederick Street is an equestrian memorial to officers and men of the *Royal Scots Greys* who fell in the South African War (1899–1902).

On the Garden Walk, farther west, facing the Castle Rock, will be found the *American Memorial* to Scots who laid down their lives in the 1914–18 War, presented by subscribers in the United States of Scottish blood or sympathies. The work (1927) of Professor R. Tait McKenzie, this shows the seated figure of a young kilted soldier, gazing upward, and emblematic of youthful aspiration, military ardour and patriotic devotion. The background takes the form of a frieze of Scottish troops and volunteers from every walk of life and grade of society, led by pipers and drummers, all marching in answer to 'The Call'.

Near the western end of the gardens are bronze statues of *Sir James Young Simpson* (1811–70), the eminent physician and popularizer of chloroform as an anæsthetic, and of the *Rev Dr Thomas Guthrie* (1803–73), the founder of Ragged Schools.

At the west end of Princes Street is **St John's Episcopal Church,** a fine Later Gothic structure. It has a beautiful interior (*open daily* 7.45 am–9.30 pm). At the rear, facing Princes Street, is a Celtic cross in memory of *Dean Ramsay* (1793–1872; author of *Reminiscences of Scottish Life and Character*, a classic of humorous literature), who was for many years incumbent here. Scott's mother and Sir Henry Raeburn (1756–1823), the portrait-painter, are buried at the east end of the church. Round St John's—as along Princes Street—benches have been placed. Those on the south side look out on Lothian Road and the Churchyard of **St Cuthbert's** or the **West Kirk** (described on p. 128), with the massive Castle Rock as background.

Up the Mound

Having gained a first impression of Princes Street, we branch off at the foot of the Mound and ascend the slope which leads to the Old Town. Where Market Street and Bank Street meet is a monument to the memory of General Wauchope and officers and men of the *Black Watch* who fell in the South African War.

Overlooking Princes Street is **New College,** the seat of the Faculty of Divinity of Edinburgh University, and a Theological College of the Church of Scotland, designed by W H Playfair. Constructed (1846–50) round a large open quadrangle, the edifice contains lecture rooms, a senate hall, students' hall, dining hall (Rainy Hall) and Martin Hall. Since 1936, the adjacent High Church building has been adapted as the College Library, a notable collection of 150,000 books or more. In the quadrangle is a *Statue of John Knox*, by John Hutchinson, R.S.A., erected 'by Scotsmen who are mindful of the benefits conferred by John Knox on their native land'. A broad flight of steps leads to the **Assembly Hall,** wherein the annual General Assemblies of the Church of Scotland take place during May, attended by the Lord High Commissioner as the representative of the sovereign. The hall, erected in 1859, as reconstructed, is capable of holding over 2,000 persons, and has been used, during the Festival, for apron-stage productions. The architect utilized with rare skill the noble spire (240 feet in height) of the Tolbooth Parish Church—long used as the Established Church Assembly Hall—on the Castle Hill immediately behind, so that it seems at a distance to be an integral part of the building, a happy anticipation of the Union of the Churches seventy years later.

Emerging from the quadrangle through the barbican-like groined archway, we climb the steep slope of Mound Place and Ramsay Lane. Adjoining Ramsay Lane on the right are Ramsay Garden and **Ramsay Lodge,** where Allan Ramsay, the poet, retired to spend the evening of his life, in what his friends teasingly called the 'Goosepie'. The house was enlarged by Allan Ramsay, the painter, after his father's death. Incorporated (1887) in a University Hall of Residence by Sir Patrick Geddes and after the Second World War taken over as a training college by the Royal Bank of Scotland, Ramsay Lodge, viewed from Princes Street, presents an imposing appearance.

The Castle and Lawnmarket

At the top of Ramsay Lane we reach that fine approach to the fortress, the **Castle Esplanade,** about 140 yards in length and 100 in breadth. For centuries this was the scene of executions by axe and by stake. Lady Jane Douglas (Lady Glamis)—one of the most beautiful women of her time—who was accused of attempting James V's life by poison and sorcery, was here burned to death in sight of her son and her second husband, Archibald Campbell of Skipness. The real crime was that of being a Douglas. Here, too, scores of witches were 'worryit at the stake' (strangled and burned), often after scanty or no trial. A small tablet fountain (on the right as we step on to the Esplanade) commemorates their sufferings.

The open space was for long the favourite promenade of the citizens; and many eighteenth-century songs refer to 'Walking on the Castle Hill'. The Esplanade assumed its present form between 1816 and 1825. (There is no direct access from the adjoining Princes Street Gardens. On the south side steps mount to the Esplanade from Johnston Terrace. The only vehicle entrance is by Castle Hill, which leads up from where the Lawnmarket and Johnston Terrace meet.)

On the right-hand side of the Esplanade as one approaches the Castle are half a dozen monuments to Scottish regiments and soldiers, including one to *Field-Marshal Earl Haig,* Commander-in-Chief of the British Expeditionary Forces in France and Belgium during the 1914–18 War—an equestrian statue by G E Wade, presented by a Bombay Parsee, Sir Dhunjibhoy Bomanji. An impressive tombstone nearer the Castle entrance covers the mortal remains of *Ensign Ewart.* 'Sergeant Ewart of the Greys' won fame at Waterloo by capturing, single-handed, the Eagle of the 'crack' French 45th Infantry Regiment (now in the Scottish United Services Museum).

A plaque on the wall of the *Moat* records that near this spot, in 1625, the Earl of Stirling received sasine or lawful possession of the Province of Nova Scotia and thereafter the Scottish Baronets of Nova Scotia likewise received sasine of their distant Baronies. For the purpose, Scottish earth and Nova Scotian earth were declared one. A handful of real Nova Scotian earth was sprinkled into the Moat by the Prime Minister of the Province when he unveiled the plaque in 1953.

Since the withdrawal of the Garrison in 1923, the picturesque sight of Highland or other regiments drilling on the Esplanade is rarely enjoyed, but the Changing of the Guard on certain days brings troops in from Redford Barracks and provides a military pageant that never fails to appeal. The old office of Governor of Edinburgh Castle was revived in 1936 and the handing over of the key at a royal visit or the Governor's

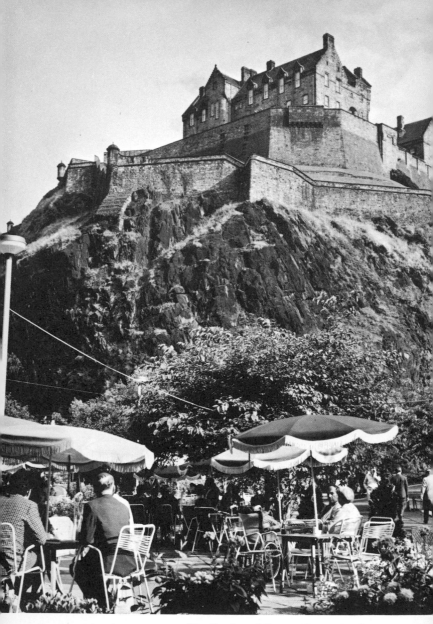

The Castle and Princes Street Gardens

installation is the occasion of another picturesque ceremony on the Esplanade. Here too, during the Festival, an impressive Military Tattoo, with Highland dancing and other displays, is held after nightfall by searchlight and floodlight.

Edinburgh Castle

(**Admission**, *see* p. 94). In the season a bus runs from Waverley Bridge to the Castle *via* the Mound and Lawnmarket.)

The Castle is entered by the **Drawbridge** over the dry Moat. In niches on either side of the gateway stand bronze statues of *Bruce* and *Wallace*, the national heroes of Scottish independence. The sculptor of Bruce was T J Clapperton, Wallace being the work of Alexander Carrick.

We pass through a strong battlemented gateway (tickets are available at the office which faces us) and leaving the Guardhouse proceed up the ascent. Gateway and Guardhouse have taken the place of the **Outer Port**. The pathway literally cuts its way through the solid rock, into which have been set commemorative panels to William Kirkcaldy of Grange, who defended the Castle for Queen Mary in 1568–73, and to Randolph, Earl of Moray, who escaladed the Rock in 1315, and took the English by surprise.

The steep narrow path leads us to the **Portcullis Gate** and about it the **State Prison**, otherwise known as **Argyll's**, or the **Constable's Tower**, a portion of the defensive works erected by David II about 1358 and destroyed in 1573. The walls are of enormous thickness–10 to 15 feet. The tower took its name from the two Argylls, father and son, Marquis and Earl, who were in turn imprisoned in the Castle preparatory to their execution, owing to their staunch adherence to the Covenant. The cell immediately over the archway, reached from above by a descending stair, was the scene of E M Ward's 'Argyll's Last Sleep' (Westminster). The son's place of confinement was a vault below the Great Hall. Montrose, Principal Carstares, and many others occupied the chamber in the Argyll Tower.

On the left a flight of stairs ascends to the Citadel, the highest part of the fortress; but if we take the 'Lang Stairs' we miss many interesting features. Let us follow the road which passes the **Argyll Battery**, on the edge of the cliff overlooking West Princes Street Gardens.

The Infirmary, Military Hospital, Governor's House, and the former Armoury are on the right, and behind, on the brink of the precipice, is the old **Sally Port**, through which the body of Queen Margaret was carried off (for sepulture in Dunfermline) by her confessor, Turgot, despite the watchfulness of Donalbain. Here took place the historic interview between Claverhouse (Dundee) and the Duke of Gordon. Dundee having climbed up the face of the rock opposite the western end of the 'Lang Gait' (now Princes Street), in the hope of inducing the chief of the Gordons to join him in raising the Highlands against William of Orange.

Passing through 'Foog's Gate', we reach the Citadel. This summit of the Castle Rock is 443 feet above sea-level, and is otherwise known as the **King's Bastion** and the Bomb Battery.

The first object of note is the monster gun, **Mons Meg.** An inscription on the carriage (a replica of the original carriage) states that the gun was made at Mons, in 1486; others say its construction was due to a Galloway smith, and that it was first used at the assault of Threave Castle. It was employed at the siege of Norham Castle, but burst on being fired in 1682, on the visit of the Duke of York, afterwards James II. Removed to the Tower of London in 1754, it was restored to the Castle by George IV in 1829, at the request of Sir Walter Scott. This

EDINBURGH CASTLE

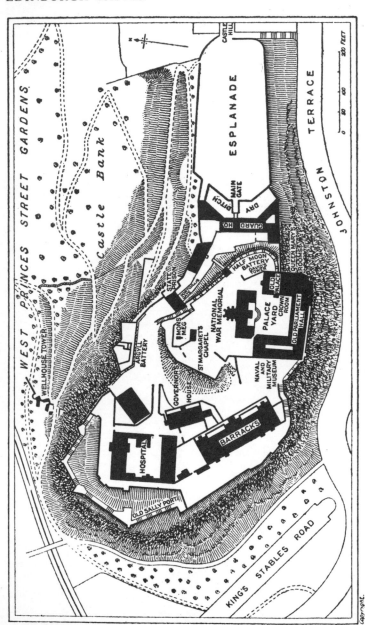

EDINBURGH CASTLE

famous gun is made of thick iron bars, held together by massive rings of metal; its length is fully 12 feet, its calibre 19½ inches, its weight 5 tons. (On a ledge of the Castle Rock below the site of Mons Meg is a modern Cemetery for Soldiers' Dogs.)

St Margaret's Chapel, erected at the instance of the good queen of Malcolm Canmore–memorable on account of her part in introducing the Roman form of Christianity into Scotland–adjoins the battery. She married Malcolm in 1069 and died in 1093, immediately after receiving news of the death of her husband and her eldest son at Alnwick. The interior of the Chapel is only about 17 feet by 11. It was restored in 1853, by command of Queen Victoria. The plate-glass windows (by Douglas Strachan) show figures of St Andrew, St Ninian, St Columba, St Margaret and William Wallace. It is an interesting example of Early Norman work and may be the oldest extant church of the Roman rite in Scotland. It contains a facsimile of Queen Margaret's copy book.

On the **Half-Moon Battery** (dating from 1574), the eastern front of the citadel, are a beacon basket and the **Well**, cut through rock to a depth of over 100 feet, and covered by a grating, which formerly supplied water to the Garrison; and the **Time Gun** (established in 1851 as a time-signal to ships on the Forth), fired each weekday at one o'clock, Greenwich or Summer time, by an electrically-controlled clock which is connected to the Royal Observatory on Blackford Hill. The ruins of **David's Tower** (begun by David II in 1367 and said to have been 60 feet in height) came to light in 1912, enclosed in the Half-Moon Bastion, after remaining hidden since 1573, when the Tower was destroyed in the siege. Excavations by the Office of Works also revealed here the vaulted reservoirs that contained the Castle's water supply.

The apex of the Castle rock is now crowned by–

The Scottish National War Memorial, a building which has been well called 'a coronach in stone'. Designed by Sir Robert Lorimer (1864–1930), it stands at the northern end of Crown Square.

The Memorial consists of a Gallery of Honour with projecting bays and entered by a noble porch, over which is a figure representing the Survival of the Spirit. The slightly severe aspect of the exterior, with its walls of ashlar, gives no hint of the rare beauty of the interior, and the visitor can hardly fail to experience a feeling of awed surprise on entering. Straight in front is the archway of the Shrine, guarded by exquisitely designed gates.

To right and left stretches the nobly proportioned **Hall of Honour,** its walls occupied by regimental and other memorials, while the frieze bears the names of battle honours. Each Scottish regiment, whether raised in the Home Country or in the Overseas Dominions, has its own memorial and display of historic battle colours, and visitors can read, on the walls and in the Rolls of Honour, the numbers and names of those who served and fell in the War of 1914–18 and in the 1939–45 War.

The **Shrine** bears much the same relation to the Hall of Honour as the sanctuary of a church to its nave. The stained-glass windows and other decorations were designed in every case by Scottish craftsmen. On either side is a fine bronze frieze in which are depicted Scots men and women in all their varied wartime uniforms, and in the centre, below the hovering figure of St Michael, is the beautiful **Casket,** given by King George V and Queen Mary and containing the hundred thousand names of the fallen. Through the floor of the Shrine the rugged rock of the hill has been allowed to project, as if to prove on what a sure foundation is based this symbol of a nation's grief and gratitude.

The Memorial is extraordinarily comprehensive; even man's humble yet helpful animal friends that played a rôle in this first World War are not forgotten. 'The only individual remembered in the shrine by a plaque is Earl Haig who commanded the British Expeditionary Forces in the 1914–18 War.'

EDINBURGH CASTLE

The **Palace Yard**, or *Crown Square,* overlooked by the memorial, contains nearly all the historic apartments of the Castle. **Queen Mary's Bedroom**, at the south-east corner, was the birthplace, on June 19, 1566, of James the Sixth of Scotland and First of England. In these confined **Royal Apartments** are a number of portraits, plans and other early relics.

The vaulted Crown Room adjoins the Royal Apartments. Here, securely but tastefully displayed, are to be seen the **Scottish Regalia**, or the 'Honours of Scotland'–a crown, sceptre and sword of state–and other jewels. The crown was refashioned for James VI and was used at the Coronation of Charles II at Scone on January 1, 1651; its gold and pearls are partly of Scottish origin; its bonnet and ermine were renewed for the State visit of Queen Elizabeth in June 1953. The sceptre and the sword are those presented to James IV by Pope Alexander VI and Pope Julius II. With them is exhibited the golden collar of the Garter, conferred by Elizabeth on James VI, together with the George and Dragon, the badge of the Order, bequeathed by Cardinal York, the brother of Prince Charles Edward, to George IV, and sent to Edinburgh Castle in 1830. Here, too, is the oak chest in which the Regalia were deposited at the Union, and in which they lay concealed for over a century until they were 'officially' discovered in 1817 by a Commission, among the members of which was Sir Walter Scott. They had been 'lost' previously at the time of the Commonwealth, having first been hidden under the pulpit of the Church of Kinneff in Kincardineshire, after being secretly conveyed out of Dunnottar Castle by Mrs Granger, the wife of the parish minister, at the instance of the Governor, Sir George Ogilvie. Round the walls of the Crown Room are emblazoned the arms of Scottish Kings and Queens.

On the southern side of the quadrangle is the **Great Hall**, built by James IV early in the sixteenth century, with a fine timber roof. It is known also as the *Old Parliament Hall* or *Banqueting Hall*. Hereabouts earlier meetings of the Scots Estates, or Parliament, are believed to have been held; in this hall met the first Parliament of James II, March 20, 1437; here too, in 1440, was held the 'Black Dinner' given by Chancellor Crichton and Governor Livingston to William, Earl of Douglas, and his brother, whence the pair of youths were hurried to execution. The Great Hall is now used by the Secretary of State for Scotland for official banquets to visiting royalty and heads of state. The Barras or Jousting Ground at King's Stables Road is immediately below the castle.

Since its restoration the Hall has become a museum of armour, most effectively arranged on the walls and floor. The windows are filled with the arms of Scottish sovereigns and nobles. A Lower Banqueting Hall at the other end of the yard now serves as a tea-room and for ceremonial occasions at the Castle.

Another interesting collection is housed in the **Scottish United Services Museum**, the main galleries of which adjoin Crown Square on both sides. Established in 1933, it contains a unique array of relics, portraits, medals, colours, trophies, uniforms of the Scottish fighting forces through the centuries, and a standard used by the Highland Division at Alamein. The series of oak statuettes representing the development of Scottish uniforms, by Pilkington Jackson, are noteworthy.

Below the Great Hall is a double series of stone-vaulted chambers, including that occupied by the condemned Earl of Argyll. These dungeons were used as places of confinement for French prisoners during the Napoleonic Wars, as described in Stevenson's novel, *St Ives.* (At present the Dungeons and David's Tower are not open to the public.)

The higher parts of the Castle command the best views of the city and its neighbourhood. From the King's Bastion we can pass to the battlemented

The View from Castle Hill

roof of the Argyll Tower, and then descend to the Esplanade, which affords contrasting pictures of city and countryside.

Looking over the low wall of the Esplanade, we see immediately below us Johnston Terrace, at the west end of which are the city's Public Health Chambers and the Married Soldiers' Quarters. In the roadway wall of these houses is a tablet bearing the inscription, 'Erected on a site near the extremity of the Ancient Town Wall built in the reign of James II, King of Scots, A.D. 1450, for the protection of Edinburgh against invasion.'

Castle Hill

Great havoc has been made in modern times of the grand old houses on **Castle Hill,** and only one or two are left. The first as we leave the Esplanade, the *Cannonball House*, has a cannonball in its west gable. This, says one tradition, was actually shot from the Castle during the rebellion of 1745. **Boswell's Court** was the residence of Dr Boswell, uncle of the biographer of Dr Johnson. At the junction with Johnston Terrace stands the **Highland Tolbooth-St John's Church,** the former Tolbooth Church, its lofty 240 ft spire being a landmark in most aspects of the city. Built in 1842, its design by Augustus W. Pugin is believed to have been influenced by the design of the House of Commons. A magnificent Royal Coat of Arms mounted to face the pulpit is a relic of the building's use as meeting place of the General Assembly of the Church of Scotland until 1929. The chair of John Knox is preserved in the Church.

On the north side of the street is the **Outlook Tower** (*admission, see* p. 94), which was acquired in 1892 by Professor (later Sir) Patrick Geddes. It has a

107

fascinating camera obscura (which, on a fine day, 'televises', in its own way, the surrounding city), a platform (with indicator) for viewing the landscape, and interesting sections illustrating the development of Edinburgh and modern Scottish craftsmanship. Here, beside Ramsay Lane, tradition has placed the town house of Sir Andrew Ramsay, who as the Laird of Cockpen was the supposed original of Caroline Oliphant's delightful ballad. Adjoining is **Sempill's Close,** containing the house which formerly belonged to the Sempills of Beltrees, three generations of whom were writers of Scots satirical verse. We next pass the south entrance to the General Assembly Hall, standing on the site of a 'Palace' occupied by Mary of Guise, Regent of Scotland. Some of the finely-carved stone and woodwork of the palace (demolished in 1861) is to be seen in the National Museum of Antiquities, in Queen Street.

The Lawnmarket

That section of the 'Royal Mile' termed the **Lawnmarket** is said by some to derive its name from the fact that the lawn or cloth sellers of the city had their booths in it; others believe it to be an adaptation of the older name 'Landmarket'.

The opening opposite the Assembly Hall is all that remains of the old **West Bow,** in bygone days one of the principal approaches to the city. The West Bow was of ill omen as the last stage of the road to execution in the

Lady Stair's House

Grassmarket and for the house of Major Weir, hanged (1670) for sorcery, along with his sister. At the head of it stands **Free St Columba's Church** (formerly Free St John's famous for the ministry of Dr Guthrie). It is now used as the Free Church Assembly Hall. Opposite is **Milne's Court,** erected in 1690 by the King's Master Mason for Scotland, Robert Mylne, the seventh (and last) of his race who in succession held that honour now restored by University as a residence for students. Just beyond Milne's Court is **James's Court,** where, despite alterations, we can still note the house in the eastern corner where David Hume lived. When he left it to go to the New Town the flat was purchased by James Boswell, and here 'Bozzy' had the honour of receiving Dr Johnson in August 1773, prior to their journey to the Hebrides.

Adjoining the lower end of James's Court is a tall house (basement and six floors), called **Gladstone's Land.** Its front of polished ashlar, with an arcade (brought to light–as were the painted ceilings–when the house was restored after 1934) distinguishes it from the others. The house, which dates in part from at least the middle of the sixteenth century, was in 1617 acquired by Thomas Gledstanes and largely rebuilt by him. It is now the property of the National Trust for Scotland and the home of the Saltire Society. (*Entrance by ground floor or outer stone stair; Monday to Friday,* 2–5).

Lady Stair's Close takes its name from Elizabeth, Countess Dowager of Stair, who lived here from 1719 in a house originally built (1622) by Sir William Gray of Pittendrum. Now known as **Lady Stair's House** it appears to have been later occupied by Eleanor, widow of Marshal Stair, the second earl. This lady, in her day a leader of fashion, was, as Viscountess Primrose, the victim of the remarkable incident (1714) recorded in Scott's story of *My Aunt Margaret's Mirror*. Purchased and restored by the 5th Earl of Rosebery, himself a Primrose, Lady Stair's House was in 1907 presented to the Town Council for use as a museum. There are a number of interesting architectural features. The museum displays MSS, and relics of three of Scotland's most famous men of letters, Sir Walter Scott, Robert Burns and Robert Louis Stevenson. (*For admission to Museum, ring bell at door: see* p. 94).

Blackie House (late seventeenth-century), in the north-eastern corner of Lady Stair's Close, was restored as a University Hall named after the versatile scholar, Professor John Stuart Blackie (1809–95). Over the Lawnmarket entrance to the close is a tablet stating: 'In a house on the east side of this close Robert Burns lived during his visit to Edinburgh, 1786.'

On the south side of the Lawnmarket is **Riddle's Court**. In it is another of the houses which David Hume occupied. A 'pend' leads into Riddle's Close, which contains **Bailie Macmorran's House.**

This civic father lives in history because he was shot by one of the High School boys. The boys had become very turbulent, and when in September, 1595, a holiday was refused, they barricaded the doors and declined to admit their masters. They had pistols, swords, and a plentiful supply of provisions. The Town Council, the patrons of the institution, sent Bailie Macmorran to reduce the defiant scholars. While engaged in this duty he fell dead, shot through the head by a pistol bullet fired by a son of Sinclair, the Chancellor of Caithness. Bailie Macmorran's house, being one of the finest in the city, was greatly used for banquets. Its modern Orwell Hall serves for entertainment of another kind. The buildings of Riddle's Court are now used by the city's education department as an adult education centre.

Lower down the street from Riddle's Court is **Fisher's Close,** in which stood the town mansion of the Buccleuch family. This tenement (250 years old) has been reconstructed internally to house the **Scottish Central Library,** a national lending library (Carnegie UK Trust), opened by HRH the Duke of Edinburgh in 1953. In **Brodie's Close** lived Deacon William Brodie, who was a member of the Town Council as Deacon Convener of the Incorporated Trades.

Brodie had a good business as a cabinet-maker, but became the secret leader and director of a gang of housebreakers. After long escaping detection he was arrested and hanged in 1788. The turnpike stair on the right conducts us to the house (with fine ceilings of 1645 and 1646). The story is the foundation of the play by R L Stevenson and W E Henley.

Melbourne Place, at the junction of the Lawnmarket and George IV Bridge, from which the High Street continues the line of the Lawnmarket towards Holyrood—comprises the site of the town mansion and chapel of the Abbots of Cambuskenneth. Here too stood the *Bank of Scotland*, till it was moved in 1806 to its present site at the top of the Mound. The Bank was founded by Act of the Scottish Parliament in 1695. In it is preserved the Darien Chest. Prominent in Melbourne Place is the modern extension offices of the Midlothian County Council. The corner tenement at the top of Bank Street—by which the Mound and Princes Street may be regained—is one of the few remaining examples of seventeenth-century domestic architecture. An elevated plaque at No. 13 Bank Street commemorates Sir Robert Philip, who there founded the world's first Tuberculosis Dispensary in 1887.

The High Street—St Giles' to the Tron

The High Street forms the middle—but not the longest—segment of the backbone of the Old Town. In it are concentrated St Giles' and John Knox's House, Parliament House and the Law Courts, the City Chambers and the Market Cross, and a cluster of hoary closes, which combine to make the High Street the focus of the secular and ecclesiastical history of the city, the very heart of Midlothian, and indeed of all Scotland.

At the head of the High Street, on the left-hand side between Bank Street and St Giles Street, stands the **Sheriff Court** (completed 1937).

Opposite, on the right, is a quadrangular space bounded by the **Midlothian County Buildings,** the Signet Library and St Giles Cathedral. In the space stands a *Statue to Walter Francis, 5th Duke of Buccleuch* (1806–84), the founder of Granton. The statue, by Boehm, has bas-reliefs illustrating Border incidents associated with the 'bauld Buccleuch'.

A few steps farther in the direction of the Cathedral a **Heart** will be seen outlined on the causeway in parti-coloured stones. This marks the spot where stood the portal of the **Old Tolbooth,** in which the opening incidents of Scott's great novel, *The Heart of Midlothian*, took place. The superstitious still sometimes express their feeling for this prison by spitting on the 'heart'. The Tolbooth—whose site as a whole is likewise indicated by special paving-blocks—was finally demolished in 1817, the entrance gate being presented to Sir Walter Scott.

St Giles' can be reached from Princes Street by a variety of routes—by public transport up the Mound or across the North Bridge to the High Street, or on foot by the Waverley Bridge and Cockburn Street (*see* p. 117) which offers a choice of short-cuts: (*a*) from the west side of the Festival offices building at its foot to St Giles Street; (*b*) by Advocate's Close, ascending from the north side of the City Chambers; and further up Cockburn Street, (*c*) the straight steep stairway of Warriston Close. Of these the middle course, by **Advocate's Close,** is not only the least tiring but the most noteworthy, although it has lost some of its artistic appeal. This alley received its name from Sir James Stewart of Goodtrees (or 'Gutters' as it came to be pronounced), Lord Advocate from 1692 to 1713. Here John Scougal (*c.* 1645–*c.* 1730), one of the early Scottish portrait-painters, had rooms. On the eastern side and also on the house of Bishop Adam Bothwell (who married Mary, Queen of Scots, to Bothwell), which looks down on it from the west, are examples of the pious mottoes wherewith worthy citizens of Edinburgh were in the habit of adorning their lintels and dormers in the sixteenth and seventeenth centuries.

Advocate's Close comes out into the High Street opposite–

111

St Giles' Cathedral, Edinburgh

St Giles' Cathedral (High Kirk of Edinburgh)

(**Admission,** *see* p. 94).

The church is a beautiful Gothic edifice, 206 feet long and 129 feet in breadth across the transepts, 110 at the west end and 76 across the choir. The fifteenth-century tower, with its '**Crown of St Giles**', the only part not altered (except by the removal of the clock face) during all the changes which have affected the building, is 161 feet high. It terminates in the representation of an imperial crown; and, from its form and the elevation of the spot, is seen with fine effect from most parts of the city.

Over the modern West Doorway are niches containing statues of monarchs and ecclesiastics connected with the sanctuary. On the pediment are represented 'Sanct Geill (St Giles) and his Hynde', and the Four Evangelists.

Almost facing the Market Cross, the **South-East Door** (a fine entrance, dating probably from 1387, rebuilt here in 1910) leads to the **Thistle Chapel**. The Chapel of the Most Ancient and Most Noble Order of the Thistle was opened by King

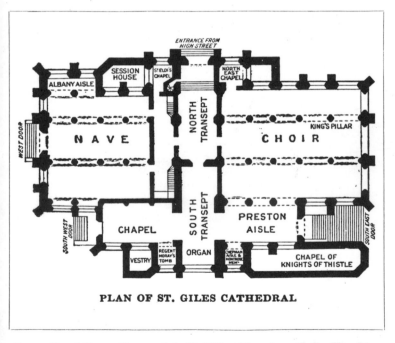

PLAN OF ST. GILES CATHEDRAL

George V and Queen Mary on July 19, 1911. Although small, the Chapel is a beautiful example of modern Gothic, designed (like the National War Memorial) by Sir Robert Lorimer, RSA, and is very richly decorated. The elaborately ribbed roof has a series of large bosses with heraldic devices. The Royal stalls are at the west end, and there are fourteen others for the rest of the knights.

To the west of the Chapel is the **Preston Aisle**, in which is the **Royal Pew**, occupied during Assembly time by the representative of the Sovereign, the Royal High Commissioner. The seats are of stained oak, according well with the antique 'atmosphere' of the building. Opening off the Preston Aisle is the **Chepman Aisle**. Walter Chepman, a notary, with Andrew Myllar, bookseller, set up the first Scottish printing press in 1507. This Aisle contains a monument to the Marquis of Montrose, whose body was interred in the vaults beneath in 1661, some years after his execution. It also contains a framed copy of the National Covenant.

Beyond is the **South Transept**, at the end of which is installed a fine organ. To the west is the **Moray Aisle** or **Side Chapel**. Underneath the oriel window in its west wall is a bronze **Memorial to Robert Louis Stevenson**, the work of *St Gaudens*, a tribute from admirers of 'R L S' in all quarters of the world. Off the south side of the Side Chapel is a small chapel formerly known as the Holy Blood Aisle, containing a monument to the 'Good Regent', James Stewart, Earl of Moray, with a Latin inscription from the pen of George Buchanan.

Outside the Moray Aisle is the *Vesper Bell,* a survival of pre-Reformation times, bearing the date 1452. At the end of the South Aisle is a display of ancient *Service-books* (including Laud's Liturgy) and a disused *Font* in Caen stone.

Crossing the west end of the **Nave**, we come to the **North Aisle**, off the west end of which is the **Albany Aisle**. It is said to have been built by Robert, Duke of Albany, in expiation of the murder of his nephew the Duke of Rothesay, in 1402. In the Albany Aisle is the Memorial Chapel commemorating those members of the Congregation who were killed in the Second World War.

Eastward, beside the High Street entrance, is **St Eloi's Chapel** (or the Hammermen's Chapel), where the craftsmen dedicated the famous 'Blue Blanket', or banner of the trades. In it is a monument to Archibald Campbell, Marquis of Argyll, who was beheaded in 1661. To the east of the High Street entrance is an ancient Chapel which was restored as a memorial to Dr William Chambers, now designed as the Chapel of Youth in which hang the colours of the Youth Organizations of Edinburgh. There is a window in memory of Chambers and his brother Robert.

The Church contains many other memorials of famous people.

The four octagonal pillars supporting the Tower of the Cathedral are said to be part of the Norman building erected in 1120. Stretching eastward from these pillars is the **Choir**, with the Pulpit, beautifully carved in Caen stone by John Rhind. At the end of the Choir is the oak Communion Table.

Hung on the walls of the Cathedral are many of the old colours of famous Scottish regiments, and to these have been added other historic flags of the Second World War.

The open space south of St Giles', originally the graveyard, is—

Parliament Square

In it is **John Knox's Grave,** but the exact spot in the former burying ground has not been traced. On the pavement in the north-west corner is a bronze statue of John Knox by *Pittendreigh MacGillivray*, R.S.A.

In the centre of the Square stands an equestrian statue of Charles II, cast in Holland and erected in 1685. Made of lead, it evinced early in its career (significantly, some would say) a weak-kneed condition which has been a recurrent source of anxiety and expense. This is probably the oldest lead equestrian statue in Britain.

Parliament House (*entrance–free–at* No. 11, *south-west corner*), in which is the Court of Session, dates from 1632–40, although in 1808 a Grecian propylæum and colonnade were erected in place of the former Gothic front. The most interesting portion of the range of buildings is the great hall in which the Scottish Parliament held its sittings. It is called the **Parliament Hall**, and is 122 feet long, by 49 feet in breadth, with a fine oak roof and floor, similar to those of Westminster Hall. The Scots Parliament met here from 1639 until the Union in 1707. At the southern end an ornate window commemorates the institution of the 'College of Justice' by James V in 1532. In this noble apartment are many statues, including those of the first Lord Melville, Lord President Blair, and Lord Advocate Dundas, by Chantrey; and one of Duncan Forbes of Culloden, another Lord President, by Roubiliac (1752)–this, next to that of Charles II (*see* above), being the oldest statue in Edinburgh. On the two sides of the principal entrance are statues of Lord President Boyle and Lord Jeffrey, by Steell. In a bay is a sandstone statue of Sir Walter Scott by John Greenshields, stonemason. Portraits of other celebrities of Bench and Bar adorn the walls.

Beneath the southern window one passes to the corridor where are four of the nine courts of the **Outer House**, each presided over by a Lord Ordinary. Farther along the corridor, to the left, is the **Inner House**, divided into the First and Second Divisions. It was in the First Division that Sir Walter Scott had his seat as Clerk. While waiting the summons that the case in which they are engaged is about to be heard–a summons delivered after the stroke of a bell from a rostrum under the great window–the advocates, gowned and wigged, pace up and down the grand old Parliament Hall.

The **High Court of Justiciary** can best be reached by a door a little farther east along the square, but it may also be entered from the corridor.

A door leads from the Great Hall on the west side to the **Advocates' Library** (*private*). In the entrance lobby is the standard of the Earl Marischal of Scotland, carried at Flodden. The Advocates' Library was founded in 1682 by Sir George Mackenzie of Rosehaugh. Most eminent of its Keepers was David Hume, the historian. By the generosity of the Faculty of Advocates, all but the Law Department of this ancient and famous library was handed over to form the National Library of Scotland. Below Parliament Hall is the **Laigh Hall**, or Lower Hall, where at one time the Advocate's Library was housed. Restoration has revealed a fine row of supporting pillars.

Between St Giles' Cathedral and the Midlothian County Buildings is the **Signet Library** (*no public admission*). It belongs to the Society of Writers to HM Signet. The upper apartment is a superb room, having a cupola, with paintings of Apollo and the Muses, and portraits of historians, poets and learned men. The library contains over 110,000 volumes. At the head of the staircase and in other parts of the building are many portraits of legal worthies.

The Hall of the **Society of Solicitors in the Supreme Courts of Scotland** is entered from Parliament House. The S.S.C. Library is open 10 till 4 (1 on Saturdays).

At the north-eastern angle of Parliament Square are the **City Police Headquarters.** In the roadway midway between these and the cathedral stands–

The Cross known in early times as the *Mercat Croce*. Here Royal proclamations are read by the Lord Lyon King of Arms and by the Heralds–a picturesque spectacle. The Cross was of old the scene of many ceremonies, gay or grim, but in 1756 the mutilated relic was taken down as an obstruction. The shaft, however, was preserved in Lord Somerville's grounds of Drum, and in 1866 was replaced outside St Giles Church. In 1885 W E Gladstone restored the Cross and had it erected near its former site (outlined in paving-blocks on the main thoroughfare at 190 High Street). The new cross, with the original shaft, or 'lang stane', forming the centre, bears a Latin inscription written by Gladstone, in which he claims 'through both parents a purely Scottish descent'.

City Chambers. In the High Street, opposite the Cross, are the City Chambers. Early in the nineteenth-century the Corporation took over what was originally the *Royal Exchange*, built (1753–61) on the design of the brothers John and Robert Adam but little frequented by Edinburgh merchants, who preferred to transact their business at the Cross as had long been their habit.

A modern arcade of seven arches admits to a quadrangle in front of the main entrance. Under the central arch is the city's Stone of Remembrance in honour of those who died in the two World Wars. In the quadrangle is Steell's *The Taming of Bucephalus by Alexander the Great*. Panels in the entrance hall record the names – many of them highly distinguished – of the Chief Magistrates in unbroken succession from William de Dederyk (1296) to the present day. The Council Chamber is a handsome room with pictures of historic events in the annals of the town.

The City Chambers also incorporate premises on the other side of Warriston Close, formerly occupied for over a century by the publishing firm of W & R Chambers. It was William Chambers who suggested the name Dunedin for that city in New Zealand, and the City Chambers of Edinburgh appropriately include a Dunedin Room, a committee room beautifully panelled with wood from New Zealand. At 343 High Street is the Corporation Publicity Department.

Historic Closes

The City Chambers embrace **Roxburghe's Close**, of amazing narrowness and steepness, and extend from Advocate's Close to **Warriston Close**, named after Sir Archibald Johnston, Lord Warriston, one of the champions of the Covenant, whose town house was situated in it. A tablet on the wall of the flight of stairs descending to Cockburn Street marks the site of a 'manse' occupied in 1560–66 by John Knox. Warriston Close now leads into the High Street through the refashioned **Writers' Court,** which contained *Clerihugh's Tavern,* one of the great 'temples of Convivialia' in the city during the eighteenth century. Bronze plates commemorate other historic closes involved in the extension scheme – **Craig's Close** (called after John Craig, the colleague of Knox), which was notable as the place where Archibald Constable, the Scottish publisher, had his first premises; and **Old Post Office Close,** the home of Edinburgh's first Post Office – also the first in Scotland.

Anchor Close contained the celebrated *Dawney Douglas's Tavern,* where the 'Crochallan Fencibles' held their meetings. William Smellie's printing-office, to which Burns was in the habit of going to revise his proofs, was here. Later the close housed the *Scotsman,* until its removal to North Bridge. At 231 High Street a medallion on the wall indicates the snuff shop of James Gillespie (1726–97). Gillespie amassed a fortune as a snuff-miller and founded a hospital and school.

Old Stamp Office Close was the original office of the Inland Revenue in Scotland. Here lived for many years the Earl of Eglinton and his beautiful Countess, the latter a great mistress of fashion in her day. In this close was *Fortune's Tavern,* where the Lord High Commissioner to the Church of Scotland held his receptions; it was the most fashionable tavern in the city in the mid-eighteenth century.

In **Fleshmarket Close**, a little farther on, Henry Dundas, Lord Melville, began to practise as an advocate.

In the lodging of the Provost, Sir Simon Preston, as recorded on a plaque at the top of Cockburn Street, Mary Queen of Scots spent her last night in Edinburgh, after her surrender at Carberry Hill in 1567.

The south side of the High Street, between St Giles and the Tron Church, also boasts its historic closes.

In **Old Fishmarket Close,** where the City Police Headquarters are located, George Heriot began his married life. In **Old Assembly Close** was situated the second set of rooms where the fashionable gatherings known as the Assemblies were held. Here the powdered belles and beaux executed their stately minuets and country dances, and here (in 1753) Goldsmith, a student of physics, paid his first and last visit to a Scots assembly.

A year or two later the Assemblies removed to the adjacent **Bell's Wynd**. This wynd had at its head that famous structure the 'Clam Shell' or 'Black Turnpike' – a mansion belonging to the Augustinian Order. It became the mansion of the Bishop of Dunkeld, and afterwards passed into the hands of the Earl of Home, who here entertained Mary and Darnley on their return from Dunbar after the murder of Rizzio. In Bell's Wynd lived Lord Advocate Crichton, father of the gifted youth known as the 'Admirable Crichton' (1560–82).

The Tron Church. The Tron Church stands in Hunter Square. Erected in 1637–47, it derives its name from the public weighing beam – the salt *tron* – which stood within a few yards of it. Beside the tron the 'kailwives' (vegetable vendors) had their pitches and it has always been one of the busiest spots in the town; here the citizens still assemble at 'Hogmanay' to 'see in' the New Year. The church underwent curtailment at the formation of the South Bridge in 1785, and in 1824, during the great fire, lost its curious wooden steeple. It was closed for worship in 1952.

A cellar below the Royal Bank at 179 High Street opposite the Tron Church is associated with the agreements towards the Act of Union of Scotland and England. We are told that commissioners began their business in an arbour still existing behind Moray House, were pursued by the infuriated mob who were opposed to the Union, and finished their deliberations in this cellar. The Act of Union was passed by the Scottish Parliament in session at Parliament House in 1707.

Cockburn Street (pronounced Cō'burn) is named after that distinguished occupant of the Scottish Bench and man of letters, Henry, Lord Cockburn (1779–1854), whose *Memorials* cast such valuable light on the Edinburgh of his day, and whose name is also perpetuated in the Cockburn Association (founded 1875), which acts as guardian of the amenities of the city. Midway down Cockburn Street, it is worth while to pause and glance up at the back elevation of the City Chambers, twelve storeys in height. At the foot of Cockburn Street is the Waverley Bridge, leading up to Princes Street.

Lower High Street, Canongate and Holyrood

At the Tron the High Street is intersected by 'the Bridges'–the North Bridge coming up from the General Post Office and the South Bridge continuing it to the University. At the corner of North Bridge and the lower High Street, down which we make our way, the Royal Bank displays a few relics, in the shape of ornamental reliefs, of Allan Ramsay's wig shop 'at the sign of the Mercury', which was swept away when the North Bridge was being reconstructed. The shop was 'opposite Niddry's Wynd', now Niddry Street, at the lower end of which is **St Cecilia's Hall**, a fashionable eighteenth-century Concert hall, recently restored and acquired by the University to house its collection of old musical instruments.

At the foot of **Carrubber's Close**, Old St Paul's Episcopal Church (built 1883) occupies the site of a smaller one, wherein worshipped the congregation ejected from St Giles with Bishop Rose after episcopacy was abolished in 1688. The American Bishop Seabury attended this church when a medical student. In Carrubber's Close, in 1736, Allan Ramsay opened the first regular theatre in Edinburgh–quickly closed by the magistrates.

Bishop's Close takes its name from Archbishop Spottiswoode (1565–1639), the historian of the Scottish Church, who was born here; in the same house, Henry Dundas, Lord Melville, was born (1742).

Paisley Close recalls a tragedy of 1861. The tenement above the close suddenly collapsed, upwards of thirty-five inmates being killed. Among those rescued from the ruins was a lad who kept shouting, 'Heave awa', chaps; I'm no' deid yet'.

Chalmers Close gives access to Trinity College Church. On the opposite side of High Street **Dickson's Close** contained the studio and residence of Sir William Allan (1782–1850), President of the Royal Scottish Academy. In **Strichen's Close** was the town house of the Abbots of Melrose. 'Bluidy Mackenzie'–Sir George Mackenzie, of Rosehaugh, King's Advocate (1677–88)–lived here for many years.

In **Blackfriars Wynd** (now Blackfriars Street) dwelt the Regent Morton, Archbishop Beaton and his nephew, the Cardinal, and the princely house of St Clair, Earls of Orkney and Rosslyn. A carved lintel in the Earl of Morton's house (No. 8) is dated 1564.

South Gray's Close held the town mansion of the Earl of Buchan, and was the birthplace (1750) of Thomas Erskine, Lord Chancellor of England, and (1746) of his brother, Harry Erskine, the witty Lord Advocate. **Elphinstone's Court**, in connection with it, was the residence of the Earl of Argyll in 1574, and of Lord Hailes, Lord Belhaven, Lord Chesterhall, and of Lord Loughborough, first Earl of Rosslyn and Lord High Chancellor of England. Nearby is **St Patrick's**

Roman Catholic Church, which possesses some fine altar-pieces by Runciman. The Scottish Mint stood–up to the Union in 1707, and after–at the foot of this close, in Mint Court. The Corporation's **Museum of Childhood** (toys, etc.,) is located in **Hyndford's Close**, which, named from the Earls of Hyndford, contained the residence of Dr Rutherford, the uncle of Sir Walter Scott, who, as a schoolboy, was a frequent visitor.

In **Fountain Close**–so called from its position opposite one of the old wells in the High Street–was the printing-office of Thomas Bassandyne, who issued his famous folio Bible in 1576; while in **Tweeddale Court** was the town house of the noble family of Tweeddale. Since 1817 it has formed part of the premises of the publishing firm of Messrs Oliver and Boyd.

We are now opposite–

John Knox's House (*Admission see* p. 94). Although doubt has been expressed as to whether the Reformer really had this as his 'manse', there is good reason for believing that he inhabited it for some time, while his own was being repaired. Before this it was, it is thought, the residence of George Durie, last Abbot of Dunfermline. But the possessor with whom it is most clearly identified is James Mossman, an Edinburgh jeweller, whose initials and arms, with those of his wife, are carved on one of the panels. He was a strong adherent of Mary Stewart and suffered death in her cause. Extending over part of the front above the ground floor are large Roman letters–'Lufe God abufe al, and thi nychtbour as thi-self'. The interior is well worth a visit, many relics of Knox being stored here. There are five rooms in all, including what may be styled a bed-closet, but the most interesting is the 'study', where the Reformer is traditionally believed to have worked until a fortnight before his death (November 24, 1572).

John Knox's House

Moubray House, adjoining, was the residence of a cousin of Mowbray of Barnbugle. Probably the oldest dwelling house in Edinburgh (fifteenth century, but mainly seventeenth), it was saved from demolition and restored in 1910. A like fate threatened John Knox's House but it was saved by purchase by the Free Church.

We have reached the limits of the ancient burgh of Edinburgh—the last close on the south side of the High Street is whimsically called World's End Close. Across the street, at the corner of Jeffrey and St Mary's Streets, formerly stretched a barbican-like structure called the *Netherbow Port*, which performed a dual office, serving as one of the city gates and dividing the burgh of Edinburgh from the ecclesiastical burgh of the Canongate. The Port was demolished in 1764; its site is outlined on the street.

St Mary's Street, formerly St Mary's Wynd, and **Jeffrey Street**, formerly Leith Wynd, branch off here, the former to the south, the latter to the north-west. They mark the ancient outlets from the city. St Mary's Wynd perhaps derived its name from an ancient hospital (the earliest recorded in Edinburgh, 1438) which stood here. It was in this area, just outside the city wall, where many of the ancient inns of Edinburgh were situated. Dr Johnson stayed at the White Horse in St Mary's Street.

Jeffrey Street runs down to the south side of the Waverley Station to meet Market Street under the North Bridge. Near the foot of Jeffrey Street is a remnant of **Trinity College Church**. The building incorporates some of the features of the original structure, which stood a little to the north-west and was taken down when the Waverley Station was formed. "The Collegiate Church of the Holy Trinity' was founded by Mary of Gueldres, James II's widow, who was buried here when she died soon afterwards in 1463. Four centuries later her remains were removed to Holyrood Chapel. The massive building was never completed. The altarpiece is in the National Gallery.

The Canongate

The last and longest section of the Royal Mile, the Canongate, extends for fully a third of a mile from St Mary's Street to Holyrood. Even more than the High Street of Edinburgh, the Canongate was formerly the fashionable residential quarter. Here dwelt the Dukes of Hamilton and Queensberry, the Marquises of Argyll and Huntly, the Earls of Breadalbane, Haddington, Dalhousie, Panmure, Moray, Mar and a host of others. For a long time it remained very shabby but recent restoration and rebuilding has rid it of much of its squalor. The Canongate was till 1856 a separate burgh, with its own magistrates. Up to the time of the Union of the Crowns it rather looked down upon Edinburgh as being nearer the Court. But its glory began to pass when the superiority of the burgh was granted to the Earl of Roxburghe, by whom in 1636 it was sold to the magistrates of Edinburgh. The Treaty of Union, the building of the New Town, and the Industrial Revolution, each in turn helped towards its decay and neglect, and only in recent years has it begun to come into its own again.

Whole stretches of the Canongate have been rehabilitated by restoration, reconstruction and new building. This scheme is in evidence on the north side at *Morocco Land* (demolished in 1950), a familiar landmark bearing the effigy of a turbaned Moor, and being connected with a romantic Canongate legend, on the same lines as 'Dick Whittington'.

Farther down on the same side is all that remains of **New Street**, formerly the residence of Lords Kames and Hailes, while opposite is the well-restored (1965) **Chessel's Court**, the scene of the last exploit of Deacon Brodie which is said to have given R L Stephenson the idea for *Doctor Jekyll and Mr Hyde*.

Near St John's Close, let into the street causeway, is a ring of stones marking the site of **St John's Cross**. The old Burgh Cross has been re-erected inside the Canongate churchyard, a few yards down the street.

A little farther on is **St John Street**, entered under an archway. In the house over the 'pend' Tobias Smollett resided with his sister, Mrs Telfer, of Scotstoun. The **Canongate Kilwinning Lodge of Freemasons**, to which Burns was affiliated, meets in the building immediately beyond the archway. The Lodge has many quaint and curious records and St John's Chapel claims to be one of the oldest masonic chapels in the world.

Immediately below St John Street is **Moray House** (*open free, on application*), of old the town residence of the noble Home and Moray families. Its pillared gatehouse, stone balcony and elaborate plaster ceilings are specially noteworthy. Moray House is now a part of the College of Education. Built *c*. 1628 by Mary, Countess of Home, the house was twice the residence of Oliver Cromwell while in Edinburgh. From its balcony, on the day of his wedding, Lord Lorne, afterwards Earl of Argyll, saw Montrose led up the Canongate to execution. Lord Chancellor Seafield resided here at the time of the Union. The building has been much extended.

In the reconstruction of the properties below **Shoemakers' Land** and **Bible Land**, opposite Moray House, the architect has reintroduced an old feature in the form of arcades. Farther down is the–

Canongate Tolbooth, which dates from 1591. It is in the French style of architecture, with turrets and projecting clock. The Canongate Tolbooth (open on weekdays, 10–5: *fee*) contained a jail and Council Chambers or Court room above, where the Bailies of the Canongate gave their decisions. Exhibitions are held in its finely panelled hall. The **Canongate Kirk** (the Kirk of Holyroodhouse), a building erected by order of James II (1688) when he wished to use the former Kirk of Holyroodhouse as a chapel, has a tastefully restored interior (1950). It was within this building that Prince Charles put his officer prisoners after the battle of Prestonpans. The church contains a Royal Pew (as the parish church of the Palace), a pew for the Governor of Edinburgh Castle, which is within the parish of Canongate, and one for the Dean of the Chapel Royal. The churchyard contains the graves of many famous Scots. There is a comprehensive list at the entrance.

Opposite, and on no account to be missed, is–

Huntly House

This fine old mansion belonged (from 1647) for over a century to the Incorporation of Hammermen of the Canongate. The building, one of the quaintest dwellings in Edinburgh surviving from olden times–parts of it date from the mid-sixteenth century–was acquired (1924) by the Corporation, and, in a reconditioned state, it now serves as the **City Museum** (*admission, see* p. 94). This is laid out in a ground-floor entrance hall (off Bakehouse Close) and some eighteen rooms. Entrance to the museum is by the new extension which houses the personal collection of F M Earl Haig; the W Ford Rankin collection of Edinburgh glass, and a unique collection of Scottish pottery. There is also an exceptionally interesting collection of maps, manuscripts, pictures and objects illustrative of the city's history, a copy of the National Covenant, besides examples of old inscriptions, panelling, fireplaces and other architectural features.

On the other side of **Bakehouse Close**, beloved of artists, is **Acheson House** (1633), reconditioned admirably by the Marquis of Bute in 1938, and now the Scottish Craft Centre.

A short distance below Canongate Church, and on the same side, is **Panmure Close**. In Panmure House on its east side, Adam Smith lived from 1778 to 1790. The house, restored, was presented to Canongate Boys' Club by Lord Thomson. Opposite Milton House in **Reids Court** stands the beautifully restored (1958) Manse of the Canongate (1690), and some modern houses by Sir Basil Spence.

Of **Milton House**, built by the celebrated Scottish judge, Andrew Fletcher of Saltoun, Lord Milton, only a fragment remains. The site (on the south side) is occupied by a school. **Queensberry House**, the tall four-storeyed building with its extensive lawn to the south, was formerly the town house of the Duke of Queensberry, and is associated with the memory of John Gay (author of *The Beggar's Opera* and verse *Fables*) and his patroness, Catherine Hyde, wife of the third Duke. For a century and more, Queensberry House has provided, on a voluntary basis and after complete modernization, graceful accommodation for the elderly and chronic sick. **Whitefoord House**, where the Earl of Winton lived, stood behind Galloway's Entry, almost opposite the Queensberry residence. Here was 'my lord Seton's lodging,' where Scott in *The Abbot* makes Roland Graeme take refuge and where Professor Dugald Stewart, the famous metaphysician, resided for several years. Whitefoord House, with Callender House, is now the Scottish Naval, Military, and Air Force Veterans' Residence.

Near the foot of the Canongate, on the north side, below rebuilt Golfer's Land (associated with a royal wager, as recorded on a tablet), is **White Horse Close**, which contains in reconstructed form the White Horse Inn, a picturesque hostelry of the seventeenth century, which figures in *Waverley*.

Today the Canongate is celebrated for its manufacture of ale, there being many breweries within the limits of the old burgh. This is due to the fact that the underground springs of water are of a peculiarly suitable quality.

We now reach **Water Gate** and the line of the **Abbey Strand** (i.e. 'gutter'), where stood the 'Girth' or Sanctuary Cross, marking the limit of the Sanctuary of Holyrood, which embraced along with the Abbey and Palace and their precincts the whole of Arthur's Seat (822 feet). The abolition of imprisonment for debt in 1880 put an end to the practice of taking sanctuary. Many exciting scenes were witnessed when debtors had to outrun the bailiff.

On the left, just before the entrance to Holyroodhouse, is a small but interesting exhibition (*open April–October, admission free*) illustrating the work of the Department of the Environment in Scotland in connection with the preservation of Scotland's ancient and historic buildings. A new exhibition comprising photographs, colour slides and plans, etc., on some particular aspect of the work is mounted from time to time. Tea-room in summer.

The Royal Mile from Holyroodhouse

123

HOLYROODHOUSE

We now move—on the site of the old Abbey Gatehouse, of which traces will be seen on the adjacent walls of the Court House along with coloured armorial stone of James V from the Holyrood buildings—from the Canongate into a fine open quadrangle, with three ornamental gateways, which gives a beautiful setting to the picturesque Palace of Holyroodhouse and the ancient Abbey. The wrought-iron gates form part of the Memorial to Edward VII mentioned below.

The western side of the square is mainly occupied by a low turreted building, the **Guard House and Royal Stables**, and the **Abbey Court House**, where judgments were dispensed in the Sanctuary days.

Facing the Chapel Royal stands the **National Memorial to King Edward VII**, designed by *Sir G Washington Browne, RSA*. In a colonnaded hemicycle of sandstone, occupying the western side of the northern forecourt, is a fine statue in bronze of Edward the Peacemaker, the work of *H S Gamley, RSA*.

The ornate **Fountain** (erected in 1859), in the centre of the Square, is a copy of an ancient one formerly in the quadrangle of Linlithgow Palace.

The Palace of Holyroodhouse

(**Admission,** see p. 94).

Historical Note—The Palace was at first intimately connected with the Abbey built by David I and dedicated to the Holy Rood, the Virgin and All Saints, in gratitude, it is said, for deliverance from danger. The story is to the effect that the King, when hunting near Arthur's Seat, had his life imperilled by the charge of a huge stag; but, a fragment of the Holy Rood being miraculously placed in his hand, the stag fled appalled. The name is much more satisfactorily accounted for by the connection of the house with the famous Black Rood (or Black Cross) brought to Scotland by the Saxon Princess Margaret, who became the Queen of Malcolm Canmore. This renowned relic was a small casket in the form of a crucifix containing a splinter of the true cross. It passed to Margaret's son, David I; captured from the Scottish King at the Battle of Nelville's Cross (1346) and taken to Durham Cathedral from which it disappeared at the Reformation.

The Abbey was richly endowed, and it gradually became a royal residence. James IV lived here and began building the Palace including the northern tower and other older parts, containing Queen Mary's apartments. In 1543 the Palace and Abbey were burnt during the English invasion, only the church and north-west tower escaping. The Palace was the principal residence of Mary, and of her son, James VI, to the time when he ascended the English throne. Cromwell quartered some of his troops here after the battle of Dunbar in 1650. A few weeks later a fire destroyed the greater portion of the edifice, the structure built by James IV again escaping. In 1658, Cromwell ordered the Palace to be restored, but all his work was pulled down in 1671, when Charles II decided on the erection of a new palace, from the plans of Sir William Bruce of Kinross, who held the office of King's surveyor in Scotland. Bonnie Prince Charlie held Court at Holyrood in September–October, 1745, before setting off on his ill-fated march on London. In 1830–32 Charles X of France lived here in exile. Edward VII, as a boy, spent some time in the Palace when studying under the Rector of the High School (1859), and nowadays the Palace is frequently and regularly used as a royal residence. Since 1929 its official designation has been, as in bygone days, the Palace of Holyroodhouse.

The general style of architecture is French, of the time of Louis XIV. The old tower remains at the northern end of the western front, and that at the southern end, built by Bruce, is a copy of it. The grand entrance, of four Doric columns, is surmounted by the royal arms of Scotland. The building surrounds a quadrangle, the northern side containing the Picture Gallery, the southern side the State Apartments.

On entering, the visitor, turning to the left, comes to –

The Historical Apartments

of which the first is the **Picture Gallery,** the largest apartment in the Palace, measuring 150 feet long, 24 feet wide and 20 feet high. Here the Young Pretender, Charles Edward, held levees and balls during his brief stay in the Scottish capital in 1745; and since the Union the gallery has been used for the election of the representative peers of Scotland and the levees of the Lord High Commissioner to the General Assembly of the Church of Scotland. Scott describes the room as 'long, low, and ill-proportioned, hung with pictures affirmed to be the portraits of kings, who, if they ever flourished at all, lived several hundred years before the invention of painting in oil colours'. The portraits were executed in 1684–86 by James de Witt or Jakob de Wet, Junior (1640–97), of Haarlem, who completed the 110 works, from 'originalls' supplied by the Government, in two years.

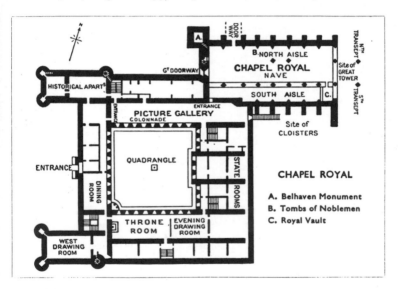

THE PALACE OF HOLYROODHOUSE

From the Picture Gallery the State Apartments on the first floor are entered. The Throne Room, Drawing Rooms, etc. contain fine paintings, tapestries, furniture, panelling and ceilings. The visitor then returns to the historic Palace and enters **Lord Darnley's Apartment**, in the old tower of the Palace. Mary was married to Henry Stewart, Lord Darnley, eldest son of Matthew, Earl of Lennox, on July 29, 1565, and thus were united two lines of succession to the English throne. Darnley's rooms consisted of an **Audience Chamber**, the room called **Lord Darnley's Bedroom**, and his **Dressing Room**. In these rooms are good specimens of ancient tapestry, and many portraits.

Holyroodhouse from Arthur's Seat

A door in the Audience Chamber leads to a staircase by which **Queen Mary's Apartments** are reached. There is also a small private staircase (closed to the public) by which the murderers of Rizzio gained access to the Queen's rooms.

Mary's Bedroom has panelled compartments with the emblems and initials of Scottish sovereigns in the ceiling; the walls are hung with tapestry illustrative of the Fall of Phaeton. Relics of Mary Stewart are to be seen in this room including authentic examples of needlework embroidered by the Queen. Adjoining the Bedroom is a small **Dressing Room**, hung with decayed tapestry. This occupies the eastern turret of the tower. A little to the west of it is a door, half hidden by tapestry, communicating with a secret staircase on the north side of the room; and near the head of this staircase is another door leading to the most interesting of all Queen Mary's apartments, the **Supper Room**, in the west turret, in which, on March 9, 1566, Rizzio was attacked by Ruthven and the other conspirators, the craven Darnley being also present, and dragged through the Bedroom and the Audience Chamber to the head of the principal staircase, where his body was left with fifty-six wounds. A brass tablet now marks the spot.

Mary's Audience Chamber is 24 feet long and 22 feet wide. In the panelled compartments of the ceiling are the arms and initials of royal persons. There is an oratory at the east end, and a portion of the frieze adorning the walls in Mary's time has been uncovered.

126

The ruins of—

The Chapel Royal is entered from the north-west corner of the quadrangle. The walls of the Chapel Royal, the nave, are the only portion of the old Abbey Church still standing, the choir and transepts having been destroyed after the Reformation. The foundations of the demolished parts of the Church, including those of the Chapter-house, have been laid bare, and along with these were discovered the remains of an earlier Christian Church, and a number of ancient graves. Of the seven pillars which once divided the nave from the north aisle only two remain, and they are broken. Externally the north wall is supported by seven flying buttresses. Of the western front only the north-western tower and the great doorway, with the remarkable west window, remain, the Palace having impinged on and obliterated the north-eastern tower. The front generally is in the Early English style, with intrusions of Later Gothic. The doorway is arched and deeply recessed. Above the lintel the space is filled with an arcade of five pointed arches. On a tablet above the doorway is an inscription placed by Charles I: '*Basilicam hanc, semi rutam, Carolus Rex optimus instauravit*', with the date 1633. 'He shall build ane house for my name, and I will stablish the throne of his kingdom for ever'. The floor of the nave is paved with gravestones, and there are several interesting tombs in the Chapel. One of the most notable is that of Viscount Belhaven (1639) in the north-west tower. Another is the tomb of Sir James Douglas of Parkhead, who killed the Earl of Arran, and twelve years afterwards (1608) was himself stabbed by Arran's nephew in the High Street of Edinburgh; and the mural monuments of Bishop Adam Bothwell, who, in this chapel, married Mary to Lord Bothwell, and of Bishop George Wishart of St Andrews, who suffered so much for the cause of Charles I, and was Montrose's chaplain and historian, attract attention. The inscription on the **Royal Vault**, in the south-east corner, restored by Queen Victoria in 1898, records that it contains 'the remains of David II; of James II and his Queen, Mary of Gueldres; of Arthur, third son of James IV; of James V and his Queen, Magdalen, and second son Arthur, Duke of Albany; and of Henry, Lord Darnley, consort of Mary, Queen of Scots'. James VII and II restored the nave as a Chapel Royal, and revived here the Order of the Thistle (*see* p. 112). The Chapel was pillaged in December, 1688, by the Revolution mob: and in 1768, during a storm, the roof fell in, leaving the building a ruin.

In the garden on the north side of the Palace is a sun-dial called **Queen Mary's Dial**, but the name is applicable to Henrietta Maria, wife of Charles I.

At the outer edge of an enclosure of grass and trees near the foot of Abbey Hill is a quaint old building (late sixteenth-century), with pyramidal or conical roof and dormer windows. This structure is known as **Queen Mary's Bath**, where, says a generally discredited tradition, the beautiful Queen was wont to bathe in white wine. In 1789, during repairs to the roof, a richly-chased dagger was found stuck into the sarking. It was probably a garden summer-house.

Grassmarket, Cowgate, Holyrood Park and Calton Hill

The Old Town of Edinburgh has much more to show besides the Royal Mile, just as Princes Street is far from being all that is worth seeing in the New Town. South of the Castle and the High Street lie the Grassmarket and the Cowgate, which are no less evocative of olden times.

From the west end of Princes Street **Lothian Road**, one of the city's main thoroughfares, leads southwards through Tollcross to the Braid Hills, Fairmilehead and beyond. In the hollow between us and the Castle is the–

West Kirk or **St Cuthbert's Church**, the history of which goes further back than that of any other religious institution in Edinburgh. As early as the eighth century the site was occupied by a church dedicated to Cuthbert, Bishop of Durham, who died in 687. It is mentioned in a Charter of David I, dated 1127, which is the oldest document in Scotland, and is preserved in the Register House. Its history during the Middle Ages is difficult to trace, although there are occasional references in papal bull, bishop's confirmation, royal charters and burgh records to St Cuthbert's, its altars, chapels and the rents it had to pay to Holyrood Abbey. On March 16, 1242 'St Cuthbert's under the Castle' was re-dedicated by Bishop de Bernham, the Bishop of St Andrew's. The pre-Reformation Church building, having been frequently damaged whenever the Castle was attacked and defended, was pulled down in 1773 and replaced by a large barn-like structure. A tower was built on to this ugly edifice by public subscription in 1789 and was so much better constructed than the main building, which survived for just over one century, that when the present Church was built in 1894 in the Early Italian Renaissance style, the tower was incorporated by the architect in his scheme. The St Cuthbert's peal of bells is known far and wide through the radio. In the burial ground are interred many distinguished men, including Napier, the inventor of logarithms, and Thomas de Quincey, the author of *The Confessions of an Opium Eater*.

King's Stables Road runs down to the Grassmarket. On a higher level is **Castle Terrace**, where was the Synod Hall of the United Presbyterian Church, first a theatre and latterly a cinema now removed to make way for Edinburgh's Opera House. It is flanked on the west by the *City Social Services Department*. A large public car park has been constructed on the slope between Castle Terrace and King's Stables Road.

The **Usher Hall**, half-way up Lothian Road, is the city's main hall. Opened in 1914, it seats some 2,750 and is the scene of big public meetings and principal concerts. The Hall is one of the finest buildings in the city, the

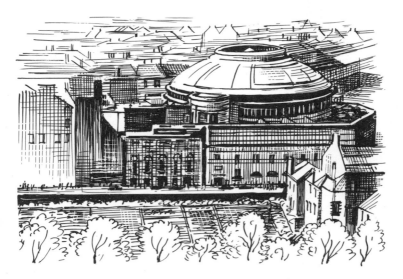

Usher Hall, Edinburgh

architecture being a mingling of the Florid Gothic and Later Renaissance styles. The cost of the building was left to the city by Andrew Usher, distiller. Behind the Usher Hall, in Grindlay Street, is the **Royal Lyceum Theatre**, today a civic theatre and still–as in 1883, when Henry Irving and Ellen Terry inaugurated it–Edinburgh's chief home of drama.

Farther up Lothian Road, on the right–where Port Hopetoun, the terminus of the Union Canal (1822) used to be –is **Lothian House**, a handsome modern structure, occupied by Inland Revenue Departments, cinemas, shops, etc. Just beyond it the thoroughfare of **Fountainbridge** runs off westward, past the factories of the North British Rubber Company, now in Uniroyal group, in the direction of Slateford or Gorgie and Sighthill, on the city's western boundary, now one of the main development areas.

East Fountainbridge takes us in the opposite direction, to the **West Port** and so back into the Old Town. A few carved stones in the West Port bear witness to bygone activities of what was 'pre-eminently the Trades' suburb', outside Edinburgh's western gateway, but the ill-famed Tanner's Close, on the north side near where the West Port enters the Grassmarket, has long since vanished. It was the abode of the notorious Irish murderers, Burke and Hare, who in 1828–29 sold the bodies of their victims for dissection in Surgeon Square. (James Bridie's play *The Anatomist* and Dylan Thomas's *The Doctor and the Devil* are both based on the ghoulish story.)

EDINBURGH

The Grassmarket

A weekly market was held here from 1477 to 1911, when the cattle and grain markets were removed to Saughton.

Time and municipal improvement schemes have swept away nearly all the ancient associations of the Grassmarket. As we stand at the western end a capital view is obtained of the grand old market-place, which can also be reached, as already mentioned, from Lothian Road, by **King's Stables Road**, where of old knights made ready for tourney in the Barras and today motorists can park their cars in modern style.

On the north side is the *White Hart Inn*, where Burns, Wordsworth and many other noted visitors stayed. The *Beehive Restaurant* nearby incorporates a strange attraction – the door of the 'condemned cell' from the Calton Jail.

On the site of the old Corn Exchange is the new Mountbatten Building of Heriot Watt University.

At the east end of the Grassmarket a small enclosed garden marks the dread place of executions. It contains a cross rather misleadingly inscribed: 'For the Protestant faith on this spot many martyrs and Covenanters died.' The Covenanters who died here for conscience' sake were the victims of fellow-Protestants; and here too many a low criminal, many a high-born leader paid the penalty. The Traverse Theatre which frequently offers *avant garde* and experimental plays is near the junction with Victoria Street (West Bow).

From the eastern extremity of the Grassmarket the West Bow leads up to the Lawnmarket, and Candlemaker Row up to the Kirk of the Greyfriars and Bristo Port, while between them begins the narrow, sombre, low road of –

The Cowgate

As the name suggests, the Cowgate was originally a rustic lane, running between hedgerows from Holyrood to the Kirk of St Cuthbert, bordered by the gardens and orchards of the Blackfriars' or Dominican Monastery. Gradually – from the fifteenth century – the Cowgate or Sou' gait ('South road') became a fashionable suburb.

On the right-hand side, as we enter the Cowgate, we pass the **Magdalen Chapel**, erected about the middle of the sixteenth century. Its stained-glass windows constitute the most notable specimens of the all too rare pre-Reformation glass in Scotland. The windows represent the royal arms encircled with a wreath of thistles, and those of the Queen Regent, Mary of Guise, within a laurel wreath, with the shields of the founder and foundress, Michael Macquhan (Macqueen) and his widow, Janet Rhynd. The chapel is interesting as possibly the place where the General Assembly of the Church of Scotland Reformed held its meeting in 1578. The tower was added in 1622 by the Incorporation of Hammermen, who administered the foundation. The chapel now serves as the University Chapel of Heriot-Watt University.

Adjoining the chapel, and incorporating its west wall, is Livingstone House, the headquarters of the General Practice Unit of Edinburgh University.

Passing under George IV Bridge, we note the Edinburgh Public Library, the National Library of Scotland and Parliament House towering above.

On the south side of the way is the **Heriot-Watt University Extension** (1934);
it houses engineering, printing and other departments. A little farther on
we pass, on the right, the remains of the **College Wynd**, now zigzag Guthrie
Street, where Sir Walter Scott was born and where formerly lived many of
the University professors; and the once spacious and fashionable **Horse
Wynd**, so named because it was the only wynd down which a vehicle could
be driven.

On the left, Blair Street leads up to Hunter Square and (beyond the arch
of South Bridge) Niddry Street and Blackfriars Street run north to join the
High Street. At the foot of Blackfriars Street Cardinal Beaton had his
palace. Opposite, on the southern side of the Cowgate, was the Blackfriars'
Monastery (1230), a Dominican Friary with extensive grounds, and
adjoining was the residence of Gavin Douglas, Bishop of Dunkeld,
translator of the *Æneid* into Scots verse (1513), the first version of a Latin
poet published in Britain. The **High School Wynd** is interesting as showing
us where the city grammar school was once located.

By Holyrood Road and under St John's Hill we reach–

Holyrood Park

(Popularly known as the Queen's or King's Park), the Royal demesne,
covering 648 acres, adjoining the Palace.

A broad road, the **Queen's Drive**, about three miles and a half long, encircles
Arthur's Seat, which forms part of the Park, and from the views it commands is
certainly one of the finest carriage-drives in Europe.

The Drive must be followed clockwise from Holyrood. On the left, behind the
Palace, is the **Parade Ground**, the scene of military reviews. North of it, is the Elsie
Inglis Maternity Hospital. On the right is **St Margaret's Well**, originally near
Restalrig and a little beyond is **St Margaret's Loch**, an artificial lake used for
boating and skating. Crowning the slope of a rugged hill behind are the remains of
St Anthony's Chapel, with his Well in the vicinity. St Anthony's Oratory is believed
to have been built about 1430, and to have been connected with the Knights
Hospitallers of St Anthony in Leith.

Near the eastern exit from the Park is **Muschat's Cairn**, the scene of an infamous
crime in 1720 when Nicol Muschat, a surgeon, murdered his wife, but our route
goes up the hill skirting **Dunsapie Loch** and **Whinny Hill**. The slopes of Arthur's
Seat here show the cultivation terraces of the Iron Age people who inhabited the
area.

On the left is a wide view of Midlothian and the Pentland Hills. **Duddingston Loch**, a fine
sheet of water, with its sedgy margin, a sanctuary for waterfowl, is seen below in the foreground;
north of it is the village of **Duddingston**, with a picturesque Norman Church, in which John
Thomson (1778–1840), the landscape painter, ministered. At the gate of the churchyard are
the 'loupin' on' or mounting stone, and the 'jougs,' an iron neck-ring used as a pillory. The
'Sheep's Heid Inn' at Duddingston claims fourteenth-century origin and has a skittle alley.
Behind the village and nestling among trees are *Duddingston House Hotel,* a straggling mansion
designed in 1763 by Sir Wm Chambers, for the 8th Earl of Abercorn, and Duddingston Golf
Course.

The road next passes over the top of the curious basaltic columns called
Samson's Ribs to dip downward to the lower road (beyond which lies Prestonfield

Princes Street and Calton Hill beyond

Golf Course) and to the **Wells o' Wearie**, celebrated in ballad literature while behind are the Pollock Halls of Residence of the University of Edinburgh and behind again the Royal Commonwealth Swimming Pool built for the Commonwealth Games 1970.

On the right a peep is obtained of the valley known as **Hunter's Bog** – a practising ground for bowmen of old and latterly for riflemen. Here part of Prince Charles Edward's army encamped in 1745.

The road then descends to the Holyrood Park Road entrance to the Queen's Park, a lower road makes for Duddingston by 'Samson's Ribs' and the 'Windy Gowl', but we continue on the Queen's Drive abreast of **St Leonard's Hill** on our right. The whole district has been rendered classic by *The Heart of Midlothian*. From Dumbiedykes Road and other points of vantage in the vicinity magnificent views are had of the vertical, red Salisbury Crags and the couched lion of Arthur's Seat.

The **Salisbury Crags** (Salisbury is said to be a corruption of Sallies brae, i.e. willows slope) present a precipitous front to the city, the highest point being 550 feet above the sea. Immediately beneath the rocks is a steep talus, on top of which is a pathway called the **Radical Road** (1820).

Ascent of Arthur's Seat – The highest of the seven hills on or round which Edinburgh is built, Arthur's Seat (822 feet), can be climbed without difficulty by a path which mounts on the Holyrood side from St Margaret's Well, passes St Anthony's Well, a deliciously cool spring gushing from below a huge boulder, and then scales the ridge overhanging Hunter's Bog. A still easier line of approach is from the side of Dunsapie Loch. The more energetic may prefer a third route *via* the 'Gutted Haddie,' a steep, narrow ravine that makes straight for the summit, from the south end of Hunter's Bog.

132

CALTON HILL, EDINBURGH

The view from the top (with its direction-finder) well repays the effort of climbing–Pentlands and Moorfoots to the south; Lammermuirs, North Berwick Law and the Bass Rock to the east; the Firth and Fife to the north; the Forth Bridges, Ben Lomond and other Highland giants to the west; and just below, 'Edinburgh Castle, town and tower,' in all their majesty. An extinct volcano, Arthur's Seat, with its red igneous rock, is a happy hunting-ground for the geologist as well as the artist.

The journey homeward from Holyrood house can be made by the familiar route up the Canongate and down the North Bridge into Princes Street, but, stimulated by the Queen's Park air, let us return instead by Regent Road and the–

Calton Hill

Abbey Hill and Abbey Mount lead up to Regent Road and so back to the General Post Office, but those on foot can gain that thoroughfare by a short-cut through the public park beyond the railway bridge or by a steep path from Calton Road.

From Regent Road we look down on the **New Calton Burying-Ground**, features of which are a watch-tower and graves protected by iron railings, erected in the days of the resurrectionists. In it are buried R L Stevenson's parents.

Farther west, we pass the old **Royal High School**, designed by a former pupil, *Thomas Hamilton, RSA*; it is a specimen of the purest Grecian Doric, and a copy of the Temple of Theseus at Athens. The School was founded about 1128 and supervised by the Abbots of Holyrood until it was transferred from the care of the Church to that of the City during the reign of Mary Queen of Scots. She took some interest in the School and bestowed an endowment upon it. James VI and I was the first to refer to it as *Schola Regia*. It was transferred from High School Yards to its present site in 1829. Among distinguished former pupils are Robert Adam, Sir Walter Scott and Alexander Graham Bell. In 1968 the School transferred again to a new site at Barnton.

Opposite is the **Burns Monument**, also designed by Thomas Hamilton. It is a reproduction (1832) of the Greek peripteral temple of Lysicrates at Athens.

The Calton Hill can be ascended by the carriage-way entered beside the High School gates, or on foot by the stairs in Waterloo Place.

The **National Monument** stands near the summit. Modelled on the Parthenon, it was designed to commemorate the gallant achievements of Scottish soldiers and sailors during the Peninsular War. The foundation-stone was laid in 1822. The work soon came to a standstill for want of funds and has never been resumed. Fortunately, the unfinished monument is more like to the Parthenon than the completed building would have been.

The elevation here is 355 feet above sea-level and a glorious view is obtained.

On the southern brow, overlooking Regent Road, is the **Nelson Monument** (1805–16), shaped somewhat like a telescope. Here are numerous relics of the hero of Trafalgar. The top of the monument, which is 102 feet in height, is surmounted by a time-ball, which falls daily throughout the year at 1 p.m. (Greenwich time).

A little to the west are the **Old Observatory** (1776) and the **New Observatory** (1818). They were transferred to the city after the Royal Observatory on Blackford

Floodlit National Memorial and Nelson Monument

Hill was built. At the south-eastern end of the City Observatory is a *Monument to Professor John Playfair*, philosopher and mathematician (d 1819); while farther west, at the top of the stairs leading from Waterloo Place, is a *Memorial to Dugald Stewart*, Professor of Moral Philosophy in the University of Edinburgh, 1786–1828. At the foot of these stairs medallions recall three great nineteenth-century Scottish vocalists–Templeton, Wilson and Kennedy (father of Mrs Kennedy Fraser, the composer and collector of Hebridean songs).

On the other side of the roadway, with a frontage of over 500 feet, lies the imposing edifice of–

St Andrew's House, since 1939 the home of the principal Scottish Government Departments. The structure was designed by Mr T S Tait. Outstanding in its conception, it nevertheless blends pleasantly both with the older architecture and with the natural rocky background of the Edinburgh scene. The main entrance contains noble bronze doors bearing in relief symbolic representations of Saint Andrew and Saints Ninian, Kentigern, Columba and Magnus. The doorway is surmounted by the Royal Coat of Arms with Scottish quartering, carved in the stone. On the fifth floor is the room of the Secretary of State for Scotland, which is panelled in Scottish walnut made from a tree planted by Mary Queen of Scots at Balmerino Abbey, in northern Fife.

A reminder of the previous history of the site, in the shape of the former house of the governor of the *Calton Jail*, stands on the brow of the cliff overlooking Waverley Station. The prison, a picturesque castellated structure, completed in 1812, served as HM County Jail for over a century, being then superseded by a new building at Saughton.

We now enter **Waterloo Place** (planned in 1815, the year of the battle), the direct approach to the Calton Hill from Princes Street, and in line with that thoroughfare. An archway leads to a flight of stairs giving access to all that is left of the historic—

Old Calton Burying-Ground. In the centre is the tall **Obelisk** raised in 1845 in memory of the political reformers, the 'Chartist martyrs,' Thomas Muir, Thomas Fyche Palmer, William Skirving, Maurice Margarot and Joseph Gerald, who were tried in 1793–94 for 'leasing-making' and 'speaking words tending to excite discord between King and people,' and sentenced to transportation for life. A few steps to the right lead to the circular and temple-like *Tomb of David Hume,* the philosopher.

Another noteworthy monument is that with a statue of *President Lincoln* (the first erected to the great American statesman in the British Isles); unveiled in 1893, it is in memory of Scots-American soldiers who fought in the American Civil War. Among others buried here are Sir William Allan, President of the Royal Scottish Academy; William Blackwood, founder of *Blackwood's Magazine*; Archibald Constable, Sir Walter Scott's publisher; Dr Candlish, the Disruption leader; and Daniel Stewart, founder of Stewart's College.

Waterloo Place crosses what is known as the Low Calton by the **Regent Bridge**, a single visible arch, with a span of 50 feet, and about the same height. In Waterloo Place are the Offices of the Inland Revenue, of British Railways and other public bodies. Princes Street is regained at the General Post Office.

The University and Around

Having now covered the oldest parts of the city, we can next turn our attention to the more or less modern districts which grew up outside the area once surrounded by the Flodden Wall. The south side adjoining the Grassmarket and Cowgate regions has first claim, on chronological as well as academic grounds.

Today, Edinburgh's main approach to the south is by the North and South Bridges.

From the east end of Princes Street, the **North Bridge**, the most outstanding of the city's many viaducts, spans the ravine between the New Town and the Old. It was first opened in 1772, widened in 1876 and reconstructed in 1897. On both sides the North Bridge enjoys magnificent views. Beneath its arches stretch the furrowed roofs of Waverley Station. On one of the piers is a sculptured memorial by Birnie Rhind, RSA, to the officers and men of the *King's Own Scottish Borderers* who fell in the South African War (1899–1902). The 'KOSB' is the only regiment that has the right to march through Edinburgh streets in peace time with bayonets fixed. This 'Edinburgh Regiment' was raised in 1688 to defend the city.

Commanding the southern end of the Bridge, on the right, are the offices of *The Scotsman* (founded in 1817: a daily since 1855) and the *Evening News*. They are among the most completely equipped newspaper premises in the world. On both sides of the street the architecture is of the Scottish Baronial type.

On reaching the point of intersection with High Street, we pass from the North Bridge to the **South Bridge**.

The scheme was first put forward two years after the opening of the North Bridge but not until 1784 did it take definite shape. The street was opened for foot passengers in November, 1786, and for wheeled traffic a year later. South Bridge is built on nineteen arches, only one of which is visible–that over the Cowgate.

Infirmary Street, running eastward, was the former site of the Royal Infirmary. The Old Infirmary in the High School Yards is now occupied by Departments of the University. The exterior of the Old High School, looking up Infirmary Street, is as it was when (from 1777) Walter Scott was a pupil. Borrow describes it in *Lavengro*.

East of the Old Infirmary runs the steep slope of the **Pleasance**, which, like other by-ways of the Old Town, has known happier days. Some improvement has been effected in the way of rebuilding, while social work is carried on by the Pleasance Trust and other bodies. The Church of Scotland *Deaconess Hospital* is at No. 148; the University owns the *Little Theatre* (No. 60) and the Pollock Institute (No. 46: Department of Physical Education, etc.).

At the corner of Chambers Street is the Old College of –

The University

(**Admission**, *see* p. 94).

Though much younger than St Andrew's, Glasgow and Aberdeen Universities, Edinburgh University is the biggest and best known. James Lawson, the colleague of Knox and minister of St Giles Church, on the downfall of episcopacy in 1576–80, pressed on the authorities the founding of the new seat of learning. The Town Council ordered a building to be prepared for the reception of students, and in 1583 they appointed Robert Rollock, professor of St Andrews, Regent or Principal of the new University. In 1617 James VI paid a visit to his native country, and was so gratified with the progress made by the 'Tounis College' that he became its patron. Only, by a characteristic lapse of memory, he forgot to endow it. Erected at intervals between 1789 and 1834, from plans prepared by Robert Adam and modified by W H Playfair, the edifice forms a rectangle, 356 feet long by 225 wide, partly Palladian, partly Grecian. The portico of the principal front has six Doric pillars, and was surmounted in 1884 by a graceful dome terminating

The University, Edinburgh

in a figure of 'Youth holding aloft the Torch of Knowledge.' Brass panels at the west end of the 'Old Quad' commemorate nearly 1000 Alumni who fell in the First World War and 250 in the Second.

The tutorial staff of the University consists of a Principal, some hundred professors and a great company of lecturers, allocated among the eight Faculties: Divinity, Law, Medicine, Arts, Science, Music, Social Sciences and Veterinary Medicine. The Chancellor is HRH the Duke of Edinburgh. The students number about 11,000 (*see* pp. 139–40, 142, 155).

Somewhere in the region of the south-east corner of the Old College stood Kirk o' Field, the house which was blown up on the occasion of Darnley's murder, February 10, 1567.

Chambers Street is named after Dr William Chambers, who was Lord Provost (1865–69) when the series of 'improvements' was started in this area. His statue stands midway in the street. Off the north side runs **Guthrie Street**, formerly the College Wynd, where, in August, 1771, Walter Scott was born. Near it, in Chambers Street, is **Adam House** (1955), with the University's Examination Halls and a charming theatre (architect, Mr W H Kininmonth, RSA), Students' Refectory and University Staff Club. On the same side used to be Minto House Medical and Surgical School, a great extramural institution, associated with the memory of James Syme, the famous surgeon, and of Dr John Brown, author of *Rab and his Friends*. It now accommodates departments of the University. Adjoining is the **Heriot-Watt University**, formerly a Technical College. In front is a statue of James Watt, while over the entrance are busts of George Heriot and Leonard Horner, one of the founders of a pioneer School of Arts (1821). In addition to day courses of instruction in engineering, chemistry, printing and other technical subjects, evening classes are held in many subjects. Its constitution consists of a combination of the two great educational agencies, the George Heriot Trust and the Watt Institution and School of Arts, formerly in Adam Square.

The **Edinburgh Dental School**, now part of the University, lies between the Heriot-Watt Buildings and George IV Bridge.

Occupying the south side of Chambers Street is an immense block in the Venetian Renaissance style–

The Royal Scottish Museum (*Admission, see* p. 94). The museum building, opened in 1866, has received additions from time to time, and is now one of the largest and most important institutions in the country. A fine Lecture Hall was opened in 1961.

The collections are divided among four major departments: (1) Art and Archaeology, (2) Natural History, (3) Geology and (4) Technology. Each major section occupies a block in the building. The first-named houses interesting remains of early civilizations, arms and armour, examples of the handicrafts of the various races of mankind and extensive collections of glass, pottery, metalwork and textiles. One of the finest possessions is the famous Paris-made Lennoxlove silver-gilt toilet service (presented to 'La Belle Stuart' by Charles II). In the Natural History Department is a wide range of mounted insects, fish, reptiles, birds and mammals, many in realistic habitat groups. The Geology Department contains minerals and fossils and is especially strong in Scottish examples. The Technology Department has a notable series of working models of various types of machinery, leading from the primitive engine to the marvels of the modern jet, and displays models of ships, bridges and lighthouses.

George IV Bridge commemorates that king's visit to Edinburgh. Where it passes over the Cowgate, two great Libraries face each other, one civic, one national.

The **Central Public Library**, an ornate pile in the French Renaissance style, was founded in 1890 by a gift from Andrew Carnegie. It includes large and well-arranged lending and reference departments (*see* p. 94)–the Edinburgh section is of particular interest–and has numerous branches in the suburban districts. It is built on the site of the mansion of Sir Thomas Hope, King's Advocate, and two of the old inscribed lintels surmount internal doorways.

Opposite are the handsome buildings (opened by the Queen in 1956) of–

The National Library of Scotland. Established by Act of Parliament in 1925, the National Library (*see* also pp. 94, 130) owes much to the munificence of Sir Alexander Grant, Bart (1864–1937). It contains the largest and most valuable collection of books and manuscripts in Scotland–upwards of three million in all–and is entitled to claim a copy of every work published in Great Britain. Designed by the late Dr R Fairlie, RSA, the edifice has a facade bearing sculptured figures (the work of Hew Lorimer, RSA) symbolic of the Arts and Sciences. Many literary and historical treasures from the Library's holdings as well as visiting and special exhibitions are on display in the Exhibition Hall and Entrance Hall on the ground floor. The main Reading Room, on the first floor, has no windows towards George IV Bridge in order to ensure silence. The Library has nine floors below street level–mostly 'stack rooms'. The well-equipped map room was opened in 1958.

Victoria Street, branching off westward–with Victoria Terrace as a balcony–joins the West Bow at its entrance to the Grassmarket, which is likewise the goal of **Candlemaker Row**, at the southern end of George IV Bridge. The Hall (1722) of the ancient Corporation of Candlemakers, at its head, has been restored. To the backs of the Candlemaker Row tenements are quaintly attached tombstones in Greyfriars Kirkyard. At the road junction in front of Candlemakers' Hall is a touching memorial to **Greyfriars Bobby**, erected by the Baroness Burdett-Coutts. Bobby was a devoted terrier that for fourteen years guarded the grave (1858) of its master, John Gray, 'Auld Jock', in the adjacent churchyard. 'American lovers of Bobby' marked the grave by a granite stone.

Through a short lane at the top of Candlemaker Row we reach the main entrance to–

Greyfriars Churchyard, anciently the garden of the Franciscan monastery which stood in the Grassmarket.

It contains many interesting monuments, including those of George Buchanan (1506–82), the humanist; Walter Scott's father; Dr Robertson, the historian; Joseph Black, the chemist; McLaurin, the mathematician; Allan Ramsay, the poet; Duncan Ban McIntyre, the Gaelic poet-gamekeeper; Sir George Mackenzie, the 'Bluidy Mackenzie'; Henry Mackenzie, the 'Man of Feeling'; William Adam, the architect; Dr Hugh Blair; McCrie, the biographer of Knox; Duncan Forbes of Culloden; James Hutton, the geologist, etc.

A flat tombstone is associated with the tradition that on February 28, 1638, the National Covenant was signed thereon by an excited multitude, but historians assure us that the stone is of later date and that the only copy available that day was subscribed by some 200 noblemen *inside* the Church, the populace signing later elsewhere. In the north-east angle of the church-yard, the former burying-place of common malefactors, the grim **Martyrs' Monument**–the original (1706) is in Huntly House Museum–pays tribute to Mr James Renwick (1662–88) and scores of other Covenanters, executed like him. The **Covenanters' Prison** is in the opposite corner; here, in an open space to the south-west, hundreds of those captured at Bothwell Bridge (June 22, 1679) were confined for weeks, over 200 who would not sign a bond not to take up arms against the King being sent off in November to the plantations, from which they were saved by shipwreck and a watery grave.

Old Greyfriars Church was opened in 1620–the first church built in Edinburgh after the Reformation. Extended in 1721, it held two congregations, Old and New Greyfriars. The building was severely damaged by fire in 1845. In 1937 the partition was removed and the united congregation now worships in the **Kirk of the Greyfriars.**

Almost opposite to the entrance to Greyfriars was the Bristo Port and fragments of the Flodden Wall survive here–one is enclosed in the Royal Scottish Museum. At the northern end of Forrest Road the Chaplaincy Centre of the University is installed in the former New North Church. Passing along Forrest Road and crossing Lauriston Place, we reach **Middle Meadow Walk**, a beautiful promenade reserved for pedestrians, which runs between the Royal Infirmary (right) and the 'New Buildings' or Medical School of the University (left). Beyond the latter is an entrance to–

George Square, named after George Brown, brother of the architect. Its erection in 1766 was one of the first overt acts to break down the prejudice against residing outside the ancient walls. James Brown here built the 'parallelogram', as it was called. George Square immediately became a fashionable locality. To No. 25–the third from the foot on the western side–Mr Walter Scott the elder removed in 1772, shortly after his son's birth, and here the novelist lived until his marriage in 1796. In neighbouring houses dwelt other famous Scots. George Watson's Ladies College (a Merchant Company School) was established here in 1871. A large part of the square is occupied by the University. At the north-east corner stands the Appleton Tower for first-year Science teaching, and at the south-east the David Hume Tower of the Faculty of Arts, flanked by the William Robertson building and the Adam Ferguson Building for the Faculties of Arts and Social Sciences. On the south side is the new Library designed by Sir Basil Spence.

In Jeffrey's rooms at No 18 Buccleuch Place (second floor), adjacent to George Square, the *Edinburgh Review* was born. No 18 now contains the Donald Tovey Memorial Rooms. Sir Donald Tovey, scholar and composer, · was Professor of Music at Edinburgh University, 1914–40. Numerous University Departments have accommodation in Buccleuch Place.

To the south of Buccleuch Place lie–

The Meadows, which cover the site of what was once a lake, or morass–the South or Burgh Loch. Early in the seventeenth century an attempt was made to drain the loch, but the scheme only resulted in reducing its dimen-

An Edinburgh sunset from Calton Hill

sions. In 1722, Thomas Hope of Rankeillor bound himself, if the loch and adjacent lands were let to him at a moderate figure, to drain the bed entirely. He fulfilled the conditions, and Hope's Park, now the Meadows, was created. **Melville Drive** skirts the southern side. The East and West Meadows, divided by the Middle Meadow Walk, are devoted to cricket, tennis, bowls, football and other pastimes.

Buccleuch Place leads into Buccleuch Street, where is the **Archers' Hall**–built in 1776–77 and modernised in 1901–the headquarters of the **Royal Company of Archers**, or Queen's Bodyguard for Scotland. This remarkable corps, which in Scotland takes precedence of all royal guards and troops whatsoever, is composed of nobles and gentlemen of position. The Society was formed about 1676, and in 1704 received a Charter under the Great Seal of Scotland making it into a royal company, reviving and ratifying on its behalf all the old laws in favour of archery. The dining-hall contains a Raeburn, and a noteworthy chandelier.

At the north end of Buccleuch Street was **Buccleuch Church**, in the grave-yard of which lie Dr Blacklock–the blind poet who befriended Robert Burns–and Mrs Cockburn, authoress of the later version of *The Flowers of the Forest*. From the **Royal (Dick) School of Veterinary Studies** (founded by Professor Dick in 1823: removed here in 1916 and now a Faculty of the University) Hope Park Terrace continues the Melville Drive eastwards and quickly takes us to South Clerk Street, part of Edinburgh's main road to the south (A7) by Galashiels and Carlisle.

On the western side of Middle Meadow Walk, with its frontage on Lauriston Place, is–

The Royal Infirmary of Edinburgh. The Infirmary, which is closely associated with the Medical School of the University, is one of the most important 'teaching hospitals' in the country, and draws many thousands of patients from near and far. It is the largest hospital under the South-Eastern Regional Hospital Board, Scotland, and has several associated convalescent homes and clinics.

Opposite the Infirmary in Lauriston Place is–

George Heriot's School (Heriot's Hospital), founded and endowed by George Heriot, 'Jingling Geordie' (*c.* 1563–1624), goldsmith to James VI, for the maintenance and education of sons of poor burgesses of Edinburgh.

The western boundary wall of Heriot's School consists of the Telfer extension of the Flodden Wall in the **Vennel**, a lane running down from Lauriston Place to the Grassmarket. This section includes entire ramparts and one of the bastions of the Flodden Wall.

In **Archibald Place** (No 16, the last on the right), on the south side of Lauriston Place, Hugh Miller resided. At the head of Lady Lawson Street is the headquarters of the Scottish South-Eastern Fire Brigade, the **Central Fire Station**. The look-out tower rises to a height of 114 feet. On the site of the Old Cattle Market rises the **Edinburgh College of Art** (1907), with over 1,000 students. A central Institution for Art Education in the city and south-east Scotland, this College is among the foremost schools of its kind in the country. Nearly opposite the Fire Station is the **Chalmers Hospital for the Sick and Hurt** (1861–64). The funds were left by an Edinburgh plumber, George Chalmers. In Lauriston Gardens stands the **Convent of St Catherine of Siena** and in Lauriston Street are Lauriston Hall and the **Church of the Sacred Heart** (Roman Catholic), which contains an image formerly in Holyrood Abbey. At its western extremity Lauriston Place reaches the busy traffic centre of Tollcross, but we return now to the eastern end.

On the eastern side of Middle Meadow Walk is the **Medical Faculty of the University**, with the splendid McEwan Hall at the north-east corner.

In Teviot Place the houses and shops opposite the Medical College occupy the site of the old **Darien House**.

Crossing Bristo Street from the McEwan Hall, we enter **Lothian Street**, where a plaque marks the house (No 42) where De Quincey died in 1859. Lothian Street is continued by South College Street. From their junction, at the back of the Royal Scottish Museum and the University 'Old Buildings', Potterrow runs southward. In the seventeenth and eighteenth centuries Potterrow, in the suburb of Easter Portsburgh, housed people of rank and wealth. Its port (called also Kirk o' Field Port) gave entry to the city from the south. All traces of this ancient suburb have now gone to make way for the Students' Centre of the University, comprising union facilities, health centre and meeting places. **Marshall Street** intersects Potterrow a little way down; the Bristo Building of the Heriot-Watt University now stands on the spot where Burns visited his Clarinda (Mrs Maclehose); and in a third-storey room in the eastern portion (formerly called Alison Square) Thomas Campbell wrote the *Pleasure of Hope*.

By South College Street we reach Nicolson Street at the Kirk o' Field corner of the University. This busy thoroughfare runs south from the Bridges, its chief feature being the pillared front of the **Surgeons' Hall** (1833). The Museum of the Royal College of Surgeons (*admission, see* p. 94) has fascinating (if gruesome) exhibits. The interiors of both the Hall and the Museum are considered among the best of Playfair's work. Opposite is the **Empire Theatre**, which, originally the home of varieties, is now used for Bingo.

The line of South College Street and of the Flodden Wall is carried on eastwards by **Drummond Street**, aforetime dubbed 'Thief Raw'. It skirts the back of the Old Infirmary and the Old Surgeons' Hall, which has unsavoury associations with the Burke and Hare murders.

The New Town

George Street and the Northern Slopes

After the Old Town, the New Town claims our attention. We have already 'done' Princes Street, as the saying goes, but Princes Street (*see* p. 95) is but the frontispiece of that entrancing production the New Town—that unique extent of grave substantial Georgian buildings, laid out in spacious streets and graceful squares and crescents, which in half a century (1770–1820) transformed the whole aspect and character of the city.

This northward extension of Edinburgh began in the region of **St Andrew Square**, at the east end of George Street. From Princes Street, just opposite the Scott Monument, the Square can be entered by St David Street—David Hume lived and died at No 21, now embodied in the London and Lancashire Insurance Company's building.

In the centre of St Andrew Square gardens is a lofty *Monument to Henry Dundas, Lord Melville,* the administrator of Scotland of Pitt's time, erected in 1821. It is modelled after the Trojan column at Rome, and is 149 feet high, the statue being 14 feet.

In the Square are the headquarters of a number of Scotland's most important financial institutions—banks, insurance companies and the like. On the east side, the **Royal Bank** (at No. 42; rebuilt 1942) occupies the site of premises once in the possession of Robert Cadell & Co, Scott's publishers after Constable's failure. The **British Linen Bank** (founded in 1746) was built in 1851 from designs by *David Bryce.* The six statues represent Navigation, Commerce, Manufacture, Art, Science and Agriculture. The **Royal Bank** (whose Charter dates from 1727) acquired in 1825 the elegant house designed half a century earlier by Sir William Chambers for Sir Laurence Dundas, ancestor of the Earls of Zetland. In front stands the *Hopetoun Monument,* in memory of John, 4th Earl of that name, who assumed command of the army at Corunna after the death of Sir John Moore. The house next the Royal Bank, to the north, is the oldest in the Square, dating from 1768; it was long Douglas's Hotel, where the dying Sir Walter Scott stayed on his return from Italy in 1832. At No. 21, on the northern side, Lord Brougham (1778–1868) was born, and here the future Lord Chancellor spent his early years.

Among the other noteworthy edifices in or adjoining the Square are the head offices of the Scottish Widows' Fund and of the Scottish Provident Institution, the premises of the Prudential Assurance Company and the Edinburgh Stock Exchange (corner of Thistle Street and North St David Street). A little way along Thistle Street—one of New Edinburgh's oldest printing centres—are the premises of Messrs W & R Chambers, the publishers, and the office of T & A Constable, the printers, where W E Henley edited the *Scots Observer*. Thistle Court, opposite, contains the first houses built (1767) in the New Town.

During the season St Andrew Square is the starting-point for many motor tours, and all the year round regular Eastern Scottish bus services leave from this centre. The bus terminal is in Clyde Street, off the north-east corner of the Square.

From the western side of St Andrew Square we enter –

George Street

Originally erected for residential purposes, it is now mainly devoted to shops and offices, but it has preserved a dignity and style of its own. George Street is half a mile in length and 115 feet wide. At its intersection with Hanover Street is a *Statue of George IV* (by Chantrey); there is a *Statue of Pitt* (also by Chantrey) at Frederick Street and one of *Dr Chalmers* (by Steell) at Castle Street – all at striking viewpoints over the Firth.

At the east end **St Andrew's and St George's Church** is memorable as the place where the Disruption of the Church of Scotland took place in 1843. Opposite is the former head office of the Commercial Bank (established in 1810; united with the National Bank in 1959 and with the Royal Bank in 1969), an imposing edifice designed by *David Rhind, RSA*. At No 22 are the rooms of the **Royal Society of Edinburgh**, with a magnificent library of scientific literature and periodicals. The 'RSE', founded in 1783, had Scott for its president in 1820–32; other distinguished Fellows have been Benjamin Franklin, Goethe and R L Stevenson. No 25, across the street, was the parental home of the novelist, Susan Ferrier (1782–1854). The offices of the Standard, the Royal, the Edinburgh, the Sun and other Insurance Companies, of the Union Bank (1830: now merged in the Bank of Scotland), of the Northern Lighthouse Board and (No 121) of the Church of Scotland (formerly those of the United Free Church) and the **Freemasons' Hall** are among the architectural ornaments of George Street.

An arcade and portico – at No 54, on the south side, between Frederick Street and Hanover Street – mark the **Assembly Rooms and Music Hall** (owned by the city), where great public functions are held. These rooms (as the 'Festival Club') serve as a focal point for the social entertainment of Festival visitors. It was at a dinner in the Assembly Rooms (February 23, 1827) that Sir Walter Scott first publicly admitted that he was the author of the Waverley novels. At No. 75 George Street, the mother of Sir Walter lived from about 1798 until 1819, and at No 108 Scott himself lived before he settled in Castle Street. The historic *Blackwood's* moved into No 45 in 1830. Shelley lodged at No 60 in 1811 (at 36 Frederick Street in 1813), and we need diverge only a few yards from George Street to find **Scott's House** (No 39 Castle Street), the first on the right-hand side of the street; here the Waverley novels were in large part written. At No 32 Castle Street (between George Street and Princes Street) was born (1859) Kenneth Grahame, author of *The Golden Age*.

At the west end of George Street is **Charlotte Square**, which ranks among the finest efforts of Robert Adam and as such is now jealously guarded against vandalism and 'modernisation'. In the gardens of the Square is the

EDINBURGH

Albert Memorial, an equestrian statue by *Sir John Steell, RSA.* On the west side of the Square stands massive St George's. Designed by Robert Reid, it was long a leading parish church (1814–1961). Its dome is modelled on that of St Paul's Cathedral. The building is now used as an additional repository for the Scottish Record Office. Nos 5, 6 and 7 are owned by the National Trust for Scotland and form the centrepiece of one of Robert Adam's finest essays in Georgian architecture. No 6, Bute House, is now the official residence of the Secretary of State for Scotland. No 9 has a memorial tablet to Lord Lister, with the dates 1870–77. That venerator of antiquity, Lord Cockburn, lived for many years at No 14 (now the Ladies' Caledonian Club). At No 17 was born (1856) Lord Haldane, who as Secretary for War (1905–12) remodelled the British Army; while No 24 was the birthplace, 1861, of Douglas Haig, British Commander-in-Chief in the War of 1914–18. Another distinguished native of this region was Alexander Graham Bell, the inventor of the telephone; his early years were spent in the corner house (No 16) at the top of South Charlotte Street, but Bell used to regard as his birthplace (in 1847) a top-storey room in Hope Street at the south-west end of the Square (almost above Earl Haig's birthplace).

For motorists the sole entrance (or exit) to the top of Queensferry Street is *via* Hope Street, from which only pedestrians can pass direct into **Shandwick Place**, the continuation of Princes Street from the 'West End.' From the foot of Lothian Road cars may go westward along one-way Rutland Street (The Edinburgh Press Club is at No. 19: Dr John Brown, who wrote *Rab and his Friends* and *Pet Marjorie*, lived at No. 23, from 1850–82) and Rutland Square (with the Scottish Headquarters of the Commonwealth Institute, Royal Automobile Club and Scottish Arts Club), and enter Shandwick Place at its western end beside Atholl Crescent.

The outstanding feature of Shandwick Place is **St George's West Church**, among whose ministers in the days when it was Free St George's, were Dr Candlish and Dr Alexander Whyte.

In Atholl Crescent is a Civil Service college. Its twin, Coates Crescent, contains the British Legion's Douglas Haig Memorial Hall and has its garden adorned by the **Gladstone Statue**, removed here from St Andrew Square in 1955. This memorial, unveiled by Lord Rosebery in 1917, represents the statesman in the ample robes of the Chancellor of the Exchequer and is the work of the eminent Scottish sculptor, Dr Pittendrigh Mac-Gillivray (1856–1938).

Haymarket Station, farther on, is on the main west and north lines from Waverley, with which it is connected by a tunnel. From the bustling roundabout of Haymarket and its Heart of Midlothian FC Memorial Clock, we turn back to gain, by way of Palmerston Place, the serene precincts of–

St Mary's Episcopal Cathedral, at the western end of Melville Street, one of the most beautiful ecclesiastical buildings erected in Scotland since the Reformation.

Built through the munificence of Barbara and Mary Walker of Coates to the designs of Sir George Gilbert Scott in the Early pointed Gothic style, it was consecrated in 1879. The total length of the Cathedral is 269 feet, the height of the nave is 58 feet, of the central spire 279 feet and the twin western spires 215 feet. There is a ring of ten bells and a fine organ. Furnishings include the original painting of 'The Presence', a bishop's chair presented by Canon H P Liddon of St Paul's, London, a recumbent figure in marble of Dean Montgomery and a hanging rood, designed by Lorimer.

The original Manor House of Old Coates north of the Cathedral was erected in 1615 by John Byres, whose town house was in the Royal Mile. It is now used as a Choir School. The Song School, which contains murals by Phoebe Traquair, was built in 1879. Here also stands the Walpole Hall, erected in memory of G H S Walpole, Bishop from 1910 to 1929, father of the novelist, Hugh Walpole. It was designed by Lorimer and built in 1931.

St Mary's Cathedral is the only church in Scotland to have its own Choir School and to have daily Choral services which maintain a tradition established in 1879.

In the streets around the Cathedral lived many Edinburgh notables of the nineteenth century. Here, today, dwell many 'specialists'; nursing-homes and private hotels and government offices abound. At 11 Rothesay Terrace are the Scottish headquarters of the Arts Council. Wide **Melville Street** leads to Queensferry Street, its old-world air heightened by the gaping metal serpent heads beside its doorsteps. These, like the cornucopias in Charlotte Square, were used by attendant link-men to extinguish their torches. In Melville Street stands a statue of the second viscount of the name and near its eastern end is **Melville College** for boys (started in 1832 as Edinburgh Institution).

Several bus services run northward and westward by way of Queensferry Street and by the **Dean Bridge**, a little lower down.

Near the Dean Bridge **Randolph Crescent** (entered by its lower end) is the only way by which traffic to or from the east can avoid the problems of the West End.

In Randolph Crescent, the French Institute (Nos 13–15) was founded by the French Government in 1946, a fresh token of the 'Auld Alliance'. The Royal Scottish Geographical Society (founded in 1884) now has its library at No 10, and at No 3 are the quarters and theatre of the Edinburgh Film Guild. By Great Stuart Street we pass into **Ainslie Place**, a graceful ellipse, where (No 23) resided Dean Ramsay, author of the humorous *Reminiscences of Scottish Life and Character*. Here we meet St Colme Street, which leads to the west end of Queen Street, and steep Glenfinlas Street, which climbs up into Charlotte Square. The northern outlet of Ainslie Place takes us into **Moray Place**, Edinburgh's most imposing circus, erected in 1822–23 to the designs of Gillespie Graham, and ever since a favourite abode, though some critics have found this monumental neighbourhood 'magnificently dull'. No 36 Moray Place, offered to Her Majesty in 1954 by Scottish Lord Provosts and other loyal subjects, is now a 'grace and favour' residence.

By Darnaway Street, to the east, we pass out to **Heriot Row**. In Heriot Row James Frederick Ferrier, the metaphysician, was born (1808); in it lived Henry Mackenzie, James Ballantyne and Sir Archibald Alison, the historian; but what makes Heriot Row a place of pious pilgrimage is its association with *Robert Louis Stevenson*, whose boyhood (from 1857), student days and apprenticeship as a writer were spent in the parental home at No 17.

Heriot Row

This whole district is rich in literary and artistic memories. Professor John Wilson ('Christopher North': 1785–1854) passed the last thirty years of his life at 6 Gloucester Place. At No. 1, Dome Terrace Robert Chambers toiled and entertained with equal zest. In Howe Street lived (at No. 11) John Ewbank, the marine and landscape painter, who produced highly-prized views of Edinburgh; and (at No. 18) Sir William Hamilton, the philosopher. Lockhart and George Hogarth, whose daughter Dickens married, stayed in Northumberland Street. At the foot of Howe Street, to the west is a fine circular sweep of houses–**Royal Circus**–where (No. 21) Robert Jameson, 'the Father of modern Natural History,' spent the latter half of his life; to the east runs dignified **Great King Street**, where (No. 72) lived and died Sir William Allan, President of the Royal Scottish Academy, and where, as a student (1879–82), J M Barrie lodged in a top flat at the far end (No. 3) with a landlady, Mrs Edwards, who was his inspiration in *The Old Lady Shows her Medals*. Round the corner, in Nelson Street, Sir Alexander Mackenzie, for thirty-six years Director of the Royal College of Music in London, was born in 1847 at No. 21. **Drummond Place**, at the east end of Great King Street, was the abode, among other celebrities, of Adam Black, the publisher–at No. 38–and at the present day the literary tradition has been maintained by Sir Compton Mackenzie (at No. 31).

Private gardens separate Abercromby Place (which contains the Royal Scots Club) and Heriot Row from **Queen Street**, on a higher level to the south. All three, like Princes Street, are one-sided, but Queen Street faces north. At the east end is the Gothic building (1890) by Rowand Anderson, gifted to the nation by J R Findlay of *The Scotsman*, which houses both the **Scottish National Portrait Gallery** and the–

National Museum of Antiquities of Scotland (*Admission, see* p. 94). The rich collections here illustrate life and history in Scotland from prehistoric down to modern times, for example the Roman occupation, Celtic metalwork and stone sculpture, relics of the Celtic saints, Norse finds, medieval art, Highland weapons. Outstanding exhibits include the Traprain Treasure, relics of Mary Queen of Scots, the 'Maiden' (a sixteenth-century guillotine). There is a branch of the museum at Shandwick Place with costume, domestic and agricultural exhibits.

Scottish National Portrait Gallery (entrance by the same door): The collection is arranged chronologically, starting with the early Stewart Kings. The great events of Scottish history are represented by portraits and groups of the most outstanding figures: Mary Queen of Scots, James VI and the Union of the Crowns, and so on to the Union of the Parliaments, and the Jacobite Rebellions of 1715 and 1745. In later rooms Burns and Scott are seen, surrounded by the men of their time. The reign of Victoria and the twentieth century are represented by portraits of men like Carlyle and Stevenson, and the later period by men like Keir Hardie and Sir Alexander Fleming. There is a large and comprehensive reference library of engravings and photographs.

Queen Street contains the BBC's Edinburgh Studios (Nos 4–6: No 5 was for many years the premises of the Philosophical Institution), the Hall and vast Library of the Royal College of Physicians (No 9: with an exquisite Adam suite at No 8). The house (No 52) of Sir James Y Simpson, of chloroform fame, is now a Youth Centre.

York Place continues Queen Street eastwards. In it are the studio of Sir Henry Raeburn (No 32) and at the corner of Broughton Street, St Paul's and St George's Episcopal Church. A plaque at 47 York Place indicates the birthplace of James Nasmyth (1808–90), inventor of the steam-hammer. Sir Arthur Conan Doyle, begetter of 'Sherlock Holmes', was born (1859) at the north-east corner of the street at what was formerly 'Picardy Place'.

In the upper section of Broughton Street are the **Roman Catholic Cathedral of St Mary** and the site of the *Theatre Royal*, on an unlucky spot where five theatres were in turn destroyed by fire in under a century (1853–1946). The old barony of **Broughton**, acquired by Edinburgh magistrates in 1636, was once notorious for its witches. The Catholic Apostolic Church, at the corner of East London Street, has remarkable murals by Mrs Traquair. St Mary's Parish Church dominates Bellevue Crescent.

The district of **Canonmills** derives its name from the mills of the Augustine Canons of Holyrood. Today it is a printing centre. It was in Tanfield Hall on the north side of the Water of Leith that the Free Church of Scotland was constituted in 1843. Warriston Road runs from Canonmills Bridge along the right bank of the river, and leads to Warriston Cemetery and Crematorium. At No 10 Warriston Crescent, on the left bank, Chopin stayed with Dr Lyschinski in 1848. A memorial plaque was unveiled in 1948. Warriston Crescent is an offshoot of **Howard Place**, where, at No 8, on the east side, Robert Louis Stevenson was born on November 13, 1850.

A short distance up Inverleith Row, which continues Howard Place, is the entrance to the –

Royal Botanic Garden, one of the finest in Britain. (*For admission, see* p. 94.) As early as 1670 Edinburgh had a 'Physic Garden'. It was located for about a century where is now the eastern part of the Waverley Station, and later had quarters at Holyrood and Haddington Place (Leith Walk). The present Garden was formed in 1820–23. Including the **Arboretum**, it covers some 75 acres and contains newly designed glasshouses (1967) as well as large Palm Houses and other ancillary houses. There is a fine new building containing library, herbarium, laboratory, offices and exhibition hall. The Rock Garden and the Demonstration Garden are specially noteworthy, as are the large collections of rhododendrons and other shrubs and trees. Here, too, is the **National Gallery of Modern Art** (*see* p. 94) installed (1960) in Inverleith House, with sculpture and tea-room in its garden.

The western gate of the Arboretum faces the **Inverleith** or **Northern Park,** with a pond for model yachts. West of the Park is Fettes College and beyond that again the **Western General Hospital**, next to the Infirmary the city's most important institution of the kind. **Fettes College**, a striking building in spacious grounds, is conducted like an English Public School. Its founder, Sir William Fettes, a wealthy merchant who was Lord Provost in 1800, left a quarter of a million for the purpose.

South of Inverleith Park lie the **Comely Bank** district and Stockbridge. Thomas Carlyle and his wife spent the early years (1826–28) of their married life at 21 Comely Bank, then a solitary street. Beyond its western end is the Royal Victoria Hospital pioneer in tuberculosis treatment, now a geriatric unit. Raeburn Place, which gives access to the Edinburgh Academy sports ground and the Grange cricket ground, links the modern Comely Bank suburb with the former village of **Stockbridge** to the east.

Henry Raeburn (1756–1823) was born in Stockbridge, beside Saunders

Dean Village, Edinburgh

151

Street; his house, St Bernard's, was in the vicinity of Carlton Street. Dean Terrace runs up the left bank of the Water of Leith to the graceful seclusion of **Ann Street** (designed by Raeburn), where Professor John Wilson had De Quincey as his guest at No 29. Within a stone's throw almost of Raeburn's birthplace was born (1796) David Roberts, RA, in a poverty-stricken house, at the foot of Gloucester Lane–the old 'Kirk Lane' to St Cuthbert's. Not far away, a third eminent Scottish artist, Robert Scott Lauder, RSA, was born seven years later in an old mansion, now dismantled, behind **St Stephen's Church**, an effective work of W H Playfair, visible from the top of Frederick Street.

From the south end of the bridge at Stockbridge, Hamilton Place conducts downstream to Henderson Row, in which are situated the former Royal Institution for the Education of Deaf and Dumb Children, founded in 1810, now a junior department of Donaldson's (*see* p. 168); and the **Edinburgh Academy** (1823), a secondary school with a proud record in scholarship and in sport. Among its alumni were such men as Archbishop Tait, W E Aytoun, Clerk Maxwell and Andrew Lang.

To return to town from Stockbridge there is a choice of routes. Comely Bank buses (24, 29) go up *via* Howe Street (*see* p. 148); another bus route (No 35) passes through stately St Bernard's Crescent and crosses the Dean Bridge; and for those on foot, a pleasant path keeps to the river side by *St Bernard's Mineral Well* (1790), runs under a lofty arch of the Dean Bridge and emerges in the old Dean Village, whence one reaches Queensferry Street by Bell's Brae.

From the village Dean Path itself, the old coach route, leads westward to join the Queensferry Road, near which it passes the main entrance to the **Dean Cemetery**. In 'the Dean' repose many of Edinburgh's distinguished sons, including Lords Cockburn and Jeffrey; Professor John Wilson and his son-in-law Aytoun, the poet and scholar; Edward Forbes, the naturalist, and James Syme, the surgeon; James Nasmyth, inventor of the steam-hammer; Paul Chambers and Sam Bough, the artists; and Alexander Russell, of the *Scotsman*. Here, too, is buried General Sir Hector Macdonald.

Bruntsfield – Braids – Blackford – Craigmillar

The two main roads connecting Edinburgh with the south pass through the suburbs of Newington and Morningside. For the latter we proceed up Lothian Road and Earl Grey Street to **Tollcross** (where are the Central Halls, belonging to the Edinburgh Methodist Mission) and turn right into Home Street and its continuation, Leven Street. At the beginning of Leven Street is situated the **King's Theatre** (1906) – the operatic fare of the Festival is dispensed here; at the other end is the **Barclay Church**, the spire of which is a conspicuous feature for miles around. It stands on the edge of a rolling stretch of common, known as the **Bruntsfield Links**, which for centuries was devoted to golf, and where the 'short game' is still played. The *Golf Tavern*, facing the Links, claims to date back 500 years. West of Bruntsfield Place and the Links, in Gillespie Crescent, is what was formerly James Gillespie's School, now the workshops and offices of the Blind Asylum, on the site of the old mansion of Wright's Houses, occupied at one time by the famous, or infamous, Duke of Lauderdale.

A High School (for girls), perpetuating Gillespie's name, beyond Bruntsfield Links occupies new buildings (1967) and incorporates **Bruntsfield House**, one of the oldest ancestral mansions in Edinburgh, housing the school offices. The estate belonged to George Warrender, Lord Provost in 1713–15, but the house is of more ancient date. Besides a ghost and secret chamber it boasts fine specimens of Norie's decorative art. Eastward along Warrender Park Road is the **Usher Institute of Public Health**, a gift (1902) to the University from Sir John Usher. Southward again, in Whitehouse Loan, are the Bruntsfield Hospital for Women (1887) and **St Margaret's Convent**, opened in 1835 – the first Roman Catholic Convent in Scotland since the Reformation – and dedicated to St Margaret, wife of Malcolm Canmore. It belongs to the Ursuline Order.

In Bruntsfield Crescent, facing the putting greens at the southern end of the Links, are the British Council Office and Centre for Overseas students and the headquarters of the **Scottish Youth Hostels Association**, with a commodious hostel (*see also* p. 93).

Bruntsfield Place runs up the western verge of the Links to **Boroughmuirhead**, the summit level of the old Burgh Muir, passing on the right Viewforth, in which is situated Boroughmuir Secondary School.

THE BRAIDS

Morningside Road, with its cluster of churches, points due south, but a short divergence westward along Colinton Road is worth while, since it brings us to **Merchiston Castle**, the home of John Napier (1550–1617), the inventor of logarithms. The school once housed round it is now at Colinton. Long derelict, this fifteenth-century tower has been restored since 1958 by the Corporation and is now enclosed in the buildings of the **Napier Technical College** (1964).

Farther down the other side of Colinton Road is **George Watson's College**, the lengthy frontage of whose main buildings cannot be missed. The College, one of the 'Merchant Company' schools, has a long and honoured tradition in Scottish education, having been founded on the death (1723) of George Watson, first accountant to the Bank of Scotland. It moved to here in 1930.

Beyond its junction with Colinton Road, Morningside Road reaches **Church Hill**. In No 1 of the street so named lived and died the noted preacher Dr Thomas Chalmers (1780–1847). The **Morningside Parish Church** (1837) was among the earliest of suburban sacred buildings. Its outer wall displays the **Bore Stone**, wherein (according to Scott's *Marmion*) was planted the royal standard when the Scottish army mustered on the Boroughmuir before marching to Flodden.

In Bank House across the road from the Bore Stone, Cosmo Gordon Lang, Archbishop of Canterbury (1928–45), spent some of his boyhood years when his father was minister of Morningside Parish Church (1868–73).

The Braids

From the foot of Morningside Road begins a long steady ascent by Comiston Road or Braid Road. Westward are Jordanburn Nerve Hospital and the **Royal Edinburgh Hospital (Psychiatry)**, comprising 'West House', and, up on Easter Craiglockhart Hill, **Craig House**, a picturesque building which incorporates an old haunted manor-house, long occupied by John Hill Burton, the historian. The valley between Easter and Wester Craiglockhart Hills contains Glenlockhart Road, a delightful avenue, and the billowy course of the *Edinburgh Merchants' Golf Club*, south of which lie an old people's Home and, behind it, the **City Hospital** (1903), the latter a many-winged block of buildings of red stone. The main road pursues its uphill course southward, across the Braid Burn, past the high-perched *Braid Hills Hotel*. The Braid Burn Valley is pleasantly laid out as a public park and has an Open-air Theatre.

Through a residential suburb, we ascend to **Fairmilehead**. Extensive water-works lie to our left; beyond, along Frogston Road, is the **Princess Margaret Rose Orthopaedic Hospital** (1932). Not far from the Fairmilehead crossroads are *Lothianburn Golf Course* and **Hillend Public Park** (opened 1924), a fine stretch of breezy Pentland slopes. At Hillend is the **Hillend Ski Centre**, with an artificial ski slope almost a quarter of a mile in length. A *chairlift* has a capacity of a thousand passengers an hour.

By a rough path skirting the Lothianburn Course, **Swanston** may be reached in a few minutes; apart from its Stevensonian associations, this charming secluded 'clachan', with its thatched roofs and quaint little cottages and 'sporty' golf course, is well worth a visit. Fairmilehead may be regained by a good road leading northwards from Swanston and by Oxgangs Road, which it joins near Hunters' Tryst (Bus 4). Off Oxgangs Road stands a rugged monolith, the **Caiystane**, now National Trust property.

At the bus stop just past the commanding hotel, a road leads steeply upwards and eastwards to Braid Hills Drive and the famous **Braid Hills Golf Course**. This, opened in 1889, is probably the most frequented of its kind in the world. By acquiring additional ground and with over 200 acres at its disposal, the Corporation provided two 18-hole courses from 1922. Many a 'crack' player has learned his golf on the Braid Hills, and especially on Sundays, when no golf is permitted, these healthy uplands with their springy turf and glorious views are a favourite resort of walkers young and old. A Ride, much favoured by horse riders, runs alongside the boundary wall that separates the Braids from *Mortonhall Golf Course* on the south. A fine motor Drive bounds the northern side of the Braids, with an admirable outlook on city and Firth, and passes close to the fourteenth-century Liberton Tower and the early seventeenth-century manor-house of Upper Liberton (restored). Two footpaths find their way down to the Braid Burn at the foot of Blackford Hill. The first of these skirts the wooded **Hermitage of Braid** estate, which, presented to the city in 1937 by Mr John McDougal as a pleasure ground, can be entered here at its eastern end beside a rustic bridge. The charming eighteenth-century mansion is leased to the local Boy Scouts Council as a hostel. (The western entrance is on Braid Road, about half a mile up from the foot of Morningside Road and is quite near a bus stop at Greenbank.)

By the side of the stream as it winds its way through this sequestered glen, we might well believe ourselves many miles from the haunts of man. Yet the city is only over the crest of the hill. If we follow the Braid Burn, where it emerges from the Hermitage, past a quarry, which has bitten deep into the hillside, and the *Craigmillar Park Golf Course*, we can soon reach Liberton Dams and a main traffic route.

Climbing the slope of—

Blackford Hill, and resting on the summit (500 feet above sea-level), we are on the very spot described by Scott as that where Marmion stood and gazed with rapt wonder and delight on the scene below. Today a viewfinder helps in the identification of distant heights. Blackford Hill was purchased by the Corporation in 1884, and opened as a public park. It has an area of 107 acres, and a pond, beloved of children for its swans and exotic ducks.

On the eastern side is the **Royal Observatory** (1896), under control of the Astronomer Royal for Scotland, who is also Professor of Astronomy in the University. The Observatory specializes in automation applied to astronomy; other sections work in space research and seismology. Near the western brow are an all too conspicuous television relay station and the City Police Wireless Station.

At the north-east corner of the hill the Harrison Archway commemorates Lord Provost Sir George Harrison (1885). Here is the Clubhouse of *Craigmillar Park Golf Course*.

Nearby, in West Mains Road, are the **King's Buildings** of the University ('KB'). Chemical Laboratories, the first of a series of Science Departments to rise on the 115 acres acquired for the purpose, were opened in 1924, the Department of Zoology following soon after. Here too are the Animal Genetics, Geology and Engineering Departments and the School of Agriculture. In front of King's Buildings is a statue (by William Brodie) of Sir David Brewster, the scientist, who was Principal of the University, 1859–68. Westwards, by Blackford Avenue, one reaches the harmoniously designed *Reid Memorial Church* (1933: open 9.30 to 4.30 daily) and the Blackford Pond entrance to the Park (No. 41 bus route). This is the valley of the River Jordan which rises in Craiglockhart Hill and here flows (now seldom seen) past streets and buildings with Biblical names, Canaan, Nile, Goschen, Eden, Hebron. In Canaan Lane is the Astley-Ainslie Hospital.

The Grange, Blackford Avenue, once noted for its trees, goes up past St Raphael's Hospital on the left and the Geological Survey Offices on the right, to Grange Loan. Originally the Grange estate belonged to the monks of St Giles. In Grange House–demolished to make room for modern residences–Principal Robertson, the historian, ended his days. It was the home of Sir Thomas Dick Lauder from 1832 to 1848–hence the names of numerous streets in the Grange district.

Walking up Lovers' Lane, we reach the Grange Cemetery, opposite which stands the Chalmers Memorial Church, of which Dr Horatius Bonar, the hymn-writer, was long the minister. In the *Grange Cemetery* are interred many distinguished persons, including Dr Chalmers, Dr Guthrie, Hugh Miller and the Nelsons (publishers). In the vicinity there are, among other public institutions, the Trades Maiden Hospital (where the Trades Standard, the 'Blue Blanket', is kept) in Grange Loan and the Astley-Ainslie Hospital in Canaan Park and adjoining charming grounds. The White House in Whitehouse Loan has memories of Robertson, Blair and Home.

By Grange Road we cross Causewayside to Salisbury Place–in which is located the Longmore Hospital for Incurables–and so into the pleasant suburb of **Newington**, at Minto Street. Northwards along Causewayside one quickly reaches (on the left) Braid Place, a small street where, at **Sciennes Hill House**, met the two greatest figures in Scottish literature. (A tablet marks the building on the north side.) Here, at the home of Professor Adam Ferguson, in the spring of 1787, the boy Walter Scott got 'a look and a word' from Robert Burns, because he alone of all the company could name the author of some lines under a print which had deeply affected the national bard. Sciennes (pronounced *sheens*) is a corruption of Siena. A Dominican nunnery, dedicated to St Catherine of Siena, was founded after Flodden beside Sciennes Road, which today contains the Royal Hospital for Sick Children–familiarly the 'Sick Kids'.

In Salisbury Road is the Jewish **Synagogue**, a modern brick building of striking design. William Blackwood lived at No. 1 when he founded his famous *Magazine* in 1817.

Beyond Salisbury Road, across Dalkeith Road, lie the Pollock Halls of Residence of the University named after former Principals, Baird, Brewster, Ewing, Fraser, Grant, Holland, Lee, Turner and including the residences of the Nelson family of Salisbury Green and St Leonards which adjoined the printing and publishing works of Messrs Thomas Nelson and Sons, Ltd.

The Royal Commonwealth Swimming Pool built 1969 for the Commonwealth Games is on the corner of the properties.

The first street on the left, down Minto Street, is Blacket Avenue, in which is situated **Newington House**, the Scottish National Institution for War Blinded. In Duncan Street is the Edinburgh Geographical Institute of Messrs. John Bartholomew & Son, Ltd, a map-making establishment of world-wide fame. Farther south, in Craigmillar Park, are the School and Braille Press of the **Royal Blind Asylum** (first founded in 1793). On the other side of the main road, off East Suffolk Road, are University Hostels for Women Students.

To the east of Newington is **Craigmillar**, reached from Cameron Toll (foot of Dalkeith Road) by Peffermill Road, which, beyond a cluster of breweries, continues as Niddrie Mains Road. The **Thistle Foundation Settlement** (1950) at Niddrie Mains is a beautifully laid-out village of about 100 houses for gravely disabled ex-Servicemen. Its inter-denominational Robin Chapel commemorates the son of the founder, Sir Francis Tudsbery. Craigmillar Castle Road leads southwards to the ruins of—

Craigmillar Castle (*Admission, daily, fee*). Built in the fourteenth century, this ancient keep has walls fully nine feet thick. The Prestons of Craigmillar were a family of note for three or four hundred years, and successive proprietors added to the Castle. Here James III's younger brother, John, Earl of Mar, was imprisoned for suspected conspiracy and, according to tradition, murdered; here Mary Stewart resided at critical times in her career; and here was planned the murder of Darnley, the 'bond of blood' being dated from Craigmillar. The historic old Castle (now in the care of the Department of the Environment) is a picturesque landmark on its hill crest and well repays a visit as the most notable antiquity of its kind in outer Edinburgh.

Portobello from Joppa

Portobello, Joppa and Musselburgh

Portobello, three miles east of the General Post Office and a part of the city, can be reached by bus from Princes Street.

At Abbeyhill, a mile from the GPO, Regent Road (bus 26) joins London Road (bus 15) near the Commonwealth Games Stadium and Sports Centre at Meadowbank (1970).

Beyond Abbeyhill lies Piershill, northward of which was **Restalrig** village. The estate, now covered by Corporation houses, was in the fifteenth and sixteenth centuries the property of the Logans of Restalrig, whose mansion was at Lochend, overlooking the Loch. Restalrig Church has a thirteenth-century font, while in the churchyard is the **Well of St Triduana** (restored). This saint blinded herself to ward off an importunate suitor and her shrine was frequented by those affected with eye troubles.

Opposite the former Piershill Barracks was the hamlet of **Jock's Lodge**, and the locality preserves that name. A bypass branches off here, by Willowbrae Road. Adjacent are the sports field of the Royal High School and its Junior Department buildings in Northfield Broadway. North of Moira Terrace, which leads on to Portobello, are Craigentinny House (*c* 1600: now a Social Centre) and the **Craigentinny Marbles**, a handsome tomb with Biblical bas-reliefs to a former proprietor, William Henry Miller (d 1848), wealthy and eccentric bibliophile, who accumulated the Britwell Court library.

We reach Portobello at King's Road, past the large red building of the Ramsay Technical Institute.

Portobello and Joppa

together form a popular seaside resort, with an extensive beach and a marine promenade, and the influx of visitors during the Trades Holidays is enormous. Portobello is supposed to have been named after Admiral Vernon's victory in 1739. In 1765 valuable clay deposits were discovered near the Fishwives' Causeway and the *Figgate Burn*, and brick-making and pottery have been carried on in Portobello since that time.

On the Esplanade are the **Open-air Swimming Pool** (hours 2–9; Saturdays 10–9; Sundays 10–6; closed mid-September to mid-May) and the **Corporation Baths** (hours 9–9 (Saturdays 6)).

The Open-air Swimming Pool, opened in 1936, ranks among the largest and best equipped in Britain. The pool (sea-water, warmed, if necessary, to a temperature of 68° F.) is 330 feet by

150, and the depth varies from a few inches to 6½ feet at the deep end. A notable feature is the artificial wave-making plant. There is accommodation for well over three thousand bathers and for three times as many spectators. Galas are held, the evening ones being enhanced by underwater illumination.

The Corporation Baths, situated eastward from the Open-air Pool, are justly regarded as among the most complete establishments of the kind. Here (besides Turkish and Aeratone Baths) a sea-water 'dip' can be enjoyed without the necessity of braving the elements.

At the west end of Portobello is the Electric Power Station. To the north of it in the grounds of the former Marine Gardens are now a bus depot and works. Golf is played in the Public Park, south of the railway. In the High Street are the Town Hall and the Public Library. Hugh Miller resided in Tower Street, off the High Street, and here he shot himself (1856). Sir Harry Lauder was born in Portobello.

Making our way eastward along the coast, we pass, almost immediately on leaving Joppa, the **Salt Pans**, where coarse salt has been manufactured for centuries. Here, at *Eastfield*, is the city boundary and the eastern terminus of bus routes through the city to Corstorphine, Juniper Green or Moredun, Gilmerton.

At **Fisherrow**, as at Newhaven (*see* p. 165), the fishing population form a self-contained community, thrifty and hard-working. Fisherrow is part of–

Musselburgh,

which adjoins **Inveresk**, where was a Roman station. Of note are the sixteenth-century Tolbooth, No 7 High Street (restored) reputed residence of the French Ambassador in Stuart times, the ancient bridge (frequently referred to, incorrectly, as 'Roman') over the river *Esk*, and the site of the Chapel of **Loretto** (on which Lord Clive built himself a residence–occupied since 1829 by a well-known public school, for boys) where alleged 'miracles' were wrought before the Reformation. In **Pinkie House**, now part of Loretto School, Prince Charles Edward, on his way to invade England, spent the night of October 31, 1745. The Battle of Pinkie, in which Hertford crushed the Scots in September 1547, was fought a mile to the south-east. At the head of High Street is a monument to 'Delta'–Dr D M Moir (1798–1851), poet and novelist. Musselburgh, proudly known as the 'Honest Toun', has historic Golf Links and a Racecourse. The Institute of Seaweed Research (at Inveresk Gate, overlooking the Esk) is said to be the only one of its kind in the world.

From Musselburgh it is but a short journey back to Edinburgh by bus.

Port of Leith, Newhaven and Granton

From the east end of Princes Street Leith Street goes off downhill to justify its title. At Union Place the road widens and Picardy Place joins it on the western side. **Greenside**, between Union Place and the Calton Hill, was of old a tourney ground and the scene of many an execution. Beyond it the stage-coaches of later times swung right for London Road, on which dignified Royal Terrace now looks down from the back of the Calton. The road to Leith here has a confusing variety of names, these differing on each side of the wide thoroughfare and changing with nearly every block of houses. Off the west side, Annandale Street leads to a Corporation Bus depot, originally the Industrial Hall.

At Pilrig Church the former burgh boundary is reached. **Leith Walk** proper continues to the centre of Leith with its statue of Queen Victoria, 1½ miles from the GPO. 'As long as Leith Walk' is a local saying. This road follows the line of entrenchment, the 'Lang Dyke', behind which Leslie defied Cromwell in 1650. Numerous buses follow this route to Leith.

Alternative access to Leith may be had by Corporation bus (No. 34) by Queensferry Street, Stockbridge, Bonnington Road (passing Broughton Secondary School, Powderhall Grounds – where foot races and greyhound racing are held – Rosebank Cemetery and Old Pilrig House) to Leith Docks; or (bus 1) from High Street by Canongate and Holyrood to Easter Road (off which lies the ground of the Hibernian Football Club) and Leith Links.

Port of Leith

From 1143 – when David I gave his charter to the monks of Holyrood – until 1832, Edinburgh exercised superiority over Leith. There had always been haven for ships where the Water of Leith joins the Forth, and in 1329 Robert Bruce took account of it by granting to the burgesses of Edinburgh 'the port of Leith, mills and their pertinents, to hold to all time.' The place was on several occasions devastated by the English, notably in May 1544 when Hertford landed at Granton with a large force to sack Leith and burn Edinburgh. After the battle of Pinkie, three years later, Leith, a rich prey, was again pillaged. During the Reformation struggles, the Queen-Regent made Leith her headquarters, and strong fortifications were thrown up to defend the town against the assaults of the Lords of the Congregation, assisted by English troops. French mercenaries made a most spirited resistance, notwithstanding famine, and held out till 1560 and the Treaty of Edinburgh. A century later, General Monk had his headquarters at Leith and fortified the Citadel. The ill-fated Darien expedition sailed from Leith Roads on July 25, 1698. Since its seizure by Mackintosh of Borlum and his Highlanders in the ''15,' Leith's history and triumphs have mostly been connected with commerce – although it played a valuable if untrumpeted rôle during both World Wars and more than once was attacked from the air. The Reform Bill gave Leith a municipal constitution of its own, which it guarded jealously till 1920. The Port greatly extended in 1968 by the opening of a new deep-water entrance lock was controlled by the commissioners for the Harbour and Docks of Leith but is not part of the amalgamated Forth Ports Authority.

From the foot of Leith Walk radiate the chief business thoroughfares–Junction Street, Kirkgate, Constitution Street and Duke Street.

Duke Street leads eastwards past Leith Academy (former High School) to **Leith Links**, a stretch of common that is a godsend to the crowded town. Charles I was playing golf here in 1641 when word was brought of the Irish Rebellion, an incident depicted in a well-known picture by John Gilbert. The two knolls, *Giant's Brae* (westerly) and *Lady Fife's Brae* (easterly), were the sites of batteries erected by the English during their attack on Leith in April 1560. Buses (Nos. 12, 25) skirt Leith Links and run along to Portobello by Seafield Road between Craigentinny (with a municipal golf course) and the Forth (with a breezy Promenade).

Constitution Street makes northwards for the Docks, among its features being St James's Episcopal Church, designed by Sir Gilbert Scott, with a lofty spire; the **Old Town Hall** (built in 1827), a mixture of Ionic and Doric styles; on the east side of the street. On the west side is the beautiful **Roman Catholic Church** known as *Maris Stella*, in the mixed type of Early Gothic. At the northern end of Constitution Street are the **Assembly Rooms** or **Exchange Buildings** (1788), an imposing pile with Ionic pillars, and opposite, in Baltic Street, is the **Corn Exchange**.

From the statue of Robert Burns (the work of D W Stevenson, RSA) **Bernard Street** takes one to The Shore.

Off Bernard Street run Quality Street (where at No 29 was born the Rev John Home, author of the tragedy *Douglas*) and Water Street–the ancient Water Lane–which contains **Andro Lamb's House**, ably restored and accounted the finest historic dwelling in Leith. Mary Queen of Scots rested in it in 1561.

The **Kirkgate**, into which we pass at the end of Water Street, was formerly the main street of the burgh, and here leading residents had their mansions. This area was rebuilt from 1966 onwards and is now a traffic-free pedestrian shopping and residential area right through to Tolbooth Wynd (*see* p. 163). On the west side is **Trinity House**, a modern edifice in the Georgian style, but with a Grecian portico and pilasters.

Almost opposite Trinity House is **St Mary's Church**, the parish church of South Leith from 1609, originally a chapel under the parent church of Restalrig.

The nave dates back to the fifteenth century. The choir and transepts are later, having been destroyed by the English in 1544 and 1547. While Cromwell's men held Leith, his chaplains, and on one memorable occasion Oliver himself, took part in the services. In the graveyard are interred the Bartons, the great sailors of the fifteenth century; the Balfours of Pilrig (whose old mansion is still extant), ancestors of R L Stevenson; Captain Gibson, leader of the Darien expedition; and the Rev John Home (1722–1808). His verse tragedy, *Douglas,* evoked extraordinary enthusiasm when produced in Edinburgh in 1756, but gave such offence to the anti-theatre Presbytery that Home resigned his ministry.

St Anthony's Street, on the western side of the Kirkgate, commemorates the Austin Friary of St Anthony.

At the southern end of the Kirkgate we turn up **Great Junction Street**, a busy thoroughfare connecting South with North Leith. Near the farther

Lamb's House, Leith

end, at the head of Mill Lane, stands **Leith Hospital** (founded in 1850). Mill Lane opens into Sheriff Brae, and finally into Coal Hill, on the margin of the old harbour. These are all historic localities. **Coal Hill** has interesting associations, for the Scottish ancestors of W E Gladstone were connected for over a century with this locality. In Peter Williamson's 'Directory' for 1786 is the record: 'Thomas Gladstone, flour and barley merchant, Coal Hill'. He was the father of Sir John Gladstone, afterwards of Fasque, whose youngest son was the famous statesman. Sir John Gladstone was himself born in Coal Hill. **St Thomas's Church** was built by him in Sheriff Brae.

The **Shore** is a continuation of the Coal Hill, and also an historic locality. Abutting on Coal Hill stood the Old Council House (sixteenth century). In the **Tolbooth Wynd** was the Tolbooth of Leith, erected by order of Mary Queen of Scots. The chief points of interest in 'The Shore'—which is really the bank of the Water of Leith where it debouches into the Forth—are two ancient hostelries, the *Old* and *New Ship Inns*.

Both were in existence in 1680. The former (still in use as a hotel) probably goes back to the sixteenth century. Above the entrance is carved in bold relief an ancient ship. Only a heavily-moulded doorway, surmounted by a Latin motto, remains of the *New Ship*. The taverns of Leith are frequently mentioned by the Scottish poets, including both Robert Fergusson and Burns.

PORT OF LEITH–NEWHAVEN

A stone on the quay wall, opposite the *Old Ship Inn,* records the date, 1822, when George IV stepped ashore.

The Shore joins Tower Street near the spot where stood the Signal Tower, a prominent object in all old views of the Leith Harbour area. The Inner Harbour is a good vantage-ground from which to ascertain the 'lie' of the complete system of **Docks**. On the west side of the river mouth is the Victoria Dock (1852). On the other side of the Outer Harbour are the Albert Dock (1869), the Edinburgh Dock (1881), farthest east, and the Imperial Dock (1901), farthest north. This last is the largest dock on the East Coast of Scotland, covers about 75 acres, and cost about a million sterling. It is 1,900 feet long and 550 feet wide. The docks are fitted with all the latest appliances for the handling and transmission of goods. The existing docks system has been reclaimed entirely from the sea during the last 150 years and is constantly being expanded. In the Western Harbour area reclaimed land is being used by industrial concerns for grain importing, flour milling and storage. To the north of Imperial Dock are fertilizer and oil installations. A new sea-lock has made it possible for Leith to accommodate much larger vessels.

By the bridge at the end of Bernard Street, we cross the river to **North Leith**. Or the passage may be made higher up, near the site of the first bridge built over the Water of Leith, by Abbot Bellenden, in the fifteenth century. He founded a chapel here and in the seventeenth and eighteenth centuries **St Ninian's** (in Coburg Street) was the parish church of North Leith. Only the graveyard and the old church tower, now incorporated in a warehouse, remain. Some of the gravestones bear quaint epitaphs, and many of the older navigators of Leith lie here. Coburg Street is a continuation of the Ferry Road, at the east end of which is the new **Town Hall**, with Library attached. The old **Citadel** of Leith, erected by Monk, which stood in Commercial Street, the leading throughfare of North Leith, is still represented by some ancient buildings called Cromwell's Barracks. Continuing westward along Commercial Street, we pass **Leith Nautical College** and lofty blocks of flats which now cover the site of the old Leith Fort.

Newhaven

The village of Newhaven is a quaint old place, dating from the fifteenth century, when it was called 'Our Lady's Port of Grace', from a chapel dedicated to the Virgin Mary and St James. James IV built his fleet here (including the *Great Michael*, of which a model will be found in the Royal Scottish Museum), and insisted on manning his warships with as many as he could get of 'ye fischeris of ye New Haven'. Newhaven has a harbour and fishmarket and a lengthy breakwater. •

At Newhaven a speciality is made of fish dinners and fish suppers, and Newhaven fishwives, with their creels and their distinctive petticoats and shawls, are picturesque figures.

To the south, bordering the Newhaven Road, is the pretty **Victoria Park**. The Starbank Public Park overlooks the sea on the way past Trinity and Wardie to–

Granton

A charming view is gained of the Forth and its islands. **Inchkeith**, with its lighthouse and formidable fortifications, defends the passage of the Firth. The spacious **Granton Harbour** was begun by the fifth Duke of Buccleuch in 1835. It is a busy commercial port with large petrol, fuel oil, esparto grass, and wood pulp imports. The East Breakwater is a favourite objective for a brisk walk.

The ruins of **Granton Castle** have been removed by quarrying, and the mansion of **Caroline Park** (formerly Royston Castle), a short distance west of the harbour. It has a fine seventeenth-century staircase balustrade of hammered iron. The huge Scottish Gas Works lie still farther to the west. A marine promenade has been constructed between Granton and Cramond.

From the foot of Granton Road, in Granton Square, numerous routes lead back to Princes Street. This interesting and important part of Edinburgh's sea coast can also be readily reached by way of Inverleith Row and Goldenacre, west of which, on Ferry Road, are the old Scottish International Rugby Football ground (Inverleith; now the Sports Ground of Daniel Stewart's College), the *Northern General Hospital*, the Bruce Peebles and Ferranti Works (Electrical Engineering) and the Pilton and Muirhouse housing schemes – today a vast aggregate of new dwellings.

Granton Square can be reached (*a*) via Goldenacre by bus No. 8 or 9 or (*b*) round by Leith and Newhaven by bus No. 16 or 22. No. 8 continues to Silverknowes, as also does bus No. 16.

West from Edinburgh

Lauriston Castle – Cramond – Corstorphine – Colinton – Pentlands

Just within the city's western bounds, three villages, Cramond, Corstorphine and Colinton, all invite a visit.

To Cramond

Cramond (5½ miles) nestles at the mouth of the *Almond* and is reached by leaving the Queensferry Road (A90) at Davidson's Mains or at Barnton. (Bus No. 41.)

At the end of the Dean Bridge the picturesque **Trinity (Episcopal) Church** is now an electricity sub-station. To east and west, Eton Terrace – Professor George Saintsbury, critic and gourmet, lived at No 2 – and Belgrave Crescent look down across wooded gardens on the Water of Leith and are good examples of the modern fashionable residential quarters of Edinburgh. **Daniel Stewart's College**, a Merchant Company School for boys, was opened, as a 'Hospital', in 1855; its founder was a 'Macer' in the Court of Exchequer. The architect, David Rhind, used the design, Elizabethan in style, with which he won second prize in the competition for the Houses of Parliament. From **Craighleith Quarry**, to the north, about a mile westward along the Queensferry Road, a large part of the New Town was built.

A loop road at Blackhall leads past **Craigcrook Castle**, where Jeffrey entertained Tennyson, Dickens, Thackeray and other celebrities. This Craigcrook road rejoins the Queensferry Road just where we leave it, by Quality Street, to cut northward through **Davidson's Mains**, where the Ferry Road from Leith ends. Across the old railway track has been built the new Royal High School. Cramond Road runs between *Bruntsfield Golf Course* and –

Lauriston Castle (*Fee. Closed Fridays*. Access, bus 41). Beautifully situated on a terrace overlooking the Firth of Forth, this historic mansion, with its contents, was bequeathed to the nation by the last owner, Mr W R Reid, and since 1926 has been administered by Edinburgh Corporation as a public demesne and museum.

Most of the existing building belongs to the early nineteenth century, but it incorporates a sixteenth-century castle. In the later seventeenth century Lauriston was acquired by the Law family and it was the early home of John Law (1671–1729), the celebrated financier who founded the forerunner of the Bank of France and whose 'Mississippi Scheme' turned out to be a 'bubble', which burst in 1720.

Lauriston Castle

The Castle has its secret staircase and 'hidey-hole' and the rooms are full of collector's pieces, tapestries, portraits and the like. The grounds are charming and make a perfect setting for garden parties.

The Corporation acquired the land lying between Lauriston Castle and the sea and **Silverknowes** as a housing area and a pleasure ground with a golf course and a wide highway to and along the coast, where are sands, parks, a Caravan Site, and a hotel.

About a mile beyond Lauriston Castle is **Cramond**. The Romans had a station here and excavations have yielded some interesting 'finds'. The most easterly section of the fort can be seen in outline in an area of open ground beside the church which is built over much of the remainder. A portion of one wall has been left exposed. The church (restored) and church-yard take one back to the seventeenth century. In Cramond House grounds is now a College of Education. The village, down a very steep hill with a sharp turn, has the air of an erstwhile smuggler's den. Quaint old *Cramond Inn* is a small but much-favoured stopping place. Off the mouth of the Almond lies Cramond Island.

Cramond is the western extremity of the Marine Promenade, which links it with Granton, but on foot one can continue westward along the coast, as far as South Queensferry and the Forth Bridge, by hailing the boatman in charge of the private ferry across the river–a delightful walk (4 or 5 miles) through Dalmeny Woods and grounds. The path passes the Eagle Rock (perhaps carved by a Roman legionary), old Barnbougle Castle and Dalmeny House (seat of the Earl of Rosebery).

The road between Cramond and **Barnton** adjoins, for part of the way, the golf course of the Royal Burgess Golfing Society, with Braehead House on the west side.

Old Cramond Brig across the River Almond built in 1619 a picturesque structure rebuilt and widened is associated with the rescue of James V by Jock Harvieson from a band of ruffians. (A mural in Cramond Church commemorates the event.) A new bridge upstream, half a mile west of Barnton Hotel, replaces one by Rennie (1820) and carries the main road (A90) to the Forth Road Bridge.

To Corstorphine

Corstorphine is reached from Princes Street by a broad highway, which forms the first part of the Glasgow Road (A8). Turning west at Haymarket we pass on the right stately Donaldson's Hospital (1851) – now **Donaldson's School for the Deaf**. At Coltbridge the Water of Leith is crossed, near the whitewashed *Roseburn House*, which bears the date 1582. At the railway bridge at Roseburn Terrace is the **Railway Museum** housing documents, maps, badges and other relics from Scottish railways, first of its kind in Scotland, run by the Scottish Railway Preservation Society (*Admission, daily*). Behind Roseburn Park is the Scottish Rugby Union's Stadium (1925) – **Murrayfield** – where 'Internationals' and Highland Games are held. Adjacent is Murrayfield Ice Rink.

Beechwood House (1780) – today occupied by the Scotus Academy, a Roman Catholic boys' school, looks across to **Carrickknowe** municipal golf course. And now, some 3 miles from Princes Street, we come to –

The Scottish National Zoological Park (*Admission, see* p. 94). The Park extends to over 70 acres, and is laid out in grassy, tree-shaded grounds on the southern slope of Corstorphine Hill, affording splendid views of Edinburgh, the River Forth, and a wide extent of country bounded to the south by the Pentland Hills. The collection of animals occupies natural enclosures and represents most of the animal groups throughout the world. There is a fine colony of Antarctic penguins which breed regularly each year. There is a Children's Farm, a complete steading in miniature where everything is scaled to Shetland ponies representing Clydesdale cart-horses. Close to the main entrance is the beautiful Carnegie Aquarium of three halls, exhibiting both marine and fresh-water animals. There is a Fellows' club house and a public licensed restaurant and cafeteria. A glorious prospect of the city, the Pentlands and the Firth of Forth is obtained from the summit of the Zoo grounds on Corstorphine Hill.

The Royal Infirmary's Corstorphine Hospital adjoins the Zoo. Though a suburban ward of the city, **Corstorphine** retains not a little of its village character. (The accent is on the second syllable: the name may mean Cross of Torphin.) Its chief pride is a fifteenth-century church, with tombs of the Lords Forrester. Near the church are a seventeenth-century circular dove-cote and a studio where remarkable tapestries are made. Corstorphine

At Corstorphine

stretches out westward to the Maybury Roadhouse, about a mile beyond which are the golf course and the aerodrome of **Turnhouse**, the civic airport for Edinburgh.

From the top of Kaimes Road (which starts beside the Corstorphine Hospital) and of Clermiston Road (farther west) delightful paths run through **Corstorphine Woods** to Rest and be Thankful—where David Balfour parted from Alan Bryck. Like Clermiston Tower, which crowns Corstorphine Hill (520 feet), Rest and be Thankful is a magnificent viewpoint. From it a public path, intersecting Murrayfield Golf Course, runs down to Ravelston House and Ravelston Dykes (terminus of bus route 13). **Ravelston House** (long held by the Keith family) with its quaint old garden and sixteenth-century 'doocot,' 'contributed several hints' to Scott for Tully-Veolan in *Waverley*. In 1960 the Merchant Company bought the estate for a new Mary Erskine School.

The villas and gardens of Ravelston Dykes make a very pleasing approach to town. We pass the new Mary Erskine School, a Merchant Company school for girls, to the north of St George's School for Girls and at the back of Daniel Stewart's College turn south by Belford Road, between John Watson's School (1828) and the Dean College (formerly an Orphan Hospital: now used as a training centre). Beyond old Bell's Mills and the west entrance of the Dean Cemetery we cross the Water of Leith by the Belford Bridge, and so up into Queensferry Street.

Just beyond Corstorphine and the city boundary is the Royal Highland Showground at Ingliston, 86 acres, with grandstand seating for 5,000. The Show is held in the third week of June but motor racing and other events are held through the year.

COLINTON–THE PENTLANDS

To Colinton

Colinton (4 miles from the GPO) bestrides the *Water of Leith*, and can be reached by either side of the river. The northern route–that of bus 44–is by the Lanark Road, which from Haymarket runs through rather dreary Dalry to the eastern end of Gorgie Road. Gorgie Road adjoins **Tynecastle**, the 'Heart of Midlothian' Football ground, and *Saughton Park* (including a superb Rose Garden) and is the way to *Sighthill*, a development area, and to Dalmahoy and Ratho (with golf courses). But we turn up Ardmillan Terrace for Slateford–beyond the Corn and Cattle Markets–where the Union Canal passes over the valley of the Water of Leith and a riverside walk to Colinton begins. Farther west along the Lanark Road is **Kingsknowe**, with still another golf course, and, opposite, **Hailes House**, now a *Youth Hostel*. Through the upper part of Colinton the road proceeds to **Juniper Green** (just within the city's western boundary), Currie and Balerno, starting-points for Pentland tramps. At Juniper Green is the *Baberton* golf course.

The alternative route to Colinton is by **Craiglockhart** (bus 9 or 10). Opposite the King's Theatre Gilmore Place strikes off to the west and we take it to meet Colinton Road at Myreside, the sports ground of George Watson's College. Nearby, the University and the Corporation Schools have their fields where we skirt the Union Canal at the old suburban line station (line closed). Then up, past what was known as the 'Happy Valley' (with a pond) and the East of Scotland tennis courts, to the Sacred Heart Convent and Training College and Firrhill. From Firrhill a bus route (No 4) goes off to Hunter's Tryst (at an entrance to the War Department's Dreghorn Grounds), Oxgangs Road (for Swanston) and Fairmilehead. We, however, turn right at Firrhill and pass between the extensive Redford Barracks and Merchiston Castle School to Colinton.

As a lad, R L Stevenson spent many of his holidays at Colinton Manse, with his grandfather, Dr Lewis Balfour. The Church and Manse are down in the valley of the Water of Leith, in picturesque **Colinton Dell**, along which winds one of Edinburgh's favourite woodland walks. Spylaw Park, below Colinton Bridge, and Gillespie Road, which goes up to join the Lanark Road, remind us that here the Laird of Spylaw, James Gillespie, had his snuff-mill. Meal-mills and paper-mills today maintain the milling traditions of the Water of Leith.

With its memories of the Covenant and of Stevenson, Colinton is a natural introduction to the Pentland Hills, R L S's 'Hills of Home'.

The Pentlands

The northern tip of the Pentland Range lies within the city boundary, which runs along the summits of **Caerketton** and its neighbour, **Allermuir** (1,617 feet), Edinburgh's loftiest point. The Pentlands offer the walker a choice of delightful and not too arduous paths–old Kirk roads and drove roads–while the motorist can put a girdle round them by taking the Lanark road (A70) as far as Carnwath (26 miles), in Lanarkshire, and there striking eastwards (by A721) for some 8 miles to join the Biggar road (A702), south of Dolphinton (22 miles from Edinburgh).

The Old Lanark road skirts **Balerno** (8 miles: with noted paper mills) and Harperrig Reservoir (14 miles) and reaches Carnwath by the desolate moorland stretch of the 'Lang Whang'. The Biggar road, on the east side of the range, is more sheltered and pastoral in its surroundings. **West Linton** (18 miles), on the Lyne Water, is a health and holiday resort, and **Carlops** (15 miles) is a charming hamlet, with Habbie's Howe, scene of Allan Ramsay's *Gentle Shepherd,* in the Newhall grounds nearby. On the hill slope about 8 miles from Edinburgh, is the site of *Rullion Green,* where on November 28, 1666, the Covenanters were defeated by General Dalyell and the Pentland Rising was crushed. On Bush estate Edinburgh University School of Agriculture has teaching farms. Breezy Hillend Public Park (4 miles from the GPO) is just outside the city boundary. The adjoining Lothianburn Golf Course stretches upward and westward to Swanston (*see* p. 154).

Pentland Walks–From Colinton (reached by Corporation buses), Currie and Balerno (Eastern Scottish buses) inviting tracks cross the Pentlands to Flotterstone or Nine Mile Burn (both on an Eastern Scottish route). The hill paths are indicated by guide posts of the Scottish Rights of Way Society–in places by irksome fences. The nearest, shortest (between 5 and 6 miles) and perhaps the most popular crossing starts from Colinton by way of Woodhall Road, and turns up **Bonaly Road** (bus route 9) in under half a mile. (A little farther along Woodhall Road, Fernielaw Avenue leads up to Torduff and Clubbiedean Reservoirs, a charming walk.) **Bonaly Tower** was the home of Lord Cockburn and here he wrote his *Memorials.* By Bonaly Reservoir and the back of Capelaw Hill the path climbs over to **Glencorse Reservoir**, before reaching which it is joined by another path, the Kirk Road from Currie. From Glencorse Reservoir, beneath whose waters are buried the ancient ruins of St Katherine's in the Hopes, a road runs down to Flotterstone Bridge, on the Biggar road. Castlelaw Hill, to the north, has a Fort of the Iron Age and an earth-house. The road to Glencorse Reservoir continues besides the clear Logan Burn to the far end of another Compensation Reservoir, Loganlee, on which **Scald Law** (1,898 feet), the highest of the Pentland Hills, looks down from the south. By the Green Cleuch a path links this point with Threipmuir Reservoir and the road down to Balerno, passing Bavelaw Castle.

Farther west there are somewhat longer paths crossing the Pentlands, from the Old Lanark road: (*a*) by the *Bore Stone* and North Esk Reservoir to Carlops; (*b*) by Harperrig and the *Cauldstane Slap* to West Linton.

Short Excursions from Edinburgh

Of the many attractive spots within easy reach of the city, two—the Forth Bridges and Roslin—are of outstanding interest and demand special description.

The Forth Bridges and Hopetoun House

The most spectacular and most popular short excursion from Edinburgh is to the Forth Bridges (9 miles) railway or road. In addition to the Eastern Scottish buses to South Queensferry—many of which proceed to Bo'ness *via* Hopetoun Cross Roads and across the new Road Bridge to Dunfermline and Leven—coaches run daily during the season from St Andrew Square. A delightful approach to the railway Bridge on foot is from Cramond through the Dalmeny Woods.

At Cramond Bridge the Queensferry road (A90) crosses the *Almond* and the city bounds and enters Linlithgowshire or West Lothian. A little way up the beautifully tree-lined river is **Craigiehall**, with an old bridge and grotto; it is now in War Department hands. On the right stretch for miles the grounds and woods of the Earl of Rosebery, whose seat, **Dalmeny House** (1819), contains many treasures. The village of Dalmeny lies to the left, about half a mile from the Queensferry road; Dalmeny railway junction is three-quarters of a mile from the Forth Bridge.

Dalmeny Church, dating back to the twelfth century, has a fine doorway and arch, and is one of the best examples of Norman architecture in Scotland. It was restored by the parishioners with their own hands. In the northern vault lie members of the Rosebery family, from its founder in the seventeenth century, Sir Archibald Primrose, to the eminent statesman and *littérateur* who was Premier in 1894–95.

A steep hill, Hawes Brae, leads down to the old-world burgh of **South Queensferry**, the site of a ferry from time immemorial. Margaret, Queen of Malcolm Canmore, often crossed here on her journeys between Edinburgh and Dunfermline —hence the name. The old Hawes Inn figures in Scott's *Antiquary* and in Stevenson's *Kidnapped*.

South Queensferry is an ideal spot from which to view—

The Forth (Railway) Bridge. Seen from below, the Bridge is infinitely more impressive than when one crosses it in the train.

The wide and deep Firth of Forth narrows to a mile where the North Queensferry peninsula projects and midway is the rocky island of **Inchgarvie,** the channels on each side of which are

The Forth Road Bridge

570 yards wide and over 200 feet in depth. What was necessary was a structure having spans of over 1700 feet, capable of resisting the great wind pressure of this exposed estuary, and of supporting heavy traffic. To meet the difficulties of the case, the cantilever, or bracket, principle was adopted.

The Forth Bridge consists of approach viaducts and three vast double steel cantilevers, the brackets of which extend 680 feet north and south, with tubular towers rising to 361 feet above the water – as high as St Paul's Cathedral. Each cantilever is supported on four huge main piers. The 350 feet between the extremities of the opposing arms, in mid-channel, are bridged by lattice girders, fastened at one end to the cantilever, the outer end being left free, to allow for expansion or contraction.

The length of the Bridge is 5350 feet, or with the approaches 8100 feet, i.e. over 1½ miles. The permanent way is 150 feet above high water. The cost of the undertaking was nearly three and a quarter millions sterling. The chief engineer, Sir John Fowler, was assisted by Sir Benjamin Baker, the contractor being Sir William Arrol. Begun in 1883, the Bridge was opened on March 14, 1890.

The Forth (Road) Bridge. To meet the ever-growing demands of road traffic, the **Ferry Service** for cars, etc., had been improved from time to time and by the opening (1936) of a bridge at Kincardine-on-Forth, higher up the Firth, Fife was brought considerably nearer to Edinburgh by road and the long detour *via* Stirling was obviated. But frequent congestion of traffic and consequent delay at Queensferry accentuated the need of a road bridge at this point. The first pile of the **Forth Road Bridge** was at last driven into the bed of the Firth in November 1958, and the Bridge finally opened to traffic in September 1964. The new bridge crosses the Forth from beside Port Edgar, half a mile west of the railway bridge, to North Queensferry, near the Mackintosh Rock, and is the longest suspension bridge in Europe (1½ miles, with approach viaducts). The central span is 3300 feet, the two side spans 1340 feet each; the steel towers rise 500 feet above the water. The cost was nineteen and a half million pounds.

One and a half miles west of South Queensferry is **Hopetoun House** (home of the Marquess of Linlithgow), a huge and magnificent building begun in 1699 by Sir William Bruce, enlarged by William Adam and completed by his famous sons. *During the season* (*usually May to September inclusive*) *it is open* (*1.30 to 5.45, closed Thursdays and Fridays*). The house has fine interior decoration and furniture, superb picture collection, and beautiful grounds. There are two deer parks with deer and St Kilda sheep. Afternoon teas are available.

Farther west, between the Bo'ness road (an Eastern Scottish bus route) and the Firth, are **Abercorn Church**, on the site of a seventh-century bishopric; and **Blackness Castle**. Of old an important fortress, Blackness served as a prison for Covenanters in the seventeenth century. (*Open 10–7, in winter 10–4; Sunday, from 2; Admission 5p.*) About a mile south of it is **The Binns**, home of the Dalyells, now under the National Trust. (*Open on Saturday and Sunday 2–5; additionally weekdays in summer.*) Here was born Tam Dalyell, the scourge of the Covenanters; here he started the Royal Scots Greys; here he grew his legendary beard after the execution of Charles I.

Nearly opposite, on the Fife side of the Forth, is **Rosyth Naval Base**. In 1903 the Government purchased from the Marquess of Linlithgow the shore lands surrounding Rosyth Castle (1560) and constructed a Base, which became one of the largest in the world, capable of docking and repairing all classes of war vessels, minor craft making use of Port Edgar on the south shore. The Firth of Forth, with its succession of powerful batteries along both sides and on the islands, was generally considered impregnable and the strategic value of the Base was fully proved during both World Wars.

For municipal purposes Rosyth's Garden City, close neighbouring Inverkeithing, forms part of **Dunfermline**, a couple of miles to the north. With its noble Abbey, where Robert the Bruce and Queen Margaret (*see* p. 105) are buried, and the remains of a royal palace, Dunfermline is of primary historical interest and, thanks to the bequests of Andrew Carnegie, who was born here in 1835, it emjoys many amenities, including the beautiful Pittencrieff Park.

Roslin and the Esk Valley

Buses run regularly from St Andrew Square to Dalkeith, Lasswade, Rosewell (for Hawthornden), Roslin and Penicuik in the Esk Valley.

The Old Dalkeith road (A68) runs north of the new (A7)–by **Little France**, where lingers the stump of an old sycamore tree, known as 'Queen Mary's Tree'. At Little France were lodged Mary Stewart's French retainers when she resided at nearby Craigmillar Castle. The usual route to Dalkeith, however, is now through Newington–down Minto Street from Salisbury Place–turning left at **Nether Liberton**, the site of a Braid Burn mill, bestowed by David I on the monks of Holyrood. On the right is a fine old dovecote. We pass the public park of **Inch House**, embodying an ancient tower and a Jacobean mansion erected in 1617. The Liberton golf course is skirted, and we see on high ground to the right, crowned by its church tower, **Upper Liberton**, or 'Leper town', formerly a place of resort of pilgrims to *St Catherine's Holy Well*, which lies a little beyond the church, on the Penicuik highroad.

Dr Guthrie's School for Girls is in Gilmerton, which is reached beyond Greenend and the new suburb of Moredun (with the Animal Diseases Research Institute). The Guthrie School for Boys is up in Liberton. These 'approved' schools are the descendants of the philanthropist's Original Ragged Schools (1847). Farther on, past Gilmerton, is (left) the entrance to Drum, an Adam house, the seat for three hundred years of the Lords Somerville. On the right are Messrs Dobbie's magnificent nursery beds, in season a mass of colour, and the gates of Melville Castle, renowned in Scottish song—and now an hotel.

At the point where the Old and New Dalkeith roads meet is the northern entrance to **Dalkeith House** or **Palace**, the seat of the Duke of Buccleuch. The House (*not open to the public*) stands in spacious grounds, in which the *North Esk* and *South Esk* join. General Monk is said to have planned the Restoration while resident in Dalkeith House, which was reconstructed, from Sir John Vanbrugh's designs, by the Duchess Anne, after the execution (1685) of her husband, the rebel Duke of Monmouth.

Dalkeith, a burgh with an interesting history, and remembered in Scots literature as the scene of 'Delta's' *Mansie Wauch,* retains few relics of its past apart from the old collegiate Parish Church on the north side of the High Street. In the unroofed choir of this are tombs of the old Earls of Morton, and of the Buccleuch family.

Newbattle Abbey, a mile to the south, incorporates remains of a Cistercian abbey, founded by David I, the monks of which were the first to work coal seams in Scotland. Long the seat of the Kerrs, Marquesses of Lothian, it contains a valuable library, many fine paintings, painted ceilings and historical relics. Donated by its owner, Newbattle Abbey since 1937 is a residential College of Adult Education. Outside the grounds is Newbattle golf course.

By way of Dalkeith's pleasant suburb Eskbank, we pass on to **Bonnyrigg**, a mining community. In the background to the left are **Dalhousie Castle**, whence the Earl of Dalhousie takes his title, and the square tower of **Cockpen Church**, a locality which yields at least a title to Lady Nairne's humorous song, 'The Laird of Cockpen'.

United with Bonnyrigg is **Lasswade**, to the north-west. In Lasswade Cottage Sir Walter Scott resided (1798–1804) after his marriage. The village is supposed to be the original of Gandercleuch, in the *Tales of My Landlord.* The churchyard contains the tomb of Drummond of Hawthornden and that of Henry Dundas, Lord Melville. De Quincey in his old age resided at Mavisbush, Polton, farther up the North Esk. Polton has paper-mills.

Lasswade, Polton and their neighbour, **Loanhead**, on the other side of the river, are directly accessible from Edinburgh by bus.

Hawthornden, on the site of a still older house, of which a ruined tower remains, stands on the right bank of the *North Esk,* a couple of miles south-west of Bonnyrigg. It was the home of William Drummond (1585–1649), the poet, sometimes called the 'Scottish Petrarch'. 'Rare Ben Jonson' paid him a memorable visit in 1618–19.

Roslin

The walk to Roslin (there is a regular service of buses from St Andrew Square to Roslin, *via* Loanhead) along the left bank of the *North Esk,* from Loanhead or Polton, is enchanting and gives a good view of Hawthornden House. After rain, however, the path is apt to be treacherous and it may be closed as the result of flooding. The wooded banks of the stream are bounded by lofty sandstone cliffs, decked with foliage and wild flowers. The rocks have been worn into picturesque and fantastic shapes, and there are caves, one said to have been a retreat of Wallace.

Roslin (or **Rosslyn**) **Chapel** (*daily, but Sundays for services only*) was founded in 1446 by William St Clair, Earl of Orkney and Roslin, a descendant of one of the Norman companions of William I. The founder's death in 1484 hindered its completion, but the remains are extremely beautiful. The choir is a fine example of florid Gothic, there being thirteen different styles of arch. The exquisitely carved **'Prentice's Pillar** is said to have been constructed by an apprentice in the absence of his master, who, on his return, burning with envy, ruthlessly slew the young artist. The Chapel, below which there is a more ancient crypt, sustained much injury at the Revolution of 1688. Restored in 1862, it is now used as an Episcopal place of worship. It contains a memorial window to the versatile 5th Earl of Rosslyn, actor, soldier, journalist and gambler.

Roslin Castle (*apply caretaker*) was built by the founder of the Chapel. The more ancient parts of the Castle are indicated by huge fragments. It must have been a place of great strength, moated, and only accessible by a drawbridge. The Castle is finely situated on a steep promontory overhanging the river. *Roslin* means the 'Fall at the headland.' In the Castle garden is a venerable yew tree.

At Roslin, on February 23, 1302, took place the famous triple engagement with the army of Edward I, under Sir John de Seagrave–the Scots, under Sir Simon Fraser, defeating each of the three divisions of the English in turn.

Some 4 miles south-west of Roslin and accessible by numerous buses from Edinburgh (10 miles), is **Penicuik**, signifying 'The Hill of the Cuckoo'. It is a paper-manufacturing place, standing on the North Esk. With the neighbouring Glencorse Barracks it was used for the detention of prisoners-of-war during the conflict with Napoleon. Three hundred of them died here, and were buried at a spot indicated by a simple memorial in the grounds of Valleyfield House. In the finely-wooded grounds of **Penicuik House**–the seat of the Clerks, burned in 1899 and never rebuilt–are an obelisk in memory of Allan Ramsay and the ruins of Ravensneuk Castle.

Howgate, a couple of miles south-east of Penicuik, has a quaint old inn, from which Rab and his friend, the carrier, set out daily for Edinburgh, as recorded by Dr John Brown.

A View near Crawford

Carlisle to Glasgow

Route via Beattock, Abington and Hamilton

This route has been described as far as Abington on pages 79 and 87.

A mile or so from Abington a good little road goes off on the left for Sanquhar (*see* p. 183) by way of **Crawfordjohn**, of old noted for its curling stones.

But the Glasgow road (A74) climbs north-westward to just on 1,000 feet and then drops to **Douglasdale**, a valley extending from the foot of Caintable to the confluence of *Douglas Water* with the Clyde. The valley was the cradle of the great Douglas race, who played such a prominent part in the history of Scotland and were at once the glory and the scourge of their country.

Sir Walter Scott made his last pilgrimage in Scotland to this locality, while preparing for his last novel, *Castle Dangerous*, and he has described with a master hand the ruins of the famous old castle, and the choir of the ancient Church of St Bride, under which the chiefs of the princely race of Douglas were buried for centuries.

From Douglasdale the road climbs north-westward again, and then by Lesmahagow descends finally to the increasingly industrial vale of the Clyde and so by Hamilton (*see* p. 219) to **Glasgow**.

From Abington via Lanark

The road which keeps to the west side of the Clyde below Abington soon comes in sight of **Tinto**, 'the hill of Fire', celebrated through Lanarkshire for its conspicuous height (2,335 feet). The easiest ascent of the hill is up the north-east slope by an obvious path commencing about half a mile west of Thankerton. There is an excellent view-indicator on the summit. The name recalls the Beltane fire of the Druids, whose altars crowned its summit, and the beacon fires of later ages. A hole in a large stone on the summit is said to be the impress of Wallace's thumb! *Fatlips Castle*, on the eastern flank of the hill, is likewise said to be the haunt of a brownie.

Beyond Tinto the road curves round towards the north-west and runs for 9 miles to **Lanark**, the county town of Lanarkshire (described on p. 223). At the west end of the town the road forks. The right-hand branch is the direct road to Stirling and the North. It passes through **Carluke** to the east of Coatbridge and Airdrie, joins the busy Glasgow–Stirling road at Cumbernauld, crosses the Forth and Clyde Canal, and then passes through Denny and on to Stirling.

The left-hand branch descends to the Clyde, which is crossed at Kirkfieldbank, and then follows the west side of the river for three miles to Crossford, half a mile to the west of which are the extensive ruins of **Craignethan Castle**, the original of Tillietudlem in Scott's *Old Mortality*. Tradition says that Queen Mary sheltered here after her escape from Loch Leven. In the neighbourhood is *Lee Castle*, where was kept the Lee Penny, which figures so prominently in *The Talisman*. The ancient Pease Tree at Lee even in Cromwell's time was hollowed with age and capacious enough to permit him to dine with a party of friends.

Opposite Motherwell, on the west side of the Clyde, is Hamilton (*see* p. 219) some 11 miles south-east of Glasgow. On its eastern side are extensive parks. Places on the upper Clyde and into Glasgow are described in the Clyde section of the Glasgow pages of this book (*see* p. 216).

Carlisle to Glasgow

Route via Dumfries and Kilmarnock

This route, slightly longer than others, passes through the heart of the Burns Country. Road and rail maintain close company throughout. It has already been described on pages 79–80 as far as Gretna, where the lefthand turning is taken. As the road runs westward along the shores of the Solway Firth, there are distant views of Criffel (1,866 feet), far away in the west, and of the Lakeland mountains to the south. Nine miles from Gretna is the busy town of **Annan** (*Central, Queensberry, etc.*), offering golf and fishing and a number of interesting trips into the hinterland, no fewer than half a dozen roads radiating from the vicinity. Annan was the birthplace of the celebrated preacher Edward Irving (1792), and it was here also that he was deposed by the local presbytery for his heretical opinions. Thomas Carlyle was a student and later teacher at Annan Grammar School.

The more interesting route from Annan to Dumfries is that *via* **Ruthwell**, in the parish church of which is a cross that is said to be the most ancient, as it is certainly the most graceful, of Runic monuments. From Ruthwell a devious road leads to **Caerlaverock Castle** (*open*), on the shores of the Firth. Of Edwardian type, the castle is triangular in plan, with two towers at the gatehouse and one at each of the other two angles. Parts of the screen walls are original; others represent successive rebuildings. Over the gateway are the Maxwell arms and the motto 'I bid ye fair'. Caerlaverock Church contains the grave of R Paterson, the original of *Old Mortality* (*see* p. 196). From Caerlaverock, Dumfries may be reached by a road skirting the pleasant estuary of the Nith and passing through the little resort of Glencaple (*Nith Hotel*).

Dumfries

Angling–In River Nith.
Distances–Carlisle 33 m; Castle Douglas 18 m; Edinburgh 73 m; Glasgow 74 m; Kirkcudbright 27 m; Lanark 55 m; London 332 m.
Early Closing Day–Thursday.
Golf–Two 18-hole courses.
Hotels–*County* (45 rooms), *Cairndale* (42 rooms), *King's Arms* (60 rooms), *Station* (25 rooms), *Waverley* (17 rooms), *Winston* (16 rooms), *Balmoral* (11 rooms), and many others.
Museums–Town Museum, Corberry Hill, Old Bridge House, Folk Museum, Ellisland Farm.
Population–29,400.
Railway–Station on Carlisle-Kilmarnock-Glasgow main line.
Swimming pool–By river at Greensands.

The busy county town of Dumfries stands on a wide loop of the Nith, about 5 miles above the point where that river empties itself into the Solway

Firth. Its interests for some visitors are bound up with Burns, who is buried in St Michael's Churchyard; but it is also a good holiday centre, and offers golf (2 courses), boating, river and loch fishing and a fine indoor swimming pool. Those who approach Dumfries by the road from Caerlaverock enter the town by St Michael Street, at the eastern end of which is the Churchyard. The Burns mausoleum is at the farthest corner from the entrance, while his original grave, marked with a wooden sign, is at the north-east corner of the churchyard. The monument within (restored 1935) represents 'the genius of Coila finding her favourite son at the plough'. Jean Armour and other members of the poet's family are also buried here.

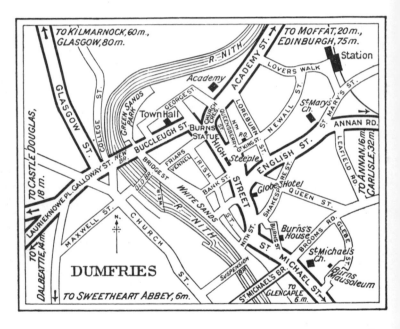

A hundred yards westward of the Church, Burns Street branches off to the right from St Michael Street; on the right of it is **Burns's House**, the poet's home from 1793 until his death in July, 1796. The House (*Admission fee*) has been renovated and fitted up as a Museum of books and relics. Turn to the left at the far end of Burns Street and then to the right, and on the right will be seen the *Globe Inn*, Burns's 'Howff', where he often for-gathered with his friends. Here are shown his chair, a windowpane with verses traced by his hand, and other interesting relics.

Those entering Dumfries by the direct Annan road pass on right the County Buildings, in front of which is a monument to the Duke of Queensberry (d 1778), and will find the *Globe* and Burns Street by bearing left at the fountain at the end of English Street.

From this fountain High Street goes on past the lofty Midsteeple (erected 1704). Near the end of High Street, marked by a statue of Burns, stood the old Greyfriars Monastery in which Bruce slew the Red Comyn for his adherence to the English. A tablet on the wall in Castle Street records the event. The continuation of High Street is named after the Academy, standing a little to the north and numbering among its 'old boys' Sir J M Barrie, OM.

Our road bears left at this point, and by Buccleuch Street reaches the New Bridge (1794). The Old Bridge (fifteenth-century) succeeds one of Devorgilla's day (*see* below).

Maxwelltown, now amalgamated with Dumfries, stands across the river. Its fine old windmill, once an observatory, is now part of the Burgh Museum (*free*; camera obscura, *fee*) which includes an interesting Burns collection and some archaeological exhibits.

For Sweetheart Abbey, 6 miles to the south, *see* p. 186.

The Kilmarnock road is the first turning to the right beyond the New Bridge at Dumfries and makes for Lincluden. Lincluden College, or Abbey, can be reached by car by that road, turning off Jock's Loaning. Alternatively there is a way by cutting through the Lincluden housing estate.

Lincluden College (*weekdays, 10–4; summer 7; Sundays from 2; fee*). The ruins stand where the Cairn flows into the Nith, and comprises a small portion of the twelfth-century Benedictine Nunnery and more considerable remains of buildings erected in the fourteenth–sixteenth centuries when the Abbey had become a College. They are seen from the main road about 2 miles from Dumfries. In the transept of the little church note the tomb of the Provost, with the inscription, 'You who tread on me with your feet remember me in your prayers.' The chief feature in the chancel is the canopied tomb of Margaret, Countess of Douglas.

The Moniaive Valley–Less than 3 miles from Dumfries the Glasgow road crosses the Cairn, and a road goes off on the left for Moniaive, passing almost immediately on the right a circle of standing stones known as the *Twelve Apostles*, though only eleven are present. A mile or so farther along this road a divergence to the left runs to **Irongray**, where, near the south-east corner of the Church, is buried the original of 'Jeanie Deans', the gravestone bearing an inscription written by Sir Walter Scott. A little farther west is a Covenanters' Stone, the last object of the renovating care of 'Old Mortality': as with so many of these stones, the inscription is uncompromisingly blunt.

The main road next comes to Dunscore, about 6 miles to the west of which, and reached by a rough road, is the farm of **Craigenputtock**, 'Cacophonious Craigenputtock', the abode of Thomas Carlyle from 1828 to 1834. Here he entertained Emerson and wrote *Sartor Resartus* and several of his essays. Four miles above Dunscore the Moniaive road passes

MONIAIVE

Maxwellton House, the birthplace of Annie Laurie, the subject of the famous song, who is said to have been buried in the neighbouring churchyard of Glencairn.

Moniaive (16 miles from Dumfries) is a pleasant little place with a seventeenth-century market cross and a monument to the Rev J Renwick, the last of the Covenanting martyrs, who was executed at Edinburgh, 1688. The road between Moniaive and Thornhill passes the hill of *Tynron*, where the Bruce is said to have taken refuge after the murder of the Comyn at Dumfries.

A little more than 3 miles beyond the bridge over the Cairn, the Dumfries–Kilmarnock road passes the farm of **Ellisland**, where Burns lived for three years and where he wrote 'Tam O'Shanter', 'Ye Banks and Braes' and other poems. The farm is now a national possession in the care of the town of Dumfries; there is admission to the display rooms in the farm, and through the stackyard and beside the river. Beyond Ellisland is Friar's Carse, the scene of the bout described in 'The Whistle': it is now a convalescent and holiday home.

On the other side of the river is *Dalswinton*, with a small loch on which, in October, 1788, was launched 'the first really satisfactory attempt at steam

The Midsteeple, Dumfries

navigation in the world'. William Symington was the engineer and Robert Burns one of the passengers. The bridge over the Nith at Auldgirth was built by Thomas Telford.

Thornhill (*Buccleuch & Queensberry*), an attractive little place spread out along the main road, has a seventeenth-century cross, and a tall column (1714) topped by the winged horse emblem of the Queensberrys. Across the river slightly north of the village is Drumlanrig Castle (Duke of Buccleuch): there is a pleasant walk or drive through the policies. In the park are the ruins of *Tibber's Castle*, well worth visiting.

The road under the railway (station closed) leads, in a series of turns, to *Crichope Linn* in about 3 miles–a secluded little spot well worth visiting. Half a mile upstream from the Linn is a fall known as the *Grey Mare's Tail*, not to be confused with the much finer fall of that name above Moffat. By turning to the left after passing under the railway one can reach in 2 miles the ruin of *Morton Castle*, of thirteenth-century date.

At **Carronbridge**, 1¾ miles beyond Thornhill, there goes off on the right the 20-mile road to Elvanfoot and Crawford, in Clydesdale, by way of the Dalveen Pass, a fine run through striking scenery which also provides part of the most direct route from Thornhill to Edinburgh. Three miles from the fork a road goes off on the right to **Durisdeer**, with a church containing memorials of the Queensberry family; the village has a strange, out-of-the-world appearance. Beyond it the Well Path ascends the hills and rejoins the main road at the far end of the Dalveen Pass.

Some 6 miles from Carronbridge the road swings sharply to the right and enters the Dalveen Pass. A farm road strikes off on the left at this point for Nether Dalveen Farm, where is a monument to Daniel McMichael, the Covenanter, from which it is less than a mile over the dip in the hill to the **Enterkin Pass**, whence the way is clear to Leadhills. The pass is a long V-shaped defile seen at its most striking aspect from the Leadhills end (*see below*).

Through the **Dalveen Pass** the road winds between steep, treeless hillsides which rise to nearly 1,000 feet above it and seem to close it on every side. The summit, where the road passes into Lanarkshire and enters the Clyde basin, is 1,140 feet above the sea, a rise of 930 feet from Carronbridge. Hence to **Elvanfoot** the road bears company with the Potrail Water and, later, the Daer Water, the two chief tributaries of the Clyde, and very 'fishful' streams. It should be noted that the road bridge across the railway is some distance north of Elvanfoot village; motorists should be on guard against a premature turning out of the road opposite the station (*closed*). For Elvanfoot and routes hence, *see* page 87.

The main Kilmarnock road keeps to the left at the Carronbridge fork, and with views of Drumlanrig Castle (Duke of Buccleuch) on the left it descends to the Nith, which bears it close company for several miles. Then the valley opens out and we come to **Sanquhar** (pronounced *Sanker*), a name well known to students of history.

The Mennoch Pass

A monument in the main street bears an inscription recording the 'Declarations of Sanquhar', wherein Richard Cameron (1680) renounced allegiance to Charles II and James Renwick repudiated James II. Sanquhar Castle, a fine ruin to the south of the town, was once the seat of the Queensberry family; it now belongs to the Marquis of Bute, one of whose titles is Earl of Sanquhar.

By the **Mennock Pass** to **Leadhills** (10 miles from Sanquhar) – The route leaves the Thornhill road about 2½ miles south of Sanquhar and for a while winds up a beautifully wooded glen, which is succeeded by a deep hill-gorge. For several miles the narrow valley is level and presents a charming scene of simple beauty. Then comes the ascent to **Wanlockhead** (*Youth Hostel*) and **Leadhills** (*Hopetoun Arms*), two villages which owed their existence to the former nearby lead mines. Lying as they do some 1,300 feet above sea-level, they yield only to Flash, near Buxton, Princetown on Dartmoor, and Nenthead in Cumberland on the score of altitude. Leadhills was the birthplace of Allan Ramsay (1686–1785), author of *The Gentle Shepherd*. A stone in the churchyard marking the death of one Taylor, who died at the age of 137, suggests that the situation of the village is healthy enough. Near the churchyard is a monument to William Symington, the pioneer of steam navigation.

Near Elvanfoot (*see* p. 87) on Clydeside is the farm of *Hole*, near which was found the gold from which James V coined his 'bonnet-pieces', so called from the fact that they were impressed on one side with a portrait of His Majesty wearing a bonnet.

From Sanquhar a road runs up beside the Crawick Water for 14 miles to **Crawfordjohn** (p. 177). On the west side of the Nith is the Euchan Glen, with a chalybeate well and a rocky gorge called the Deil's Dungeon.

Above Sanquhar the Kilmarnock road runs pleasantly beside the Nith, by Kirkconnel, to **New Cumnock** (*Crown*, *Threave*), where Burns's 'Sweet Afton) comes down on the south from the slopes of Blacklorg Hill (2,231 feet). Just beyond the bridge over the Afton Water a cross-country road goes off left, to Dalmellington (p. 197); our road turns right through the town and at the north end turns left, in 5 miles reaching **Cumnock**, with many memories of 'The Killing Time'. Hence a road on the right goes up beside the Lugar Water to Muirkirk, near the head waters of the Ayr river, and thence past the Glenbuck reservoirs to Douglas (p. 225). Westward is the road *via* Ochiltree to Ayr. A mile or so beyond Cumnock the road passes the house of *Auchinleck* (pronounced *Affleck*), a mile or so to the west. This was the residence of Boswell's family, and as such was visited by Dr Johnson on his return from the Hebrides. Thence by wooded country to Mauchline (p. 247), and so to **Kilmarnock** (p. 236).

From Kilmarnock Cross, Portland Street and Wellington Street lead out and on to Fenwick, and so over the hills to **Glasgow** by a road which climbs to over 700 feet and commands grand views across the Lower Clyde to the distant mountains around Loch Lomond. Glasgow is entered by way of Giffnock.

Carlisle to Stranraer and
Glasgow by the coast

Distances–Carlisle to Stranraer, 110 m; thence to Ayr, 50 m; thence to Glasgow (direct), 32 m; (by coast) 70 m.

As far as Dumfries this route has been described on page 179.

From Dumfries to Castle Douglas (18 miles south-west) there are three routes: the main road by Crocketford (whence a branch crosses the hills by Balmaclellan to New Galloway, p. 196), the more interesting route *via* Dalbeattie, and that which comes to Dalbeattie by way of a wide sweep around the base of Criffel. All three routes start from the western end of the New Bridge of Dumfries; the Criffel road going off on the left in about 400 yards and the Crocketford road to right at the fork 400 yards farther along the Dalbeattie road.

The Criffel road is the most picturesque of the three, running near Sweetheart Abbey and then round the base of Criffel and by Kirkbean.

The road turning left beyond the bridge over the Nith leads southward in about 6 miles to the remains of–

Sweetheart Abbey (*weekdays 10–7; Sundays from 2, admission fee*) a beautiful Cistercian foundation of the thirteenth century which derives its name from the fact that the foundress, Devorgilla, ordered the heart of her husband, John Balliol, which she had cherished in a casket, to be buried in her tomb. John Balliol was the father of the puppet-king Balliol and the founder of Balliol College, Oxford. The arches of the nave and the massive central tower are in good preservation, and there are considerable remains of the transepts and chancel; the only part roofed over is part of the south transept. The style is Early English and Decorated.

In a westerly direction is the Waterloo Monument on a northern spur of Criffel.

Criffel (1,866 feet). Southward of the village of New Abbey is Loch Kindar, and beyond that is the lane which forms the beginning of the ascent of Criffel which, for its height and the comparative ease of the climb, gives a greater width of view than any other eminence, though it is even more noted as a feature of views from

Sweetheart Abbey

distant points, such as the Lakeland mountains, the Isle of Man, the Cheviots, etc. At the south-eastern foot of the mountain are the ruins of *Wreaths Castle,* once the property of the Regent Morton. The slopes of Criffel are a good point from which to observe the extraordinary tidal range of the Solway: from the shore southward of the mountain the waters ebb and flow over at least 4 miles of sands.

Arbigland, on the shore near Kirkbean, was the birthplace (1747) of the notorious Paul Jones. Thence by a succession of picturesque and popular villages including **Rockcliffe** (*Baron's Craig*), and **Kippford** to Dalbeattie.

Dalbeattie

Distances—Castle Douglas 7 m; Dumfries 14 m; Edinburgh 87 m; Glasgow 88 m; Kirkcudbright 14 m; London 346 m.
Early Closing Day—Thursday.

Golf—9-hole course.
Hotels—*Galloway Arms* (5 rooms), *Maxwell Arms* (8 rooms).
Population—3,250.

Dalbeattie is a bright and attractive little place built of grey granite from its own quarries and situated among very pleasant scenery. It stands where the stream known as the Kirkgunzeon Lane runs into the Urr Water, which a mile or so lower down forms what is known as the Rough Firth.

The **Moat of Urr** is situated 3 miles north of Dalbeattie. It is one of the most perfect relics of its kind, of Saxon or early Norman date, in Britain. A resemblance has been traced to the Tynwald Hill in the Isle of Man, and it has been conjectured that it formed an open-air seat of justice when Galloway was an independent kingdom. It consists of three distinct terraces surrounded by a fosse.

Castle Douglas

Distances – Dalbeattie 7 m; Dumfries 18 m; Edinburgh 91 m; Glasgow 84 m; Kirkcudbright 10 m; London 350 m; New Galloway 14 m; Newton Stewart 33 m.
Early Closing Day – Thursday.
Golf – 9-hole course.

Hotels – *Douglas Arms* (20 rooms), *Ernespie House* (16 rooms), *Imperial* (15 rooms), *Crown* (10 rooms), *King's Arms* (15 rooms), *Market Inn* (9 rooms).
Population – 3,300.

Castle Douglas is a modern market town owing its foundation to the marl in Carlingwark Loch, which was formerly used as a fertiliser. It is a busy little place at the north end of the loch which is noted for its good fishing.

Threave Castle (*daily except Thursdays in summer, fee*) lies 2 miles west on an island in the river Dee and is reached via Bridge of Dee on the A75 road. The ruin is of a fourteenth-century keep built by Archibald the Grim, 3rd Earl of Douglas, whose character as a host may be inferred from an inspection of the granite knob projecting from the front of the Castle and known as 'Gallows Knob', which, the founder was wont to boast, 'never wanted a tassel'. The castle (National Trust) is in the care of the Department of the Environment.

Threave House, a late nineteenth-century mansion, and its fine gardens, are used as a gardening school but the grounds are open daily throughout the year, *fee*.

On the Threave estate is a *Wildfowl Refuge* of the National Trust. *Conducted parties are admitted by prior arrangement from November to March daily except Mondays.*

For the road to Ayr *via* New Galloway and Dalmellington, *see* p. 196.

The main Wigtown road from Castle Douglas keeps on the north-western shore of Carlingwark Loch, but those with time to spare may be recommended to take the road down the eastern side of the loch and join the road from Dalbeattie near Palnackie. Above the road hereabout is a picturesque rock known as the *Lion's Head*, and a mile southward is *Orchardton Tower*, the last remaining Round Tower in Galloway. The best viewpoint in the neighbourhood is *Ben Gairn* (1,250 feet), to the west of the road from Castle Douglas, and forming with the neighbouring height of Screel a very attractive walk.

From Auchencairn the road goes towards Kirkcudbright *via* Dundrennan with its picturesque ruined Abbey.

Dundrennan Abbey

Dundrennan Abbey (*open daily, fee*) was where in 1568 Mary spent her last night on Scottish soil after the defeat at Langside had dashed hopes raised by the escape from Loch Leven. The abbey was founded in 1142 by David I and Fergus, Lord of Galloway, for Cistercians from Rievaulx in Yorkshire.

The ruins are considerable and of great beauty. They include much Norman and Transitional work and there is a rich chapter-house dating from the end of the thirteenth century. Only the transepts and west end of the church remain. A number of fine monuments are preserved, one of them, rather gruesome, of an abbout murdered, possibly by an inhabitant who disliked the incoming Latin monks.

Port Mary, on the coast south-westward of the Abbey, is said to be the spot from which the hapless Mary took boat for England.

Kirkcudbright

Distances – Castle Douglas 10 m; Dalbeattie 14 m; Dumfries 27 m; Edinburgh 100 m; Glasgow 89 m; London 359 m; New Galloway 19 m; Newton Stewart 27 m.
Early Closing Day – Thursday.

Golf – 9-hole course.
Hotels – *Royal* ((22 rooms), *Selkirk Arms* (25 rooms), *Mayfield* (30 rooms), *Ardam House* (16 rooms).
Population – 2,500.

Kirkcudbright (pronounced *Kirkoobrie*) is the capital of Galloway, the patron saint being St Cuthbert, hence the name of the town.

It is one of the most ancient towns in Scotland, and is beautifully situated on the river Dee, near the head of Kirkcudbright Bay. In medieval days the port was among the first six in Scotland, but it greatly decayed during the seventeenth century. The royal castle, situated at the Castledykes, was one of the national fortresses which figured in the War of Independence. Among the remains are the **Tolbooth**, with its beautiful spire, built from stones taken from Dundrennan Abbey, and the castle of the McLellans, Lords Kirkcudbright (*weekdays, 10–4 or 7; Sundays, 2–4 or 7; charge*). Among the public buildings are the Town Hall and the interesting Stewartry Museum, while **Broughton House** (*Mon–Fri 11–1, 2–4; April 2–4 only; Winter, Tues and Thurs, 2–4 only*) is a delightful Georgian House with large library and art collection. The river, which is tidal for about two miles above the town, is spanned by a bridge affording easy access to western Galloway.

At Gatehouse of Fleet

The district has many literary associations, particularly with Burns. In Borgue parish, on the western side of the bay, is laid the scene of Stevenson's *Master of Ballantrae*, and the shores of the bay were the haunt of Dirk Hatteraick and his smugglers in Sir Walter Scott's great romance, *Guy Mannering*. Paul Jones, the 'Father of the American navy', was a native of the district, and commanded ships belonging to the port. Kirkcudbright Bay was one of the places selected for the landing of the Spanish Armada and also for French invasions in aid of the Stewart dynasty. At **Tongland**, about 2 miles north of Kirkcudbright, is a very large hydro-electric power station (*see* p. 196).

From Kirkcudbright we continue westward to Gatehouse, which soon comes into view in the valley below, and to the left the Water of Fleet is seen widening to form Fleet Bay.

Gatehouse of Fleet

Distances—Castle Douglas 15 m; Dumfries 33 m; Edinburgh 106 m; Glasgow 89 m; Kirkcudbright 8 m; London 365 m.
Early Closing Day—Thursday.
Golf—9-hole course.

Hotels—*Clydesdale Cally* (112 rooms), *Murray Arms* (29 rooms), *Anwoth* (14 rooms), *Angel* (8 rooms).
Population—830.

This is a very pretty town nestling in the wooded valley of the Water of Fleet amid green hills that rise on the west almost to the dignity of mountains. A mile south of the town is a conspicuous Monument to Samuel Rutherford (1600–61) one of the great preachers of the Covenant. Near the foot of the monument on a rocky platform over the Water of Fleet is—

Cardoness Castle (*open daily, fee*), an ancient home of the McCullochs. This well-preserved fifteenth-century tower-house is of four storeys and has a vaulted basement. The fireplaces in the great hall and upper hall are notable.

To the north-west of Gatehouse is the old Kirk of Anwoth (built 1626), with a picturesque graveyard containing a Covenanter's tomb with characteristic inscription.

From the Kirk an old Military Road provides a good walk over the hills to Creetown, 7½ miles west of Gatehouse of Fleet in a direct line, but 12 miles by the pretty road past Anwoth and along the coast. Six miles from Gatehouse the shore shows a rocky ridge, beneath which is Dirk Hatteraick's Cave, one of several in the vicinity. Barholm Tower, among woods on the right, is one of the places reputed to be the 'Ellangowan' of *Guy Mannering*—another is Caerlaverock Castle (p. 179). This, too, is the country of *Redgauntlet*.

Above **Creetown** (*Barholm Arms, Ellangowan*) the bay contracts to the estuary of the Cree.

NEWTON STEWART

Newton Stewart

Distances–Castle Douglas 33 m; Dumfries 44 m; Edinburgh 104 m; Glasgow 84 m; Kirkcudbright 27 m; London 376 m; New Galloway 19 m; Stranraer 25 m; Wigtown 7 m.
Early Closing Day–Wednesday.
Golf–9-hole course at Kirroughtree.

Hotels–*Belhotel* (24 rooms), *Crown* (17 rooms), *Galloway Arms* (24 rooms), *Glencairn* (11 rooms), *Kirroughtree* (18 rooms), *Cairnsmore* (12 rooms).
Population–1,880.
Fishing, bowls, tennis.

Newton Stewart can vie with any town of its size in Scotland. It is an attractive little town busy with weaving, and has attractions with some good fishing. Its one irregular street runs for nearly a mile alongside the river; on the west the ground rises gently, but on the east the loftiest range of hills in the south of Scotland begins with *Cairnsmore of Fleet* (2,329 feet), whose summit is not more than 6 miles from the town. Across the river is **Minnigaff**, the town's more ancient suburb.

From Newton Stewart a hilly but wildly beautiful road runs over the hills to **New Galloway** (18 miles). Eight miles out is a granite monument to Alexander Murray (1775–1813), who from a shepherd boy on these hills rose to be Professor of Oriental Languages at Edinburgh University. Beside the Upper Bridge of Dee, some 12 miles from Newton Stewart, is the dam of the Clatteringshaws Reservoir of the Galloway scheme (*see* p. 196). From the Bridge a track goes off on the left to **Loch Dee**, which is also approached on foot from Newton Stewart by a path beside the Penkill Burn at Minnigaff.

Newton Stewart to Girvan direct. A road runs north-westward for 30 miles to Girvan on the west coast, passing the entrance to Glen Trool, where lie Loch Trool, a gem, and a National Forest Park (*Youth Hostel*).

A road leaves the Girvan highway at Bargrennan (*Inn*; 9 miles from Newton Stewart). In about a mile and just beyond the village of Glentrool, a right turn leads through woods to beautiful Glen Trool. Loch Trool lies to the right of the road, but neither the glen nor the loch is fairly seen until one is close to them. Three miles to the north of the head of Loch Trool stands **Merrick** (2,764 feet), the highest mountain in the south of Scotland. It may be ascended by the path from Buchan Farm to Culsharg and thence over the lower top of Benyellary (2,360 feet) to the highest point.

From Bargrennan Bridge the Girvan road climbs to some 500 feet above the sea, crosses the headwaters of the Cree and enters Ayrshire, still climbing until the highest point (558 feet) is reached, 1½ miles farther. Beyond Barrhill (whence the railway from Stranraer keeps company with the road) a very pretty valley is entered. **Pinwherry Castle**, the ruins of which are seen on the right, was a stronghold of the Kennedies, and from Pinwherry station there is a good view down the strath of the Stinchar stream to the peaked hill of Knockdolian, near Ballantrae. Then the descent to **Girvan** (*see* p. 247) begins.

Machars Promontory

Southward from Newton Stewart the promontory of the **Machars** extends for some 25 miles to Whithorn and Isle of Whithorn. **Wigtown** (*Galloway*) is a quiet little town with a ruined old Church, in the burying ground of which are the graves of Margaret MacLachlan and Margaret Wilson, the Wigtown Martyrs. In striking contrast to the sad suggestiveness of this monument is the inscription on a stone opposite the south-west transept of the old kirk:

> ' And his son John of honest fame,
> Of stature small and a leg lame,
> Content he was with portions small,
> Keep'd shop in Wigtown and that's all.'

The *Martyrs' Monument* perpetuates the memory of the two women already named, who were tied to a stake and drowned by the tide in the never-to-be-forgotten 1685, and of three men who were hanged without trial. The inscription is more remarkable for simple fervour than for grammatical flourishes.

The *Torhouse Stones*, 3 miles west of Wigtown, comprise a circle of 19 monoliths, each about 5 feet high, enclosing three central blocks. South of Wigtown is **Baldoon Castle**, the parental home of David Dunbar, the Bucklaw of *The Bride of Lammermuir*. From Sorbie, with a square old tower, a road goes eastward to **Garliestown**, busy with the milling and timber trade.

At **Whithorn** (*Grapes, Castlewigg*) the main feature of interest is the ruin of the Priory Church, supposed to occupy the site of St Ninian's Chapel, the first Christian Church in Scotland. An interesting collection of early sculptured monuments is housed in the adjacent museum (*admission, fee*) (*open weekdays only, 10–7 or 4*). South-east from the village is the so-called *Isle of Whithorn*, actually a peninsula. Near the south end of the harbour are the ruins of St Ninian's Kirk, which disputes with the Priory Church the honour of standing upon the site of St Ninian's Chapel (early fifth century).

On the west coast of the promontory, some 4 miles from Whithorn, is **St Ninian's Cave**, with crosses cut in the rock by pilgrims.

Port William (*Eagle, Monreith Arms*) is a quiet little resort (population 550), on Luce Bay. There is a sandy beach and there are fine views across the bay. To the south-east is **Monreith House** with its notable rhododendron gardens and in the park, the old Monteith Cross, an ancient free-standing wheel-headed cross about $7\frac{1}{2}$ feet high and displaying elaborate interlacing.

Glenluce (*King's Arms* (9), *Judges Keep* (11)) is a pretty Galloway village placed near the head of Luce Bay. Two miles to the north is the twelfth-century **Glenluce Abbey** (*daily, fee*) in its beautiful situation. A Cistercian house founded in 1192 by Roland, Earl of Galloway, the ruins are of considerable architectural interest. Of the church, in the First Pointed style of the late fifteenth century, the south aisle and south transept are the principal remains.

Almost a mile west of the village is **Castle of Park** a tall castellated mansion dating from 1590. Built by a son of the last Abbot of Glenluce it looks out over the village from its prominent position on the brow of a hill.

Five miles westward the road skirts the extensive grounds of Lochinch and the gardens of **Castle Kennedy** (*gardens daily, April to September, 9am to 5 pm. Admission fee. Free car park.*) Castle Kennedy is the home of the Earl of Stair and one of the show places of Galloway. Here between the two lochs of Inch are fine lawns, terraces and shrubberies with a lily pond, and a notable avenue of 'Monkey Puzzle' trees.

Three miles farther is –

Stranraer

Angling – For trout in nearby lochs.

Bathing – From East Shore and Broadstone, both having sandy beaches.

Bowls – Stranraer Bowling Club, Bowling Green Lane; and West End Bowling Club in Park Lane. Visitors welcomed.

Distances – Edinburgh 123 m; Girvan 30 m; Glasgow 84 m; London 401 m; Newton Stewart 25 m; Wigtown 27 m.

Early Closing Day – Wednesday.

Golf – 18-hole course at Creachmore.

Hotels – *North West Castle* (29 rooms), *George* (30 rooms), *Buck's Head* (17 rooms), *Lochnaw Castle* (6 rooms).

Population – 9,850.

Sailing – Loch Ryan Sailing Club. Regatta.

Tennis – Courts in Stair Park.

Stranraer is the chief commercial centre in South-west Scotland west of Dumfries. It stands at the head of **Loch Ryan**, which is 8 miles long and nearly 3 miles wide, and provides a sheltered harbour for the car ferry making the short sea trip across to the Irish coast at Larne, 30 miles away. In addition to the inevitable interests of the waterside, there is golf, boating, bathing, fishing, tennis, etc., and the town is a good centre for the exploration of the peninsula terminating southward in the Mull of Galloway.

The remains of Stranraer Castle in the centre of the town date from the early sixteenth century. It was long used as a jail.

From Stranraer the road strikes southward to Luce Bay near **Sandhead**. At Kirkmadrine, near Stoneykirk, are three of the earliest Christian monuments in Britain (fifth or sixth century). From **Drummore** (*Queen's*), prettily situated in front of a little bay, the chief excursion is to the lighthouse at the Mull (5 miles). There is a motor road, but the best walking route is along the coast by Portankill, where are the ruins of **Kirkmaiden** Old Church, the most southerly parish in Scotland, the greatest north-south measurement of the country being popularly 'Frae Maiden Kirk to John o' Groats'. The path then climbs the cliff past *St Medans's Chapel* (a cave with remains of walls) and joins the road across the Tarbet to the Lighthouse.

Port Logan, on the western coast, is at the head of a pretty bay and has a tidal fish-pond inhabited by remarkably tame fish. The beautiful **Logan Gardens** (*April–September, daily, fee*) display many sub-tropical plants and shrubs.

The most important place on the west coast is **Portpatrick**, 7 miles from Stranraer by road. (*Cross Keys, Fernhill, Portpatrick, Melvin Lodge, Roslin; several boarding-houses; golf.*) It is picturesquely situated overlooking the remains of a harbour built by Rennie.

View over Ballantrae to Ailsa Craig

Stranraer to Girvan by the Coast

The first few miles are along the southern and eastern shores of Loch Ryan past Cairnryan (*Lochryan Hall*). Near the mouth of the Loch the road turns inland up **Glen App**. **Glenarn Castle**, home of the Earl of Inchcape lies on this road. The extensive gardens contain a notable collection of plants and shrubs, rose garden, borders and hothouses (*open daily except Saturdays, May to August, fee*).

Ballantrae (*Royal, King's Arms*) is a fishing village with golf links and other attractions for those who like unsophisticated holiday resorts. When R L Stevenson visited the village in 1878, his eccentricity of costume caused the people to stone him. *The Master of Ballantrae* was laid at Borgue (p. 191) and not here.

Some 5 miles beyond Ballantrae is the ruined tower of **Carleton Castle**, where May Cullean, the eighth wife of a wicked baron who had disposed of seven wives by pushing them over the cliff, turned the tables on her liege lord and threw him instead–a feat not undeservedly commemorated in a well-known ballad.

Girvan and the coast northward to Glasgow are described on pages 216–47.

195

Castle Douglas to Ayr (direct)

This is a splendid run of 51 miles comprising some of the best scenery in South-west Scotland.

As the road leaves Castle Douglas the monument to Neilson, inventor of the hot-blast, is conspicuous on a hill to the left. Along by Crossmichael the Dee widens to several loch-like reaches and beyond Parton forms the long *Loch Ken*. Near the head of the loch is Kenmure Castle, a modified fifteenth-century house in which Burns stayed.

Beyond the loch is **New Galloway** (*Kenmure Arms, Cross Keys*), a neat little burgh which is the centre for some pleasant excursions among the hills. There is good fishing. The burgh is in the parish of Kells and the church is half a mile away on the brow of a hill. There are some curious gravestones in the burying ground, notably one to a sportsman named John Murray (d. 1777).

One cannot travel far in this neighbourhood without being aware of the **Galloway Hydro-Electric Scheme**, a huge undertaking comprising five power stations, seven reservoirs and the necessary dams, tunnels, aqueducts and pipelines to impound and convey the water. One of the reservoirs – an enlargement of Loch Doon – would normally discharge down the River Doon to the Ayrshire coast, but by means of a dam and tunnel 6,600 feet long its waters are diverted to the Deugh watershed to pass in turn through the power stations at Kendoon, Carsfad, Earlstoun and Tongland.

These four power stations are in series, Kendoon, Carsfad and Earlstoun being in the hills between the villages of Carsphairn and Dalry, and Tongland at the head of the estuary near Kirkcudbright, the capital of the Stewartry. The fifth station, Glenlee, is supplied (by means of a tunnel 19,000 feet long by 11 feet 6 inches in diameter) from an artificial loch, Clatteringshaws, on the upper reaches of the Blackwater of Dee, the water afterwards discharging into the Ken and flowing to Tongland along with the water from the other three stations. The storage represents an aggregate capacity equivalent to about 35,650,000 units of electricity, which is one-fifth of the estimated annual output of the whole scheme.

From New Galloway there is a pleasant route over the hills westward to Newton Stewart (p. 192).

The road eastwards to Dumfries passes **Balmaclellan**, charmingly situated. Here is a monument to 'Old Mortality' (*see* p. 179) who devoted so much time to furbishing up the inscriptions on the tombs of the Galloway Covenanting martyrs and who provided the title for Scott's novel. His real name was Robert Paterson and he died in 1800, aged 88. The Covenanters' Stone found near the south side of the church is remarkable for the bluntness of its inscription. From near the Church a path leads northward to the road from Dalry to Moniaive, passing the ruins of Barscobe Castle.

Dalry (*Lochinvar, Milton Park, Commercial*) on the *Ken*, is a very popular little centre with anglers and walkers. It slopes steeply up from the riverside in one street. In the kirkyard are some Covenanters' tombs with the customarily blunt inscriptions, but more notable examples of these outpourings are at Balmaclellan (*see above*) reached by a path or a road over the hills south-eastward.

From Dalry to Carsphairn there are two roads–the old one, hilly, but commanding the best views, and the new one, which passes through the best valley scenery. About 2 miles from Dalry, Earlstoun Tower will be seen in the valley. Some miles farther a mountain route from Moniaive comes in on the right.

Carsphairn (*Salutation*) is a small village of one street, on a tableland 600 feet above the sea and flanked by lofty green mountains, all easy of access and affording views that are wide rather than striking. From the north end of the village a track goes westward across the meadows beyond the river, and some 2 miles farther passes the abandoned Woodhead Lead Mines, the ridge beyond which commands a good view of *Loch Doon* (now a reservoir under the Galloway Scheme: *see* p. 196). The loch is some 5 miles long by half a mile wide; fishing is free. A remarkable early castle, which would have been submerged by the artificial raising of the loch, has now been removed from its island site to the shore of the loch. The actual work of transference, stone by stone, was carried out by the Ancient Monuments Department of the Department of the Environment. At the foot of the loch, which is more easily reached from the road near Dalmellington, is little *Ness Glen*. The path from Carsphairn descends to the head of the loch, but the walk down the western side to the glen is monotonous.

It is some 6 miles on from Carsphairn to *Loch Muck*, from which a track runs up to the foot of the Ness Glen. From **Dalmellington** (*Eglinton, Ladywell House*), 6 miles farther, roads run eastward to New Cumnock and westward to Maybole and Girvan, but we follow the Doon through the hills to beyond Patna, whence the river sweeps away on the left and the road goes straight ahead towards **Ayr** (p. 241).

The Kelvin and Glasgow University

Glasgow

Banks – *Bank of Scotland*, 110 St Vincent Street, C.2; *Clýdesdale*, 30 St Vincent Place, C.1; *Royal Bank of Scotland*, 98 Buchanan Street, C.1; *Savings Bank*, 177 Ingram Street, C.1.

Bus Tours – The Scottish Bus Group and associated companies run regular services of buses to all parts of Scotland. Services for places north and east of Glasgow leave from Killermont Street and from Dundas Street, and for other places from Anderston Cross. Coach tours start from the Travel Centre in Buchanan Street.

Car Parking – Within the central area street parking is controlled by meters and the kerbs are marked with signs indicating restrictions. There are car parks at the Central and Queen Street stations, and others include Broomielaw, Buchanan Street, Maitland Street, Mart Street, Shuttle Street and St Enoch. There are many private garages where cars may be left.

Cinemas – Numerous cinemas throughout the city. Among the principal are *Bedford*, *Coliseum*, Eglington Street; *Cosmo*, Rose Street; *Odeon 1, 2 and 3*, *Playhouse*, *Regent*, Renfield Street; *ABC 1 and 2*, *La Scala*, *Gaumont*, *Curzon Classic*, Sauchiehall Street.

Dancing – *Albert*, Bath Street; *Barrowland*, Gallowgate; *Majestic*, Hope Street; *Plaza*, Eglinton Street; *Tiffany's*, Sauchiehall Street.

Distances – Aberdeen 144 m; Ardrossan 29 m; Ayr 33 m; Callander 36 m; Carlisle 94 m; Dumfries 74 m; Edinburgh 44 m; Gourock 26 m; Hamilton 11 m; Lanark 25 m; Largs 30 m; London 394 m; Manchester 212 m; Peebles 50 m; Prestwick 31 m.

Early Closing Day – Tuesday or Saturday.

Football – *Celtic*, Celtic Park; *Partick Thistle*, Fishill Park; *Queen's Park*, Hampden Park; *Rangers*, Ibrox Park; *Clyde*, Shawfield Park.

Golf – Municipal courses (18-hole): *Deaconsbank*, Rooken Glen; *Linn Park*, Cathcart, *Littlehill*, Bishopriggs; *Lethamhill*. Municipal courses (9-hole): *King's Park*, *Knightswood*, *Ruchill*.

Greyhound Racing – Carntyne, Shawfield and White City.

Hotels – *Central* (240 rooms), Gordon Street; *North British* (80 rooms), George Square; *St Enoch* (146 rooms), St Enoch Square; *Bellahouston* (46 rooms), Paisley Road West; *Lorne* (87 rooms), Sauchiehall Street; *Tinto Firs* (30 rooms), Kilmarnock Road; *Blythswood* (56 rooms), Argyle Street; *Newlands* (15 rooms), Kilmarnock Road; *Royal* (47 rooms), Sauchiehall Street; *Shawlands* (20 rooms), Shawland's Centre; *Stepps* (50 rooms), Stepps Road; and many others.

Ice-Rink – Crossingleaf, Titewood, S.1.

Information – Municipal Bureau, George Square.

Libraries – Municipal lending libraries in all districts. Important reference libraries include *Mitchell Library*, North Street; *Stirling's Library*, Queen Street; *Commercial Library*, Royal Exchange Square.

Police – Headquarters at 21 St Andrew's Street.

Population – 898,000.

Postal – Head Office, George Square. Numerous branch offices.

Railway Stations – *Central Station*, Gordon Street; *Queen Street Station*, George Square.

Sports Centre – Bellahouston Drive.

Theatres – *Citizen's*, Gorbals Street; *King's*, Bath Street; *Metropole*, St George's Cross; *Pavilion*, Benfield Street.

Underground – There is an underground electric railway, 6½ miles long, running round the city and its western suburbs. Frequent service from 6 am until 11 pm.

For a city of its size and antiquity Glasgow is not very rich in objects of architectural or historical interest – the Cathedral, Provand's Lordship and the Corporation Art Gallery and Museum with the neighbouring Univer-

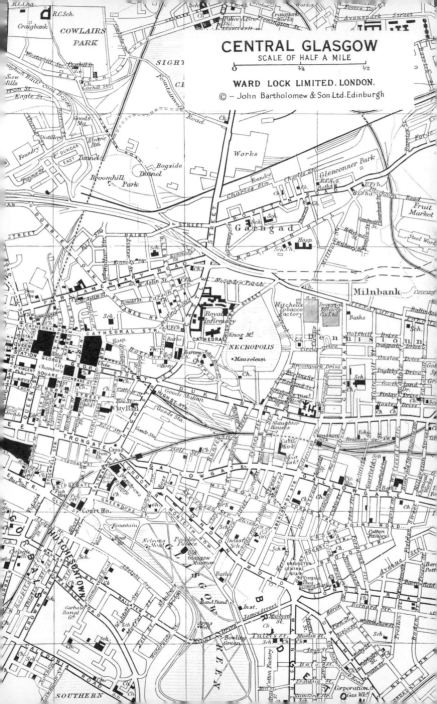

sity nearly exhaust the list in that direction. Any lack of archaeological show-places is, however, amply compensated by the industrial and human interest of the city. Clyde shipbuilding yards have led the world since the momentous day when Henry Bell's *Comet* introduced steam propulsion; Clydeside engineers are to be found wherever there are engines to be nursed, and if in less prosperous years the achievements of Clydeside shipyards have been less spectacular than in the flourishing days just before the 1914–18 War, the influence of other great Glasgow industries has been potent in many directions.

The stranger who wanders along the quays and wharves of the Broomielaw will realize, if he has not done so before, how great is the interdependence between this, the third most populous city in Britain, and the wild country stretching almost from the municipal boundaries to Cape Wrath and the farthest Hebrides. Flocks and herds and the abundant produce of the seas are poured into Glasgow daily, and in return almost every artificial requirement of life is sent to every hamlet in the western Highlands accessible by steamer–for notwithstanding the railway and the development of the motor, boats still play an important part in the transport system of western Scotland: a fact which tourists, unless they are motoring will quickly realize.

The city is well equipped with public transport, and all the major places of interest may be reached by this means with no difficulty.

For places on the river and Firth of Clyde, see pages 216–31.

The focal point of Glasgow's business life is **George Square**. The two main railway termini are close at hand; here are the **Bank of Scotland**, the **Merchants' House** (the meeting-place of the Chamber of Commerce), the head **Post Office**. The eastern side of the Square is filled by the frontage of the **Municipal Buildings** (the elaborately decorated Banqueting Hall and other apartments may be seen Monday, Tuesday, Wednesday and Friday). Glasgow has a well-merited celebrity for its municipal administration, and a hint of the complexity of the task may be caught by walking eastward from George Square and noting how far back this immense block of buildings extends. The Municipal Information Bureau is in the Square.

Of the monuments in the Square the two most notable are the *War Memorial,* at the eastern end, and the lofty monument to *Sir Walter Scott.* In connection with Chantrey's statue of *James Watt,* we may recall the tradition that Watt, a native of Greenock, solved the practical application of the steam-engine during a Sunday afternoon walk on Glasgow Green in 1765.

From the south-west corner of George Square busy Queen Street leads to Argyle Street, passing on the right the **Royal Exchange**, a Grecian building designed by Hamilton, now housing Stirling's Library and the Commercial Library.

Ingram Street, on the left, leads to **Hutcheson's Hospital**, a wealthy foundation which originated in the bequests of two brothers Hutcheson in the seventeenth century. Of the net annual income, which is a substantial amount, three-fifths are devoted to pensions and two-fifths to education.

The hospital buildings are now occupied by the Glasgow Educational Trusts.

Queen Street terminates in **Argyle Street**, which to the left leads into **Trongate**, a bustling thoroughfare which has changed considerably since the days when it was haunted by Burns, Sir Walter Scott, Adam Smith, David Hume and other great men of the day. Not long since, however, something of its historic appearance has been recaptured by the successful reproduction of the old Cross, standing at the junction of the Trongate, High Street, Saltmarket and Gallowgate. The **Tron Steeple** straddling the pavement a little west of the Cross is all that remains of St Mary's Church–the Tron Church was burnt down in 1793.

High Street, on the left, leads up past the Tolbooth Steeple (1627) to the Cathedral; but those with time should pass down the **Saltmarket**–its glories sadly departed since the days when Bailie Nicol Jarvie and other douce Glasgow merchants of olden time here won their crowns, kept their crowns and counted their crowns and flavoured their punch with limes grown on their own little farms 'yonder awa' ' in the West Indies. At the lower end of Saltmarket is an entrance to **Glasgow Green**, dating back to 1662. It has an area of 136 acres and the drive round it describes a circuit of $2\frac{1}{2}$ miles. Provision has been made for most games. In the *People's Palace* is the **Old Glasgow Museum** with exhibits and pictures of the history and life of Glasgow.

From the foot of Saltmarket, buses run up past the Trongate and by **High Street** to the Cathedral. It is difficult to believe that at one time the High Street was quite monastic in character; two plaques near the gates of the railway goods station are the only evidence of the former old College on the site which housed the original Glasgow University. Adam Smith laid the foundations of modern economic science while Professor of Moral Philosophy at this College; while James Watt was attached to it as philosophical instrument-maker he made his experiments which led to the steam-engine; and in the College gardens Francis and Rashleigh Osbaldistone fought (*Rob Roy*).

High Street climbs steadily to Cathedral Square, the final few hundred yards being known as the 'Bell o' the Brae'.

The Cathedral

The Cathedral is open everyweekday, April to October, 10–7; October to March, 10–5; Sundays, 10.30–8 except during service hours.
Sunday services at 11 and 6.30.
Permission to photograph the interior can be obtained from the local office of the Department of the Environment, Argyle House, Lady Lawson Street, Edinburgh, EH3 9SD.

This, the Parish Church of Glasgow, is a perfect specimen of Early English Gothic architecture. It and the Cathedral of Kirkwall are the only churches in Scotland in the condition in which they were before the Reformation, except that, in 1846 and 1848, two western towers of Glasgow were pulled down, a sadly misguided action.

About the year 543 St Kentigern, better known as St Mungo, now the patron saint of the City, built a simple Church on the present site. It is a forgotten but

George Square, Glasgow

noteworthy fact that he brought Christianity to Glasgow twenty years before Columba brought it to Iona. On the holy site the Cathedral was founded in the days of Bishop John and dedicated in 1136. Of this Norman church a few stones remain. A second Cathedral was dedicated in 1197. Of course the Cathedral was not built at one period, but spread over centuries, and owes its completion to many builders and the generosities of many churchmen.

After the Reformation the beautiful building suffered much through sheer neglect, being divided up into no fewer than three distinct Parish Churches; but in the first quarter of the nineteenth century a restoration was completed. The Munich painted glass has been replaced by modern stained glass, and there is some sixteenth-century Flemish and seventeenth-century Swiss glass. The Cathedral is now maintained by the Department of the Environment as property of the Crown.

The **Nave** has a peculiar charm of simple majesty, folded in stillness. The very fine rood screen is one of the few solid stone screens remaining in Scotland, and bears a close resemblance to the one in Canterbury Cathedral. The sculptured figures upon it represent the Seven Ages of Man.

Behind the Altar is the fine **East Chapel**—in medieval times four separate chapels; in one of which is to be seen an ornamental tombstone of 1633.

Near the Sacristy door, in glass case, note the old Bible of the Reader's Lectern, of date 1617: it disappeared in 1745, but was restored to the Cathedral in 1849. It is bound in oak boards, covered with native sealskin. The preacher's hour-glass—an object once common to all pulpits—stands on the pulpit. The sand takes thirty-eight minutes to run out, suggesting a longer sermon than is commonly acceptable today!

In the **Sacristy** may be seen the chair said to have been occupied by Oliver Cromwell during Divine Service.

The **Crypt**, acknowledged to be one of the finest Gothic vaulted crypts in Europe, is entered by steps beside the Rood Screen. Here is the Shrine of St Mungo, where the saint was buried on January 13, 603. Here, also, is an ancient well. At its source on the hillside St Mungo is said to have baptized his converts when all around was wild forest and moorland. The well is closed, but the water of the spring is still quite fresh. In the Chapel of St Andrew is the effigy of Bishop Wishart – the friend and supporter of Wallace and Bruce – a great Scottish patriot whose help was valued highly by those leaders, and whose influence was acknowledged fully by the English enemy of the time. Also in the crypt is a tombstone of some Covenanters of the seventeenth century – 'The Killing Time' – who were put to death for the faith, at the corner of the Cathedral.

Opening from the Crypt at its north-east corner is the **Chapter House**, recently restored and furnished.

Until the beginning of the nineteenth century the Crypt was used by the congregation of the Barony Kirk. It is described in Chapters 19 and 20 of Scott's *Rob Roy*, and one of the pillars is known as Rob Roy's pillar, from the assignation there between him and Francis Osbaldistone.

Another vaulted crypt, known as Blacader or **Fergus's Aisle**, is the last piece of building before the Reformation. The grave of the holy man was there, surrounded by a grove; and a quaint carving on the arch near the entrance, just above the stair, shows the body of Fergus on a cart – the legend being that he was so conveyed, by a yoke of wild oxen to the place where, when they stopped of their own accord, he was buried.

Overlooking the Cathedral, and separated from it by the valley down which once flowed the Molendinar Burn, is –

The Necropolis, access to which is gained by an Elizabethan portal (sculptured with the arms of the city and of the Merchants' House on a double shield), and a single arch bridge.

The site of the Necropolis, anciently the Fir Park or Merchants' Park, attains a height of three hundred feet. The most conspicuous monument on the summit is that of *John Knox*, in his Geneva cap and gown. The figure, twelve feet in height, was wrought by Robert Forrest, a self-taught sculptor, and surmounts a massive and lofty Grecian column of Doric architecture. Among other monuments of general interest are those of *Sheridan Knowles*, the dramatist; *Michael Scott*, author of 'Tom Cringle's Log'; *William Motherwell*, the poet; *Dr MacNish*, 'The Modern Pythagorean'; *William Miller*, author of 'Wee Willie Winkie', and other well-known rhymes for children; and a marble statue of the first *Charles Tennant* of St Rollox.

The **Jews' Sepulchre**, in a secluded corner at the northern extremity of the ground, is indicated by a beautiful architectural façade, a copy of the tomb of Absalom, in the King's Dale, Jerusalem, with an ornamental Roman column, inscribed with Scriptural quotations and the well-known lines of Byron's Hebrew melody –

'Oh, weep for those who wept by Babel's stream,
Whose shrines are desolate, whose land a dream!

The wild dove hath her nest, the fox her cave,
Mankind their country – Israel but the grave.'

GLASGOW

At the corner of McLeod and Castle Streets stands –

Provand's Lordship

Admission, *fee*. Open every day except Sunday; April to September, 10 am to 12.45 and 2 to 5 pm; October to March, 11 am to 12.45 pm and 2 to 4 pm.

Now the only surviving medieval domestic building in Glasgow, Provand's Lordship dates from about 1471.

The building was probably the residence of the master or Preceptor of the almshouse for twelve aged men founded by Bishop Andrew Muirhead (1455–73) and known as St Nicholas Hospital. The remainder of the buildings have vanished, for the hospital shared the common fate of such establishments at the Reformation; but it is interesting to note that the Lord Provost of Glasgow is still *ex officio* Preceptor of St Nicholas Hospital.

At all events the building came to be, or contained, the town house or 'manse' of one of the canons of Glasgow Cathedral, whose *prebend* (or living) lay outwith the boundary of the city, in Lanarkshire near the present Baillieston. The lands in question came to be called 'Provan' or 'Provand' – 'Provand' may just be '*prebend*' in another form.

Like other lands they were secularized at the time of the Reformation; the 'canon' of the day whose name was William Baillie, obtained a charter from Queen Mary in 1562, became a lay laird, and ultimately a person of consequence.

In pre-Reformation days both James II and James IV became honorary canons, but there is no evidence that James IV ever stayed in the house now called Provand's Lordship.

For another legend, namely, that Queen Mary once lived there, some sort of case can be made. When she came to visit the ailing Darnley for a few days in January 1567 there was no obvious house to receive her. Darnley's father Lennox, pleading illness, stayed in Crookston Castle and, in any case, the Hamiltons who escorted her were at deadly feud with the Lennox Stewarts. Mary did not stay with Lennox and obviously she did not stay in the infected house wherein her husband lay.

Many of the ecclesiastical buildings had been damaged or lost in the troubles of the Reformation, but there was no reason why the prosperous William Baillie, to whom the Queen had already given a charter, should not have preserved his house in order good enough to house the Queen.

After Baillie's death the fortunes of the house declined. Its situation, which had been very near the centre of the old city, became less desirable; ownership passed from hand to hand and the building was in a poor state when it was taken over by the Glasgow Corporation.

In 1906 a body of Glasgow Citizens formed a little society to take over the feu, for which they paid themselves and in succeeding decades generous gifts from members and from fellow citizens have enabled the Society to acquire ownership of the house and to enrich it with furniture, Scottish domestic appurtenances and pictures, which illustrate Scottish domestic life for about four centuries.

The collection, which includes a very charming portrait of Mary Queen of Scots as a girl (attributed by some to Holbein) and a portrait of James VI and I by George Jamesone (1586–1644), is well worth a visit.

On the same side of the Square is the Barony Parish Church, a successor to the building so long associated with Dr Norman Macleod. An old cottage which stood just to the west of the church was rather doubtfully

Provand's Lordship

connected with Darnley's visit to Glasgow, referred to above. The name of Rotten Row invites comparisons between this drab thoroughfare and the tree-shaded lane in London. Yet odd fragments of buildings hint at times that were very different, and indeed one need go no farther than the pages of Scott for reminders that Glasgow has a history, however carefully it may conceal evidences of it. George Street leads back to George Square, passing on the right the former Royal College of Science and Technology, now **Strathclyde University**. This was founded by Professor Anderson as a true 'People's College'; the medical schools were in 1889 removed to Dumbarton Road, and are now incorporated in the University.

An exploration of the western half of central Glasgow might begin with a bus ride from the north side of George Square, by St Vincent Street and Argyle Street to Kelvingrove Park and the –

Art Gallery and Museum
Open free daily: Mondays to Saturdays, 10–5; Sundays, 2–5.

The collections are housed in a striking French Renaissance building, which is, however, best appreciated when viewed from the vicinity of the University, on the northern side of the Park. The block was built in 1901 from the plans of John W Simpson and Milner Allen, of London, with money from the Glasgow International Exhibitions, 1888 and 1901, and by public subscription. Twin central towers, rising to 172 feet, form the principal feature of the exterior. The building, of red sandstone, is 448 feet long and 256 feet wide, and is two storeys in height. On entering, the visitor finds himself in a great central hall, extending upwards through the two storeys. On each side is a court 106 feet long and 64 feet wide. These give access to the galleries, about twenty in number, those on the ground floor containing the **Museum**.

The East Court contains natural habitat groups of the mammals and birds from Africa, Australia, India, Scotland and the Polar Regions. The West Court houses a collection of ship models illustrating the history of shipping. The rooms round these are devoted to various sections, illustrating Arms and Armour, Engineering, Archaeology, Ethnography, Geology and Birds in their natural habitat. A section of Egyptology is included which contains many important exhibits. There is also a fine collection of metal-work, pottery and glass.

The *Art Collections*. The upper galleries contain the collection of pictures belonging to the city. The Venetian, Roman, Florentine and other Italian Schools are represented by the works of Titian, Giorgione, Giovanni Bellini, Botticelli, Canaletto, etc., while included with the collections relating to other great Schools are creations of such men as Mabuse, The Master of Moulins, Rubens, Vandyck, Velasquez, and others too numerous to mention. These galleries are specially rich in choice pictures of the Dutch School. There are some fine examples of Rembrandt, particularly the 'Man in Armour'; and characteristic pictures by Ruysdael, Hobbema, Ostade, Jan Steen, Wouverman, and Cuyp. Among many notable modern British works of art, Whistler's portrait of Carlyle will attract special attention, as will also certain outstanding canvases of Reynolds, Raeburn, Allan Ramsay and other portraitists of that period. Richard Wilson and Morland, with their illustrious contemporaries, Sir David Wilkie and J M W Turner, are also in evidence, the latter particularly by his renowned work, 'Modern Italy–The Pifferari.' There is also the well-known painting, 'Christ of St John of the Cross,' by Salvador Dali.

The galleries were, a few years ago, enriched by a gift from Sir William and Lady Burrell. It included items of outstanding importance among tapestries, pictures, porcelain, stained glass, furniture and silver, etc. Glasgow is recognized as one of the most important and progressive art centres in Britain.

Kelvingrove Park is in two sections, which slope more or less steeply to the Kelvin River as it hurries down to lose itself in the busy Clyde. Facing the Art Gallery and Museum across the valley is–

The University of Glasgow

an excellent example of Sir George Gilbert Scott's Early English work, to which have been added various features in Scottish baronial Gothic, notably the splendid gateway, surmounted by a crocketed spire, of which the top is 300 feet above the ground.

The University was founded in 1451, and a Pedagogy was soon in use. In the middle of the seventeenth century, the College in the High Street (*see* p. 203) was built, and this was its home until 1870, when classes were held for the first time in the building before which we stand. The entrance lodge on University Avenue was built from the stones of the High Street college gateway. The balustrade of the Lion and Unicorn Staircase, facing the Principal's House, also came from the College in the High Street.

The University includes faculties of Arts, Divinity, Law, Medicine, Science, Engineering and Veterinary Medicine; there is a teaching staff of a thousand, and the average number of students on the rolls is about nine thousand, of whom nearly a third are women. Many extensions to the buildings have been made and several large new buildings added including a striking new library.

On application to the porter in the gateway tower one can usually (except Saturday afternoons and Sundays) be shown over the *Randolph Hall* and the *Bute Hall*, in which the principal University functions are held, and the impressive War Memorial Chapel.

The University *Library* contains well over 900,000 volumes and is especially rich in theological and philosophical literature.

The **Hunterian Museum** (*open free daily, 9–5*; Saturday, 9–12) originated in a valuable collection of anatomical specimens, paintings, manuscripts, etc., bequeathed by William Hunter, MD, brother of the more celebrated John Hunter. The museum is strong in Zoology, Geology and Archaeology and contains many valuable prehistoric and Roman remains.

The medical work of the University is fostered by association with the **Western Infirmary**, the Royal Infirmary and other large hospitals in Glasgow.

West of the University, easily reached by public transport, is **Whiteinch**, famous for the *Fossil Grove* in its Victoria Park. All who visit the West of Scotland should make a point of seeing this unique series of the bases of fossilized trees *in situ*. (*Admission free*.)

A short walk northward from the University leads to the Great Western Road in the vicinity of the well-kept **Botanic Gardens** (*open free daily until dusk*). There are to be seen a large variety of trees and shrubs, both native and foreign. There is an extensive range of glasshouses, and in its Kibble Palace a unique collection of tree ferns. Beyond the Gardens stretches suburbia, so we return along Great Western Road, which presently crosses the Kelvin by a bridge just short of Woodlands Road, on the right, by which one can reach *Sauchiehall Street*. Those who do not visit the Botanic Gardens will find Sauchiehall Street at the south-east side of Kelvingrove Park. **Sauchiehall Street** is a busy and popular thoroughfare for shopping and promenading, and its air of alert prosperity is a refreshing antidote to the atmosphere of some of the poorer parts of the city. Here or near at hand are the principal shops, cinemas and theatres, and near the eastern end are Queen Street station, and George Square, from which we started the tour. In North Street, a few yards south of the important cross-roads known as Charing Cross, is the **Mitchell Library**, the largest public reference library in Scotland. The library, which originated in a bequest by Stephen Mitchell, a wealthy tobacco manufacturer (*d* 1874) was opened in 1877 and moved to its present site in 1911. The stock of the library, which is now approaching 900,000 volumes, includes special collections of music, Glasgow local histories, and Scottish poetry, particularly the poetry of Robert Burns.

The West End

The West End of Glasgow, though entirely modern, abounds in features of varied interest. From **Central Station** in Gordon Street we have a choice of two routes. We may take transport for the Botanic Gardens and Kelvinside by Bothwell Street, a western continuation of Gordon Street, reaching Sauchiehall Street near Charing Cross. The Renfield Street route is the more attractive; but some of the points of interest on the Bothwell Street route may be indicated.

Before starting, it may be well to look southward down Hope Street, where is **Record House** where the *Daily Record* and *Sunday Mail* are published.

Bothwell Street, by which we may set out on our westward tour, is rapidly rising into importance, and contains many palatial business offices and in particular numerous car showrooms. On the left is the **Conservative Club**. Farther westward, on the right, are extensive Gothic buildings connected with the **Young Men's Christian Association**. The eastern portion, known as the **Bible Training Institute**, is a resident college for men and women training for missionary work abroad, and for Evangelistic and Ministerial service. The central and original portion is the **Christian Institute**, opened by the seventh Earl of Shaftesbury in 1879. The western portion is the **Young Men's Christian Association Club**, which provides accommodation at reasonable prices for young men engaged in business in the city. One block farther on **St Vincent Street Church** comes into prominent view on the hill to the north. It is considered one of the finest churches in the city. It is in the Corinthian style, and was erected in 1858. The architect was Alexander Thomson, well known as 'Greek Thomson' from his partiality for the Grecian styles of architecture. On leaving Bothwell Street we turn into Elmbank Street and on the right we see the **Ear, Nose and Throat Hospital**, and then the **High School**, an imposing building in the Florentine style. On the left at the corner of Bath Street is the **King's Theatre**.

Visitors who wish to see the West End of Glasgow in a limited time will proceed from the Central Station up **Renfield Street,** a continuation of Union Street and Jamaica Street, one of the busiest commercial avenues of the city.

Continuing northward, Renfield Street is intersected by West George Street, West Regent Street, and Bath Street. Near the top of Renfield Street is the **Pavilion Theatre of Varieties**. At approximately 79 Renfield Street a plaque may be seen high up at the corner of the building denoting the fact that Thomas de Quincey lived at one time in a house on that site.

On the Transport Buildings at the corner of Bath Street a plaque commemorates William Harley who constructed public baths there in 1804. Also in Bath Street is **St Matthew's Church**, a fine Gothic structure with a lofty steeple. 'Ian Maclaren' and Professor James Stalker were at one time ministers at this church.

Turning westward out of Renfield Street we enter **Sauchiehall Street** (*see* p. 209), which runs in a direct line from Buchanan Street to Charing Cross and the West End Crescents. Between Rose Street and Dalhousie Street are the **McLellan Galleries**.

South of Sauchiehall Street at this point is **Blythswood Square**, in which are the **Royal Scottish Automobile Club**, the West of Scotland Agricultural College and the *Lady Artists' Club*. Also in the Square are the **Baillies' Institution Library** and Fanum House, headquarters of the **Automobile Association**, crowned by its radio transmitting mast.

Immediately north of Sauchiehall Street is **Garnethill**, crowned by the **Glasgow School of Art**, the finest example of the work of the famous architect, Charles Rennie Macintosh, and by **St Aloysius' Church and College**, belonging to the Jesuit fathers. Here also is the **Glasgow Dental Hospital**.

Proceeding westward the **Scottish College of Commerce** may be seen in Pitt Street. **Charing Cross** is reached at the junction of St George's Road with Sauchiehall Street. In North Street, which strikes off to the left, beyond the Cross, is **Charing Cross Station** and the Mitchell Library (*see* p. 209).

Behind the Mitchell Library, facing Granville Street, is the site of the former St Andrew's Halls, where the Scottish National Orchestra held its principal concerts. The Halls were destroyed by fire in October, 1962. The orchestra now plays at a new hall in Argyle Street.

Turn up Woodside Crescent, opposite North Street. On the left is Woodside Place, where, at No. 17, the great Joseph Lister lived and worked for 9 years from 1860, and on which there is a tablet denoting the fact. Continuing up the crescent, and taking the second turning on the right, we mount a flight of steps beside the **Church College** of the Church of Scotland, with **Park Church** opposite on the left. Turning left, we proceed along Woodlands Terrace and Park Terrace, its continuation, to reach the eastern entrance to Kelvingrove Park (*see* p. 208).

Those bent on seeing as many sides as possible of Glasgow's many-sided life should leave the Botanic Gardens by the western gate, and take the second turning right, noting the **Kelvinside Academy** building at the corner. Crossing Kirklee Bridge and taking Garrioch Road to the left, **Maryhill** is reached in a few minutes.

Farther westward on the right bank of the Kelvin at Killermont is situated the course of the *Glasgow Golf Club*, the oldest club in the West of Scotland and the only club in Great Britain to have both an inland and a seaside course. The car route leads to **Bearsden** and **Milngavie** (pronounced *Millguy*), and the scenery is very attractive. Near Hillfoot Station, about a mile north of Canniesburn Toll the road crosses the line of the **Roman Wall** of Antoninus Pius, which extended from the Forth to the Clyde. In the Cemetery on the high ground to the east of the road two portions of the stonework have been uncovered and may be seen.

On the borders of Milngavie are the immense **Reservoirs** in which is stored the water-supply from Loch Katrine for Glasgow. The grounds, which are open to the public, command beautiful views.

Buses run eastward to the centre of the city by Maryhill Road and New City Road. Opposite Maryhill Public Hall a road under the Canal leads to the *Western Necropolis,* in which is situated the *Glasgow Crematorium,* the property of the Scottish Burial Reform Cremation Society.

From the main gate of the Botanic Gardens, Great Western Road runs westward out of Glasgow. This is the main route by road to the Western Highlands. A short distance past the Botanic Gardens, on the left, can be seen Great Western Terrace, by Alexander (Greek) Thomson, and, half a mile further, the large gates of the **Royal Mental Hospital** at Gartnavel beside the Anniesland Boating Pond. A little further on is **Anniesland Cross**, with several important athletics grounds in its vicinity, including the University ground. The road to Bearsden and Milngavie leads off to the right, over the Forth and Clyde Canal, and past **Dawsholm Park**, with its bird sanctuary. The road ahead leads out of the city to Clydebank and Dumbarton, Loch Lomond and Helensburgh, and those on the left to Partick and Scotstoun.

For the return to the city centre, a bus may be taken to either Buchanan Street or Renfield Street. The route lies eastward through the shopping centre of **Hillhead**, and across the *Kelvin*. On looking downstream, on the right, the University tower and the Lord Roberts Memorial in Kelvingrove Park can be seen. On the left is **Glasgow Academy**, and, across the bridge, **Lansdowne Church**. North Woodside Road strikes off to the left at this point, and a short distance along it is the building, marked with a plaque, where Sir William Smith founded The Boys' Brigade in 1883. The building is still occupied by the 1st Glasgow Company. The bus route is now by Park Road and Woodlands Road to Charing Cross and Sauchiehall Street to the city centre.

The South Side

Perhaps the easiest way to gain a general idea of Southern Glasgow is to take public transport at the foot of Union Street. **Jamaica Street**, lined on both sides with spacious warehouses and attractive shops, leads to the **Broomielaw** or **Glasgow Bridge**, one of the busiest spots in a busy city. The history of the Broomielaw Bridge affords a striking commentary on the growth of Glasgow in modern times. The first bridge was begun in 1767, and opened in 1772. By 1833 the bridge had become inadequate, and a new bridge, from designs by Thomas Telford, was begun. This bridge, opened in 1836, was then the widest and most spacious in the United Kingdom. Within sixty years it was in turn condemned as insufficient. The present bridge now affords accommodation for about double the quantity of vehicular traffic which could previously pass over it. A small part of Telford's bridge has been built into the new structure.

Westward of the bridge is the Railway Bridge, and to the west of that again is the **King George V Bridge**.

On the south side of the river is **Carlton Place**, once a favourite residential locality, but now largely devoted to business uses. The church with the lofty spire is **Gorbals Church**. In **Bridge Street** and its continuation, **Eglinton Street**, there are a few features of interest. On the west side, a pillared frontage is all that remains of the Bridge Street Station, which used to be the starting-place for the coast passenger traffic prior to the erection of the railway bridges over the Clyde. In Norfolk Street is the prominent red stone building of the **Gorbals Library** with an extensive foreign language collection. In Eglinton Street is the point known as **Eglinton Toll**, though all trace of the turnpike has long disappeared. Near the Toll is the Plaza, a popular dance hall. In Albert Drive, close to the Toll, is Glasgow's **Museum of Transport** almost unique in the variety of railway engines, trams, motor-cars and horse-drawn vehicles, etc., which may be seen (*open, free, daily 10–5, Sundays 2–5*).

Here we have a variety of routes to choose from.

The public transport route passes westward through the residential suburb of **Pollokshields** to **Maxwell Park**. Sir John Stirling Maxwell, Bt, presented the Park to the burgh of Pollokshields, and the Corporation of Glasgow annexed both burgh and park in 1891. The fountain executed in Carrara stoneware and erected to the memory of Thomas and John Hamilton is a special feature. Sir John Stirling Maxwell also presented to the city the beautiful **Pollok Grounds**, extending to 121 acres of woodlands, on the west side of which is the family mansion of Pollok House. The main entrance to Pollok grounds is in Haggs Road, reached from the car stopping-place at Maxwell Park and thence on foot past the ancient **Haggs Castle**, with golf course nearby.

Continuing through Dumbreck we pass along Mosspark Boulevard with the suburb of **Mosspark** on the left. On the right is **Bellahouston Park**, scene of the Empire Exhibition in 1938. The terminus is at the junction with Paisley Road. Return can be made by the same route or by Paisley Road to the city centre.

From Eglinton Toll, **Pollokshaws Road** strikes off to the right and we may drive along this thoroughfare through **Strathbungo** and **Crossmyloof** to **Shawlands Cross**. Here the bus routes fork. That to the right proceeds through the burgh of **Pollokshaws**, incorporated in the city in 1912, to **Thornliebank**, **Speirs Bridge** and **Rouken Glen Park**. The park is one of the most picturesque of Glasgow's rural possessions. It was gifted to the city in 1906 by the late Lord Rowallan, and with subsequent extensions covers 228 acres. Its features include a striking waterfall, a boating pond, an old mansion-house, woodland walks of great beauty, and a golf course. Near the Thornliebank Gate is an old ivy-grown façade which is all that remains of the mansion of **Birkenshaw**, once the residence of Lord Kelvin.

The bus route to the extreme left at Eglinton Toll proceeds along **Victoria Road**. On the left we pass the Royal Samaritan Hospital for Women and, on the right, the Girls' School under the Hutcheson Trust.

Queen's Park, with the inclusion of Camphill Nursery Gardens, is 148 acres in extent. Ample facilities for recreation include a pond for model yachts. Near the pond is *Camphill Museum*, which has a room devoted to relics and pictures of the Battle of Langside which was fought nearby. There is an old camp of ancient British origin on top of the hill. There are fine floral displays throughout the year in the park, and a range of glass-houses where plants of every description may be seen.

Close to the southern border of the Park is the battlefield of **Langside**, where Queen Mary's forces were defeated on May 15, 1568. The memorial of the battle, designed by Alexander Skirving, takes the form of a column fifty-eight feet high. Scott falls into a curious error in *The Abbot* by making Mary Queen of Scots view the Battle from Crookston Castle, whereas she actually viewed it from Court Knowe near Cathcart Castle, in Linn Park.

South of the popular residential district of Mount Florida is—

CATHCART–CATHKIN BRAES

Cathcart,

with many historic associations. In the old churchyard is the **Martyrs' Monument**, which states that three Covenanters were killed 'with shots of guns' in 'lon of Polmadie'. To the south of the Kirk is the picturesque ruin of Cathcart Castle, near which is a wood in which is a stone marking the traditional site from which Mary Queen of Scots viewed the Battle of Langside. A little distance from the Castle is the **Auld Brig of Cathcart**, spanning a romantic dell of the River Cart. There was once a Snuff Mill here.

A bus route passes through Cathcart and along Clarkston Road to Muirend Road, near the main entrance to **Linn Park**, which includes the grounds of Cathcart Castle and Court Knowe. The Park comprises 180 acres, including a beautiful pine wood, a waterfall and river, and sylvan scenery. Adjoining the park is an 18-hole golf course.

Return to the city centre may be made by bus from the Linn Park gate. It goes via Cathcart Road and Gorbals Street. From Cathcart Road can be seen on the right, **Hampden Park**, the largest football stadium in Europe, with ground capacity for 150,000. **Queen's Park Recreation Ground** is passed on the left. As we pass through the much-maligned Gorbals district, which is being steadily rebuilt by Glasgow Corporation, we pass on the right the **Citizens' Theatre**.

By a change of bus at the junction of Cathcart Road and Carmunnock Road a visit may be made to the village of Carmunnock, passing on the way, **King's Park**, with a museum with a fine collection of period costumes, and the new housing scheme at Castlemilk.

Carmunnock retains something of its old-world appearance: whitewashed buildings and narrow streets. The church is singular on account of the stairs leading to the gallery being outside the building.

From the Carmunnock road, an older route, said to be a Roman road, strikes off to East Kilbride, passing by **Mains Castle**, the simplest type of square keep and typical of many others throughout Clydesdale. It was originally in the possession of the family of Comyn, but forfeited by them after Bruce slew the Red Comyn at Dumfries.

Cathkin Braes Park. The park was presented to the city in 1886 by Mr James Dick, of gutta-percha fame. It lies one and a half miles south of Rutherglen, and since the recent extensions is now within the city boundary. It may be reached from the west end of Rutherglen by walking up Mill Street, past Overtoun Park and the cemetery; or alternatively from the east end of the burgh by bus from the city, past Stonelaw Woods to Burnside terminus and thence uphill. The park covers 49 acres and in accordance with the wish of the donor, 'remains as nearly as possible an expanse of primitive hillside, with its crags and knolls, its natural grass, and its haphazard clumps of trees, brushwood, bushes, untouched by the formal hand of the landscape gardener'. No provision has been made for games. It forms part of the picturesque ridge of **Cathkin Hills**, separating the Clyde valley from the valley of the Cart and is, at its highest point, about 600 feet above sea-level. In the upper part of the park is a large boulder known as **Queen Mary's Seat**. On a clear day this point commands an extensive view of the Clyde valley and one can see from the Ochil Hills to the mountains of the north and west, the most distant peak seen being Beinn Lui at Tyndrum, 40 miles away.

Glasgow to Edinburgh

Only 25 miles separate western Scotland at the Broomielaw from the waters of the Firth of Forth at Grangemouth, and roads, railways, the Forth and Clyde Canal and the rivers Kelvin and Bonny all crowd through the mile-wide 'pass' below the Kilsyth Hills. The pass ends at Dennyloanhead, and here is a parting of the ways. Northward the main routes to the Highlands travel up between the hills and the Forth – another 'pass', at the north end of which Stirling occupies a fine strategic position; eastward roads and railways follow the Forth to Edinburgh, passing through Falkirk and Linlithgow and giving good views of the Forth Bridges.

The Forth and Clyde Canal (closed) ran from Bowling, on the Clyde, to Grangemouth, a distance of 38 miles. The summit point is 156 feet above sea-level, necessitating 39 locks. The Canal closely follows the line of the **Antonine Wall**, a Roman rampart erected about A.D. 142 to restrict the raids of the northern tribes. Some 40 miles long, it consisted of a ditch 20 feet deep and 40 wide and a sod-and-stone rampart 10 feet high, and along the southern side ran a paved road, with forts at intervals. Extensive remains are to be seen near Castlecary, and in recent years the remains of a fort have been laid bare at Cadder, near Bishopbriggs. The local name for the earthworks is 'Grim's Dyke.'

Road routes between Glasgow and Edinburgh:

1. Leave Glasgow by Argyle Street, Trongate, Gallowgate and Tollcross Road. Bellshill is 9 miles from Glasgow, **Whitburn** 23 miles, and **Edinburgh** 44 miles.

2. Leave Glasgow by Queen Street, George Street, Duke Street and Shettleston Road. Thence *via* **Coatbridge** (9 miles), Airdrie (12 miles), **Bathgate** (25 miles), Broxburn (33 miles) and **Corstorphine** to **Edinburgh** (44 miles).

3. The A8 road via Newhouse and Harthill and the M8 motorway are fast and avoid the towns, but are scenically uninteresting.

The Upper Clyde

The **Clyde**, the third in point of size and the most important of the rivers of Scotland, has its source in the Southern Upland district, among the Lowther Hills, at no great distance from the head springs of the Tweed and the Annan. The Clyde proper is ninety-eight miles long, and the greater part is in the county of Lanark. Its course is at first in a north-westerly direction, and it receives the waters of many boisterous, rollicking little streams, dear to the angler and to the lover of the picturesque. When first seen by travellers from the south at Elvanfoot it is a tiny rivulet. It is frequently crossed and re-crossed both by road and by the railway, and each time has obviously increased in volume. About Lamington it is quite a considerable stream. It afterwards leaves the foot of Tinto, the 'Hill of Fire', and near Lanark forces its way through the rocks in a series of what were until recently magnificent falls. Unfortunately the waters have been harnessed for hydro-electric purposes and the falls are only worth seeing when the river is in high spate and aqueducts are unable to take the full rush of waters. Below Lanark the river flows quietly through the beautiful vales of Lanarkshire; and at Dumbarton expands into the famous Firth, which, turning in a southerly direction at Greenock, becomes absorbed in the ocean after passing Ailsa Craig, where it attains a width of twenty miles and more. In the latter portion numerous inlets, resembling Norwegian fjords, branch off to the north and the west, and – winding among the mountains and islands of Argyllshire – present a continuous panorama of surpassing beauty. Among them nestle a number of pleasant resorts visited year by year by thousands in search of health and pleasure.

BOTHWELL AND HAMILTON

Situation – Bothwell and Hamilton lie respectively about 10 and 12 miles south-east from central Glasgow. There are frequent bus services.

Bothwell Castle (*open daily, fee*). The ruined Castle stands on a height called Bothwell Bank, round the base of which wind the waters of the Clyde. The banks of the river on both sides and the surrounding grounds are clad with woods. The stronghold dates from the thirteenth century, but was partially demolished after the Battle of Bannockburn.

Restoration was undertaken in 1336, but further destruction followed. Archibald 'the Grim', third Earl of Douglas, was responsible for the final repairs and additions

Bothwell Castle

at the end of the fourteenth century. The walls are fifteen feet thick in many parts, and sixty feet high at the rampart facing the river. The Department of the Environment have restored to the ruin a good deal of its medieval beauty.

Bothwell is a favourite residential resort. The landscape around the village is luxuriant and beautiful, and is studded with villas.

Architecturally **St Bride's Parish Church**, with its lofty tower, is the outstanding feature of the village. Though the nave, transept and tower date only from 1833, the choir is pre-Reformation and was built in the fourteenth century. At that time a twelfth-century church (built by the Murray family referred to above) stood on the site of the present nave, and in 1398, when it was made a collegiate church, Archibald 'The Grim', third Earl of Douglas, added to it the present choir and had it dedicated to St Bride, the patron saint of the Douglas family. In the choir, in 1399, the ill-fated Duke of Rothesay, who figures so prominently in Scott's *The Fair Maid of Perth,* was married to the daughter of Archibald 'The Grim'. It will be remembered that the Duke of Rothesay–elder brother of James I of Scotland–was later starved to death in a dungeon in Falkland Palace by order of his uncle, the Duke of Albany. Dr James Baillie, afterwards professor of theology in Glasgow University, was at one time minister of the parish of Bothwell, and his famous daughter Joanna, the friend and correspondent of Sir Walter Scott, and herself an authoress of distinction, was born in the manse here. In 1933 (one hundred years after the tower was built by David Hamilton, architect of the former Royal Exchange, Glasgow) a fine scheme of reconstruction was carried out at a cost of £10,000. During the reconstruction many carved fragments of the twelfth-century church were discovered and placed in the narthex and in niches in the walls of the nave.

The stained-glass windows are particularly fine, especially one at the east end of the choir designed by Sir Edward Burne-Jones in 1898, representing the Nativity.

On the opposite side of the Clyde from Bothwell Castle are the ruins of **Blantyre Priory**, founded by Alexander II towards the end of the thirteenth century. At the village of –

Blantyre

formerly the centre of a mining district, David Livingstone, the great African explorer, was born in 1813. The mill where he worked as a lad can still be seen and his birthplace has been restored as the **Scottish National Memorial to David Livingstone** and fitted up as a museum.

Livingstone Memorial, Blantyre

The aim of the Memorial (*fee*) is to stabilize the Livingstone tradition. The old building has been transformed into a kind of biography, profusely illustrated by pictures, relics, models and maps. Each of the original rooms serves a special purpose, beginning with the Ancestry Room. The Birth Room has been restored to its old simplicity. There is a wonderfully complete collection of personal relics, manuscripts, etc. The central interest lies in the Livingstone Gallery, where under modern lighting conditions are shown eight groups of coloured statuary in bas-relief, symbolic of the great story. These are by Mr C d'O Pilkington Jackson, whose work in the National War Memorial at Edinburgh is well known. There are rose gardens and extensive playing fields. Refreshment facilities.

Less than a mile south of the village of Bothwell, on the main road to Hamilton, is the famous **Bothwell Brig**, where the Covenanters were defeated on June 21, 1679, after a fierce struggle, by the royal forces under the Duke of Monmouth and Graham of Claverhouse. There is a graphic account of the conflict in Scott's *Old Mortality*. The bridge was rebuilt in 1826, but portions of the old structure were retained. The level lands stretching along the north-east bank of the Clyde formed the estate of Bothwell-haugh, which belonged to James Hamilton, who killed the Regent Murray at Linlithgow in 1569.

Hamilton

Golf–9-hole Municipal Course, Bothwell Road. *Hamilton Golf Club* (18 holes), Riccarton, Ferniegair.
Race Course–Meetings from May to September.

Hamilton, the chief town of the middle ward of Lanarkshire, is situated near to the confluence of the River Clyde and the River Avon and is on the main trunk road A74, eleven miles south of Glasgow. The town possesses a number of fine churches, including the Old Parish Church built in 1732. Among other public buildings are the Municipal Buildings, Town Hall and Public Library, the County Court Buildings of Grecian design, and County Administration Offices, including the modern 17-storey County Building opened in 1964. Hamilton Grammar School dates from 1588, but was removed to more commodious premises in 1848 to become Hamilton Academy. Now it has amalgamated with St Johns Grammar School and re-adopted its original name.

Centrally situated between the east and west coasts, Hamilton is suitably located for visitors wishing to be within convenient reach of differing holiday centres. Edinburgh, the east coast resorts and Ayr, and the west coast resorts, are just over one hour's car journey. Within twenty minutes the visitor may reach the lovely fruit-growing district of Clydeside, where each turn of the road discloses some of the finest pastoral scenery in the country.

The town has two golf courses and the municipal parks provide tennis courts, bowling greens and putting greens. Hamilton possesses an admirable shopping centre, with two modern cinemas and a large ballroom (Trocadero, Townhead Street). Garages, representing agencies in all makes of cars, are numerous.

HAMILTON

The site of old Hamilton, the Netherton, is within the grounds where stood the famous Hamilton Palace. Also within the grounds is the Mote Hill, or ancient place of justice. Hamilton Palace was demolished in 1927 but many of its treasures are to be found in our national museums.

Magnificent in its architecture is the **Mausoleum** built in 1854 by Alexander, tenth Duke of Hamilton in imitation of the Mausoleum of Hadrian at Rome. This Duke was buried here in a sarcophagus of black marble once the tomb of an Egyptian king at Memphis. Notable features of the Mausoleum are its prolonged echo and its whispering galleries, features which made it unsuitable for one of the purposes for which it was built, namely, a family chapel. **Chatelherault**, the old hunting lodge of the Hamiltons, still stands in the High Parks. The château was built from the plans of the Elder Adam, about 1732, in imitation of Chatelherault in Poiton.

Nearby stand the ruins of **Cadzow Castle**, which in its halcyon days gave lodging to Scottish kings and queens. Mary Queen of Scots resided in Cadzow Castle during her stay in Hamilton but the Castle was dismantled by the order of Regent Murray after the battle of Langside. The situation of the ruins, surrounded by woods, darkened by ivy and creeping shrubs and overhanging the brawling torrent of the Avon far below, is very romantic.

In the forest by which the ruins are surrounded are some magnificent oaks, and Cadzow is noted for its herd of *White Cattle,* commonly regarded as survivors of the native wild cattle of Scotland.

County Buildings, Hamilton

The village of **Quarter**, about two miles south-east of Hamilton, contains within its boundaries the field where Gordon of Earlston was killed after the battle of Bothwell Brig.

From Hamilton a trip may be taken by road (bus service) to the pretty little town of **Strathaven**, nearly eight miles farther south. The town stands on rising ground almost surrounded by the *Pomilon*, a small tributary of the Avon. It is a place of considerable antiquity, and contains the ruins of the ancient **Castle of Avondale**, where Anne, Duchess of Hamilton, resided during the Protectorate of Oliver Cromwell. Strathaven has a 9-hole golf course and is known for Lauder Ha', which was the home of the world-famous Sir Harry Lauder.

Seven miles west of Strathaven is **Drumclog**, where a party of Covenanters defeated a detachment of dragoons under Claverhouse on Sunday, June 1, 1679. The dragoons would have been entirely cut to pieces but for the resolution of the Covenanters not to fight on the Sabbath, except in self-defence. Scott gave a vivid description of the encounter in *Old Mortality*. A monument on the spot commemorates the conflict.

Fully four miles north-east of Strathaven by road, is **Stonehouse**, on the south bank of the Avon, a favourite resort of anglers, on account of the excellent trout fishing to be had in the neighbourhood. The ruins of **Cat Castle** and **Ringsdale Castle**, on precipitous rocks overhanging the river, are among the attractions of the place, but nothing is known of their origin and history. The Roman military road from Edinburgh to Ayr, known locally as the **Deil's Causey**, runs through the parish.

LANARK AND DOUGLASDALE

Lying to the south-east of Glasgow is the ancient Royal Burgh of–

Rutherglen,

said to have been founded by King Reuther, who flourished two hundred years before the Christian era. The town was made a royal burgh by David I in 1126, fifty years before Glasgow was incorporated as a Burgh of Barony; and it was an important centre of trade and commerce when Glasgow was an insignificant village clustering round the Cathedral. It was in its parish church, according to Blind Harry, that Sir John Menteith entered into an agreement to betray Wallace. Its Castle, which occupied a site near the corner of King Street and Castle Street, belonged to the Hamilton family. It was burned down by the Regent Murray after the battle of Langside. In her flight from Langside Queen Mary, accompanied by Lord Herries, passed through the town, and at Din's Dykes, near Main Street, two un-gallant rustics with scythes attempted to interrupt the Queen's progress. Rutherglen was the first place at which definite steps were taken to bring about the Covenanters' rising, which led to the battles of Drumclog and Bothwell Brig, a body of eighty men having, on May 29, 1679, burned at the Cross the Acts of Parliament against conventicles.

The visitor cannot fail to notice the width of the tree-lined Main Street, which is a busy shopping centre. For many years important horse and cattle fairs were held there, but these have been discontinued since 1900. In the centre of the Main Street, due west of the Town Hall, is the ancient burial ground of the old churchyard. The church port, which dates from the seventeenth century, is notable for the two curious stone shelters by which it is flanked and which were erected to provide cover, when needed, for those appointed to receive the offerings of the worshippers. Tradition has it that St Conval, a disciple of St Kentigern, the patron saint of Glasgow, founded a church on the site of the churchyard and records show that the Church of St Mary the Virgin existed on the site early in the twelfth century. The bell of the steeple was cast in 1635 and is a good specimen of the work of Michael Burgerhys, a Dutch bellfounder.

Rutherglen is well endowed with public and private open spaces and with playing fields containing bowling greens, tennis courts, etc. and it has the advantage of being adjacent to Cathkin Braes, which lie to the south.

The town is also an important industrial centre and has large establishments concerned with the manufacture of chemicals, paper, tubes, rope and twine, steel, biscuits and oatcakes, and chenille curtains. At one time there was also a flourishing shipbuilding industry, but that has now ceased.

Near Rutherglen is **Castlemilk House**, where Queen Mary is believed to have slept the night before the battle of Langside. It is now a Children's Home and is surrounded by a new housing estate.

Cambuslang, about a mile and a half beyond Rutherglen, is a favourite place of residence for Glasgow business men, and there is a considerable resident mining population. It was, about the middle of the eighteenth century, the scene of a famous religious revival, still spoken of as 'the Cambuslang Wark'. The multitude that took part in the meetings in tents on the hillsides is estimated by contemporary writers to have amounted to thirty thousand. The place of the meetings is now included in the beautiful Borgie Park.

Away to the right of the road **Dechmont Hill** attracts attention, and on its north side stands the castellated mansion of **Gilbertfield**, interesting as having been the residence of Lieutenant William Hamilton, the translator of Blind Harry's *Wallace*, and the friend of Allan Ramsay, the poet.

After passing Cambuslang, iron and steel works are for a time the most prominent features in the landscape, but there are some scenes of beauty and interest. On the right, from the Clyde at Uddingston, a glimpse is obtained of the ruins of Bothwell Castle. About a mile north-eastward on the main Glasgow road in the village of Broomhouse are the Calderpark Zoological Gardens set among superb woodland. Beyond Uddingston the towns of Hamilton and Bothwell (*see* pp. 216–20) are seen on the right. The scenery rapidly improves, and the deeply-wooded glen of the *South Calder* is crossed. On its banks are a number of picturesquely situated mansions, one of which, **Hallside**, was the residence of Professor Wilson, the 'Christopher North' of *Blackwood's*. Half a mile down the glen to the right is the old **Roman Bridge** which carried Watling Street across the stream. Three miles up the glen on the left, in a rock under Cleland House, is a cave where, according to tradition, Wallace hid with fifty men.

The Burgh of **Motherwell and Wishaw** consists of the two formerly separated Burghs which amalgamated in 1920. With a population of 76,000, the Burgh is the second largest in Scotland with much modern development. It has a new Civic Administrative Centre in a complex combining Concert Hall, Theatre, along with Municipal and business premises. Much of the old housing has been swept away and the Burgh is in the forefront of modern housing and shopping precincts. One of the main centres of the steel and engineering industry, and at the same time a rail centre, it also has confectionery, hosiery and shirting and silk manufacturers. Perhaps a unique feature of this industrial town is the weekly market held in Wishaw where cattle, sheep and poultry are sold. Motherwell has a famous swimming pool where many outstanding swimmers have been trained. Wishaw too now has a recently erected swimming pool which is now vying with its illustrious neighbour in producing good swimmers and divers of international standards. Fir Park is the home of the well known Motherwell Football Club. Motherwell Cricket Club's ground is situated in the policies of Dalzell Estate, formerly the property of Baron Hamilton of Dalzell, now a public park, which will eventually be linked to the extensive Strathclyde Park being developed in conjunction with other Lanarkshire Local Authorities. There are two golf courses, Colville Park Course, Motherwell and Wishaw Golf Club, Wishaw, and there are numerous tennis courts and bowling greens. There are excellent library facilities which extend to record and picture lending.

Near Motherwell is the mining village of **Carfin**, noted for the Grotto dedicated to Our Lady of Lourdes. It was dedicated in 1922, and is now beautifully laid out as a garden and visited by many thousands annually. It is conjectured that the 'Forest Kirk' in which Wallace was appointed Governor of Scotland may have been at **Carluke**. From **Braidwood** Lanark is visible to the right.

Lanark

Distances–Carlisle 75 m; Dumfries 55 m; Edinburgh 33 m; Glasgow 25 m; Linlithgow 26 m; London 375 m; Peebles 28 m.
Early Closing Day–Thursday.
Golf–18-hole and 9-hole courses on the Moor.

Hotels–*Cartland Bridge* (15 rooms), *Caledonian* (6 rooms), *Clydeside* (10 rooms), *Royal Oak* (13 rooms).
Population–8,700.
Racing–Race meetings in July and September.

Lanark is believed to have been a Roman station, and had a prominent place in early Scottish history. On Castle Hill, an artificial mound at the foot of the Castle Gate, a Royal castle, which was an occasional residence of William the Lion and other Scottish kings, long stood. The town was the scene of the early exploits of Wallace. His house was at the head of the Castle Gate, and the Parish Church, which stands on the opposite side of the street, has in a niche over its doorway a colossal statue of the Scottish hero, by Robert Forrest. The town has also Covenanting memories, and it is beautifully situated about half a mile from the Clyde, on an upland plain.

Proceeding along the south road there are seen in the churchyard the ruins of **St Kentigern's**, the ancient parish church, built in the twelfth century. It is supposed that Wallace and Marion Bradfute were married within its walls. One of the church bells, now hanging in the Town Steeple, is reputed to be the oldest in Europe.

The bearings of the bell were renewed in 1925. *Braxfield*, which is a little farther on the right, was the seat of Lord Braxfield, the famous Scottish judge, depicted by Stevenson as 'Weir of Hermiston'.

New Lanark, about a mile from the old town, is reached by a branch road. It also is charmingly situated. Here, in 1784, with a view to taking advantage of the water power, Richard Arkwright, the inventor, and David Dale, of Glasgow, erected cotton spinning mills, which were afterwards the scene of the social and industrial experiments of Robert Owen, Dale's son-in-law.

Formerly Lanark was the starting point for a charming walk to the Corra Linn, Bonnington Linn, and other beautiful waterfalls, but as already mentioned, this feature of the scenery has been to some extent spoiled by hydro-electric works.

From Lanark we go westward along the road which Wallace presumably took in his flight after the scuffle with the overbearing English soldiers. A mile long, the *Mouse Water* is crossed. Up the stream to the right is a deep, densely-wooded ravine, overhung by the **Cartland Crags**, through which the Mouse forces its way to the Clyde. One of the gloomy recesses of these lofty cliffs, which is almost under the bridge, is known as **Wallace's Cave**. A ruined keep perched on the edge of the crags is known as the **Castle of Qua**.

The Mouse is again crossed, and a glimpse is had of an old, narrow bridge, supposed to date from the Roman period. The Clyde is next crossed at the lovely rural village of **Kirkfieldbank**, beyond which are fine woods and orchard lands. Both banks of the Clyde are for miles covered with fruit trees and bushes. In early summer this part of the country is seen at its best, the orchards being then one mass of blossom. Passing through the village of **Crossford**, we come to **Nethanfoot**; and taking a path along the side of the river Nethan, through a deep and beautifully-wooded ravine, the visitor soon reaches the extensive ruins of **Craignethan Castle**, in olden times the seat of the Evandale branch of the house of Hamilton. It is much better known as the *Tillietudlem* of Scott's *Old Mortality*. There is a tradition that here Queen Mary spent part of the eleven days that elapsed between her escape from Loch Leven and the battle of Langside, and a great vaulted chamber is pointed out as Queen Mary's room.

Among other places of interest in the neighbourhood of Lanark is **Lee Castle**, once seat of the Lockharts of Lee. The castle stands about halfway between Lanark and Carluke. Inside the celebrated *Pease Tree*, near the house, which was even then hollow with age, Cromwell is said to have dined with a party of friends. This gigantic oak tree is supposed to have belonged to the ancient Caledonian forest. The *Lee Penny*, reputed to act as a charm for many of the ills that flesh is heir to, and which figures so prominently in Scott's *The Talisman*, is kept at Lee Castle in a gold box, which was presented by the Empress Maria Theresa to Count Lockhart, her chamberlain.

On the south side of Mouse Water, about a mile and a half north of Lanark, is **Jerviswood**, the seat of John Baillie, who lost his estate and his life in the troubles of the reign of Charles II. His successor, George Baillie, to whom the estate was restored after the Revolution, married Lady Grizel, daughter of the Earl of Marchmont (a title now extinct) and writer of the famous song, 'Werena my heart licht I wad dee'.

From Lanark a good road follows the line of the Douglas Water through to Muirkirk, providing a direct and expeditious route between Lanark and Ayr. It has the additional advantage of opening up to tourists the beauties of –

Douglasdale,

notable as the cradle of the great Douglas race who played so prominent a part in the history of Scotland. Extending north for about twelve miles from the foot of **Cairntable**, with the **Douglas Water** as its central feature, it presents a variety of rugged hills, bleak moorland, well-cultivated farms and some pleasing woodland. Douglas can be reached from Glasgow by bus by way of either Lesmahagow or Lanark.

The locality is the setting of Sir Walter Scott's last novel, *Castle Dangerous*, a story of stirring deeds centred round the old castle and the ancient church of St Bride in the village. Part of this church was restored by the Earl of Home, as head of the House of Douglas, in 1879, and with its sculptured tombs and other memorials it well repays a visit. Near to St Bride's is the *Sun Inn*, the oldest existing house in the village and once a prison.

Tinto, 'the hill of fire', celebrated all over Lanarkshire for its conspicuous height (2,335 feet), is only 7 miles north-east of Douglas.

Glasgow to Ardrossan by the coast

Railways–Except for the short break between Wemyss Bay and Largs the railway hugs the coast all the way.

Hamilton, Lanark and other places on the Upper Clyde are described on pages 216–25. Here we go 'doon the watter' from Glasgow to where the river merges into the Firth, the Firth into the sea.

Western Scotland, more than any other part of Britain, depends for its intercommunication upon the boat, and the Clyde is starting off point for many of the passenger steamer trips to the coast and off-shore islands. From Glasgow it is necessary to travel by rail or bus to Gourock, Wemyss Bay, or Craigendoran on the north, to join the boats.

The Clyde below Glasgow is under the control of the *Clyde Port Authority*, who have jurisdiction over Clydeport, comprising the ports of Glasgow, Greenock and Ardrossan, and an area of some 450 square miles extending 55 miles down river from the heart of Glasgow to a line drawn from Gailes on the Ayrshire coast to Corrygills Point in Arran. Almost two-thirds of Scotland's foreign seaborne trade passes through Clydeport. The many docks and wharves of Glasgow are busy with the import of crude oil, iron ore, grain and other raw materials, and the export of iron and steel, machinery, vehicles, whisky and many manufactured goods.

Govan, on the south, has an old burying-ground containing early Christian monuments said by some to be coeval with the better-known monuments at Iona. At Yoker, on the north, is the site of an electricity station of great importance to the Scottish 'grid' system.

Renfrew, on the south bank, is very active, while a notable feature of the town is the fine old Steeple, a mile inland. Renfrew is interesting from its connection with the Royal House of Stewart. In 1157 Malcolm IV, confirming an earlier grant by David I, gave Renfrew Castle and adjoining lands to Walter Fitzalan, whom he appointed King's High Steward. This office remained hereditary in the family, who now assumed the name of Stewart. A descendant of Fitzalan, also named Walter, married the Bruce's daughter Marjory, whose son, the first of the Stewart line, ascended the Scottish Royal Throne in 1370. From the fifteenth century Renfrew has given the title of Baron to the Heir-Apparent to the Scottish Throne. Nothing now remains of Renfrew Castle.

Paisley Abbey

Paisley,

a few miles south of Renfrew, is known the world over as a busy centre of
the thread manufacture, being especially associated with the Coats and
Clarks concerns. It is a by no means uninteresting blend of old and new:
on the one hand such modern work as the Coats Memorial Church, and
new housing estates with their 15-storey blocks of flats, on the other the
remains of the twelfth-century Abbey, parts of which have been restored to
form the Parish Church.

Paisley Abbey (*open daily, fee*) was founded in 1163 by that Walter Fitzalan
who became first Lord High Steward, but the original building was destroyed by
Edward I, and the present Abbey dates from the fifteenth century, though much
of it is in an earlier style of architecture. The chief external feature is the fine west
front, with deeply-recessed doorway and graceful windows. Within the building
attention is caught by the triforium of rounded arches and the clerestory passage,
carried outside alternate pillars on corbels. Off the south transept is the St Mirin
Chapel, founded in 1498.

In the choir is an effigy of Marjory Bruce, whose son was the first monarch of
the Stewart line; and in 1888 a memorial was placed in the choir 'to the members of
the Royal House of Stewart who are buried in Paisley Abbey, by their descendant,
Queen Victoria'.

In High Street is a *Museum and Art Gallery* (*open from 10 to dusk ; free*) with collections of shawls, pictures, and relics of local literary figures. Accessible from the museum is the *Coats Observatory*, housing two medium-diameter telescopes. Also in High Street is the public library.

Elderslie, about 2 miles west of Paisley is the reputed birthplace of William Wallace; but the so-called 'Wallace's House' is more modern than that.

The **Braes of Gleniffer**, a mile or so south-west of the town, above the Johnstone Road, command magnificent views across the Clyde to the hills beyond.

Crookston Castle (*open daily, fee*) 2½ miles south-east of Paisley, on the bank of the White Cart River, is where according to tradition, Mary Queen of Scots and Darnley were betrothed; it is certain they stayed here after their marriage. It comprises substantial remains of an early fifteenth-century tower of unusual type within the ditch and bank of a medieval earthwork. The ruins command an extensive view of the surrounding countryside.

On the north side of the river from Renfrew is **Clydebank**, famous for the great ships built here including the liners *Queen Mary* and *Queen Elizabeth* and the more recent *Queen Elizabeth II*.

Erskine Bridge, opened in 1971, is useful for motorists travelling north or south and desiring to cross the Clyde without going through the traffic-laden streets of Glasgow. The bridge supersedes a ferry named after Erskine House, formerly the residence of the Lords Blantyre, but now a hospital for limbless sailors and soldiers. The obelisk on the hill beyond commemorates the eleventh Lord Blantyre, who passed unscathed through the Peninsular War, but was shot accidentally in Brussels in 1830.

On Dunglass Point, about half a mile farther down on the same side, is **Dunglass Castle**, an ancient seat of the Colquhouns of Colquhoun and Luss. The Roman wall of Antoninus, erected in A.D. 140, and extending from the Forth to the Clyde, terminated here. A conspicuous obelisk commemorates Henry Bell, who was the first in Europe to apply steam-power to marine purposes. His little steamer, the *Comet*, built at Port Glasgow, was launched in 1812. As was duly set forth in the newspaper advertisements of the time, it traded between Glasgow, Greenock and Helensburgh by the power of wind, air and steam.

At **Bridge of Weir** are the ruins of **Ranfurly Castle**, once the seat of the Knox family. The Orphan Homes, founded by William Quarrier in Glasgow, were opened here in 1877.

Kilmacolm is a favourite place of residence of Glasgow and Greenock business people. It has a very fine moorland golf course.

On the north bank of the Clyde is **Bowling** where are the western terminal locks of the Forth and Clyde Canal, and farther to the west–

Dumbarton a busy industrial town, though with a place in history. The huge rugged rock offshore is supposed to have been fortified in prehistoric times and has been identified with the *Theodosia* of the Romans. Its name is a corruption of Dun-Breton: 'the hill of the Bretons', and for county .

purposes the name is still spelt Du*n*barton. Dumbarton is held to have been the birthplace of St Patrick (the claim is disputed by Old Kilpatrick).

According to tradition, Wallace was confined in the Castle for some time; certainly it was from Dumbarton Castle that Mary Queen of Scots when a child was conveyed to France for safety, and it was while on her way to Dumbarton Castle that she met her final defeat at Langside. (*Castle open, charge, weekdays 10–7; Sundays 2–7; winter, 10–4 and 2–4.*)

Almost opposite Dumbarton on the south side of the Clyde is *Finlayston House*, wherein Knox first dispensed the sacrament according to the rites of the Reformed Church, in 1556. A little farther west are the round towers and battlements of *Newark Castle (open weekdays)*, an old stronghold of the Maxwells.

Port Glasgow originated in the determination of seventeenth-century Glasgow merchants to overcome the disadvantages of the shallow river. Boats could not then come up to the city, so a new port was founded where there was deep water, and although its original purpose has long lapsed, Port Glasgow is still of considerable consequence on Clydeside. Henry Bell's famous steamer, the *Comet*, was built by John Wood at Port Glasgow in 1812, and there is a memorial tablet, unveiled during the Comet centenary celebrations in 1912. A local ropeworks has the distinction of having made ropes for both the *Comet* and the first *Queen Elizabeth*. The most important industry in the town nowadays, as will be seen, is shipbuilding, and the river bank is lined with yards.

The view across the Firth at this point is most impressive. Beyond **Ardmore Point** can be seen **Craigendoran Pier**, and the popular holiday town of Helensburgh. Stretching into the highlands beyond Helensburgh is the Gareloch, which was one of Britain's major ports during the Second World War, and is now reverting to its peacetime calm, although a large shipbreaking yard has been established at its head.

Greenock

Distances–Dumbarton 19 m; Edinburgh 66 m; Glasgow 23 m; Gourock 3 m; Largs 14 m; London 416 m; Paisley 17 m.

Early Closing Day–Wednesday.
Hotel–Trinidad.
Population–70,250.

Three centuries ago a small fishing village, Greenock is now one of the most important towns of Scotland. Its industries are sugar-refining, engineering, shipbuilding, woollen and worsted manufactures, oil and cake mills, metal box manufacture and aluminium ware. The docks are very extensive; although now that the largest vessels can sail up to Glasgow, Greenock's importance as a shipping centre has diminished. Greenock was the birthplace of James Watt, the inventor of the steam-engine. The best views of the town are obtained from Lyle Road where there is a most interesting view indicator. Near it is the Memorial of unique design erected by French troops prior to their sailing from Greenock for the North African landings in the 1939–45 War. A monument in the cemetery commemorates Burns' 'Highland Mary' (*see* p. 243), who was originally interred in the

Gourock

West Kirk Burying Ground, but as that site was acquired for a shipyard extension, the remains were removed to the cemetery in 1920. On that occasion the old kirk was transferred stone by stone to its present site on Seafield Esplanade. It contains a most interesting Sailors' Loft.

The Greenock Library in the Watt Memorial in Union Street is the oldest subscription library in Scotland.

Westward Greenock merges into—

Gourock

Car Ferry–To Dunoon.
Distances–Ardrossan 25 m; Ayr 44 m; Edinburgh 69 m; Glasgow 26 m; London 419 m; Largs 14 m; Paisley 20 m; Wemyss Bay 8 m.
Early Closing Day–Wednesday.
Golf–18-hole course at Cowal View.

Hotels–*Queens* (13 rooms), *Bay* (29 rooms), *Cloch* (16 rooms), *Fairlight* (5 rooms), *Firth* (13 rooms), and several boarding houses.
Population–10,900.
Sports–Bathing, bowls, golf, tennis, yachting, boat-trips.

Gourock is a popular resort built on and around Kempock Point. It offers boating of all kinds, bathing, tennis, bowls, golf, etc, and is the terminus of British Railways' main Clyde coast line. In 1920 Clyde pilots were transferred from Greenock to Gourock, and a new Pilot House was built on the Pier. The Royal Gourock Yacht Clubhouse may be seen close to the shore towards the south end of the town.

An interesting and noteworthy feature of the town is the **Kempock Stone** (known as 'Granny Kempock'). This menhir of grey mica schist is surrounded by railings, and situated at the top of a flight of steps. To reach it take the first passage-way on the left in Kempock Street, proceeding from the Pierhead. The stone marks a site in Druid times of an altar to Baal and there are many superstitions associated with it.

Onward from Gourock to Ardrossan and Ayr by the coast is a magnificent run, taken in either direction, the road running within a few yards of the shore for nearly the whole 26 miles to Ardrossan and within sight of the sea for the remaining 25 miles. The railway also skirts the shore for some way north of Wemyss Bay and south of Largs, but between those places there is no direct rail communication.

Along the Cloch Road is the **Cloch Lighthouse** erected in 1791, a conspicuous tower 88 feet high and a familiar object on the Firth. Then the road skirts the grounds of Ardgowan House to much pretty **Inverkip** slightly inland and which can also be reached direct from Greenock via the Kip valley road.

Cloch Lighthouse

Wemyss Bay

Distances-Edinburgh 74 m; Glasgow 31 m; Gourock 8 m; Greenock 8 m; London 422 m.

Early Closing Day-Wednesday.
Hotel-*Wemyss Bay* (12 rooms).

Wemyss Bay (pronounced *Weems*) is an attractive resort with a large railway station, designed to cope with the rail-steamer excursion traffic (car ferry to Rothesay) and a really magnificent outlook across the Firth. Wemyss Bay is the starting point of steamers for Rothesay, and for Largs and Millport. The Arran excursion and Campbeltown boats also call. The foreshore is rocky but there are most of the attractions of a popular holiday place. Castle Wemyss (nineteenth century) lies on the north side of the bay; to the south the foreshore runs along by **Skelmorlie**. Here there is a golf course. **Skelmorlie Castle** partly ancient, partly modern, is well placed about a quarter of a mile inland and the ruins of **Knock Castle** on an eminence to the south attract attention.

Largs

Boating-Rowing, sailing boats for hire.
Bowls-In Douglas Park.
Dancing-*Moorings Ballroom, Marine and Curlingham Ballroom.*
Distances-Ardrossan 12 m; Ayr 29 m; Edinburgh 74 m; Glasgow 30 m; Gourock 14 m; Greenock 14 m; Kilmarnock 25 m; London 416 m; Paisley 23 m.
Early Closing Day-Wednesday.
Golf-*Rontenburn* (18-holes) to north of town. *Largs Golf Club* (18-holes), Irvine Road.
Hotels-*Castle* (20 rooms), *Elderslie* (30

rooms), *Marine and Curlinghall* (70 rooms), *Victoria* (12 rooms), *St Helen's* (21 rooms). Unlicensed: *Firth* (9 rooms), *Haylis* (8 rooms), *Mackerston* (55 rooms), *Vanduara* (15 rooms), and many others.
Information-The Cumbraen, Pierhead.
Population-9,800.
Post Office-Aitken Street. Sub-office in Brisbane Road.
Sea Angling-Excellent from boats. Weekly competitions.
Tennis-Courts available at Irvine Road.

Largs is a very popular summer resort. The town stands on the banks of two streams, the *Gogo* and the *Noddle*, and is well-sheltered by lofty hills. The bathing is good and there are putting greens, two golf courses, and other holiday amenities. Adjoining the grass-bordered promenade is a Pavilion used for film shows, dances and teas, etc. In the neighbourhood a great battle between Haakon, King of Norway and Alexander III of Scotland was fought in 1263. An imposing column marks the site. The king managed to escape to Orkney where he died. His defeat caused the cession of the Isle of Man and the Hebrides to Scotland on condition of an annual tribute, which was paid until the days of James I.

Netherhall, the residence of the late Lord Kelvin, is within the burgh. In the old churchyard are the ruins of the former **Skelmorlie Aisle**, one-time parish church and mausoleum. It was built in 1633-36 and has elaborate paintings on the roof.

Largs is the northern terminus of a branch of the railway running up from Ardrossan.

The railway and road run near the shore to **Fairlie**, well-known for its yacht-building. **Fairlie Castle**, an old stronghold of the Fairlie family, is perched at the top of a charming glen. From Fairlie, boats run to Millport and also convey cars to Brodick in Arran.

The Great Cumbrae

The island of the Great Cumbrae lies opposite Fairlie. The only town is **Millport** (population about 2,000) at the southern end of the island. It is an attractive little place with good bathing, boating, and golf. (*Hotels: Royal George, Millerston* and several guest houses.)

The Cathedral of the Isles, a part of the Scottish Episcopal Church, was built in 1849 from designs by Butterfield. In the older, parish, churchyard is the tomb of the Rev James Adams, minister of the parish of the Established Church from 1799 to 1831, and ever remembered for his habit of praying for 'The Greater and Lesser Cumbrae, Bute and Arran, and the adjacent islands of Great Britain and Ireland'.

At Keppel on the outskirts of Millport is a most interesting *Marine Biological Station,* with a modern aquarium and a museum.

Great Cumbrae is encircled by a coast road (about 10 miles) and an inner hill road which command grand views. The lighthouse on Little Cumbrae, the companion island to the south, is of interest.

South of Fairlie, road and rail follow the coast, passing the huge towers of the Hunterston nuclear power stations, to strike inland to **West Kilbride**, a charming residential community, and **Seamill** (*Hydro*) on the coast again. Two miles west of West Kilbride is **Farland Head** and **Bortincross Castle**, a twelfth-century fortress on the summit of the cliff. There is a tradition that one of the vessels of the Spanish Armada was wrecked on the coast nearby, and a cannon said to be from the wreck stands on the green of the castle.

Ardrossan

Distances–Ayr 19 m; Edinburgh 73 m; Glasgow 29 m; Gourock 26 m; Kilmarnock 15 m; London 407 m; Largs 12 m; Paisley 24 m.

Early Closing Day–Wednesday.
Hotels–*Ingledene* (5 rooms), *Kilmeny* (15 rooms).
Population–10,500.

Ardrossan, now practically continuous with **Saltcoats**, has also an increasing influx of summer visitors, though it is chiefly concerned with its busy harbours. Steamer services run from Ardrossan to Arran all the year round and there is also a daily daylight service to and from Belfast. There is a yacht pond, bathing pool, putting, tennis and a very fine sandy bay.

Ardrossan Castle, captured from the English by Wallace and finally put to ruin by Cromwell, stands on an eminence overlooking the town.

Ardrossan Castle

Glasgow to Ardrossan (inland route)

By road or by rail the route is through **Paisley** and **Johnstone**, with large engineering works. **Milliken Park** is a station for the old-world village of **Kilbarchan**, where Habbie Simpson, the famous piper mentioned in the song, *Maggie Lauder*, died some three centuries ago. **Lochwinnoch** is charmingly situated on Castle Semple Loch. **Beith** is an important centre of the furniture trade. In the neighbourhood of **Kilbirnie** are the Glengarnock Steel Works and **Dalry**. **Kilwinning** has the picturesque ruins of an ancient abbey, and is memorable as the place where Freemasonry was introduced into Scotland. Near Kilwinning, in an extensive and finely-wooded park, stood **Eglinton Castle**, where the famous Eglinton Tournament took place in 1839. At Kilwinning our line branches off from the main line to Ayr. The *ICI* Explosives Works are near **Stevenston**, as is also the Ardeer golf course. **Saltcoats** is a favourite seaside resort, with bathing pools, model yacht pond, fine sands and other holiday amenities. There is a good 18-hole golf course.

Ardrossan to Ayr

A few miles inland from Ardrossan by way of busy Stevenston, is **Kilwinning**, notable as the home of Freemasonry in Scotland. Mother Lodge Kilwinning (No 0) having been founded in 1107, at the same time as the Abbey, of which the few remains have been incorporated into the present Parish Church.

South of Kilwinning the roadside station of Bogside is passed. The Irvine golf-courses and the steeplechase course of the Eglinton Hunt adjoin the station.

Irvine

Distances—Ardrossan 8 m; Ayr 12 m; Edinburgh 70 m; Glasgow 26 m; Kilmarnock 8 m; London 399 m; Paisley 21 m. **Early Closing Day**—Wednesday.

Hotels—*Redbrun* (9 rooms), *Grange* (6 rooms). **Population**—21,400.

At Irvine, one of the most ancient royal burghs in Scotland, Robert Burns spent some time endeavouring to earn a livelihood as a flax dresser. The site of his shop, burned down during New Year festivities, is still pointed out, and, until destroyed by fire in 1925, there was also to be seen (in the state familiar to Burns) one of the houses in which he stayed during 1781–2. It has been rebuilt and bears an inscription. The Irvine Burns Club possesses some valuable Burns manuscripts. A statue of the poet, by J P Macgillivray, RSA, stands on the town common. John Galt, the Scottish novelist, was born at Irvine in 1779, in a house which stood on the site now occupied by the Bank of Scotland. James Montgomery, the poet, was also a native of Irvine.

The area immediately west of Irvine and northward to Kilwinning has been designated for development as Irvine New Town, Scotland's fifth New Town, and scheduled for an ultimate population growth to 80,000 people.

Between Irvine and Troon is Gailes, where the Glasgow and Western Clubs have golf courses. On a height near Barassie is the ruin of **Dundonald Castle**, where Robert II, the first of the Stewart kings, died in 1390. On the slopes above the plain is **Hillhouse**, a mansion wherein Napoleon III was entertained in 1839.

Inland from Irvine is—

Rough Sea at Troon

Kilmarnock

Distances – Ardrossan 16 m; Ayr 12 m; Cumnock 15 m; Edinburgh 60 m; Glasgow 21 m; Largs 25 m; London 391 m; Paisley 21 m.
Early Closing Day – Wednesday.
Golf – 18-hole course at Barassie, near Troone.

Hotels – *Broomhill* (11 rooms), *Golden Sheaf* (6 rooms), *Ross* (17 rooms), *Burnside* (11 rooms).
Population – 48,750.
Sports – Bowls, golf, pitch and putt, tennis, indoor swimming pool.

Kilmarnock is a busy industrial town that is of interest to Burns lovers as the place where 'Wee Johnny' Wilson had his printing press, by the agency of which the first edition of Burns's poems was printed in 1786. A shop now stands on the site of the famous 'Begbie's Inn' in Market Lane, which was a favourite resort of Burns and his cronies and was where the poet revised most of his proofs. Within Kay Park is the Burns Monument and Museum. The monument – of red sandstone – is one of the finest of its kind, while the Museum contains a fine collection of Burns manuscripts and first editions. The *MacKie Burns Library* in the Museum contains a copy of every known edition of the poet's works. Opposite the entrance to Kay Park in London Road, and marked by a tablet, stands Tam Samson's house.

The Dick Institute in London Road is a model of its kind. Under one roof are an excellent art gallery and lecture room, a reading room and lending library, and a splendid museum with both local and general collections. The Richmond-Paton collection of birds attracts much interest.

In the graveyard of Laigh Kirk (which dates from 1802 though the tower is much older) are numerous tombstones to the memory of martyred Covenanters and famous characters referred to in Burns' poems.

The original John Walker started to blend whiskies in Kilmarnock in 1820 and now 'Johnnie Walker' is known all over the world.

Visitors should ascend Craigie Hill, south of the town, where there is an indicator, and one of the finest view points in Scotland.

Those who wish to explore the Land of Burns thoroughly should journey southward from Kilmarnock to Mauchline by way of historic Sanquhar (p. 183) and Dumfries (p. 179).

At **Riccarton**, now part of Kilmarnock, Wallace is reputed to have passed his youthful days; and the road eastward to Strathaven (20 miles) and Hamilton (27 miles) passes **Loudoun Hill**, where Wallace defeated the English and where in 1306 Bruce with 600 men gained a striking victory over the Earl of Pembroke and his army of 6,000. At **Drumclog**, farther east, Claverhouse was defeated by a Covenanting force in 1679.

Troon

Distances – Ayr 8; Edinburgh 72 m; Glasgow 30 m; Irvine 7 m; Kilmarnock 9 m; London 398 m.

Early Closing Day – Wednesday.

Hotels – *Marine* (72 rooms), *Craiglea* (21 rooms), *South Beach* (27 rooms), *Welbeck* (14 rooms), *Ardneil*, *Knowe*, *Sun Court*, *Portland Arms*, etc.

Golf – There are five courses. The three municipally controlled courses are Darley, Lochgreen and Fullerton, and the others Troon Old Course and the Portland Course.

Population – 11,200.

Approaching Troon, on the coast, one is made aware of the local importance of Golf. There are five first-class courses around the town, but Troon has other attractions and is in fact a very popular holiday resort. There are fine sands, with good bathing (there is an excellent open-air swimming pool), boating, tennis and other sports, together with a concert hall and other places of indoor amusement. Here again the sea-front is bordered by a wide strip of turf which adds considerably to the pleasures of the sands. On the north side of the little promontory which forms the southern horn of Irvine Bay is Troon Harbour, carrying on shipbuilding and breaking. The rocky islet (a bird sanctuary) with beacon and white lighthouse seen a few miles to seaward is **Lady Isle**; far away in the westward is Ailsa Craig. The prominent building at the back of the town is *Marr College*, a senior secondary school.

About 4 miles north-east of Troon is Auchans House, where Dr Johnson visited Susanna, Countess of Eglinton, to whom Allan Ramsay dedicated his *Gentle Shepherd*. **Monkton** is an ancient village that owes its origin to a religious house in connection with Paisley Abbey. It contains the ruins of a very old church in which, according to Blind Harry, Wallace had a wonderful dream.

In the little church of **Barnweill**, 3 miles north-east from Monkton, John Knox promulgated the new form of religion. The house which stood beside it was the ancient lazar-house or hospital for lepers, called St Ninian's

Hospital. On Barnweill Hill is the Wallace Monument, a square tower 60 feet high, with a spiral staircase in the interior. From the summit one has a wonderful view of the whole of the Burns Country.

Prestwick

Distances – Ayr 3 m; Edinburgh 71 m; Glasgow 30 m; Irvine 9 m; Kilmarnock 9 m; London 393 m.

Hotels – *Auchencoyle* (7 rooms), *Carlton* (9 rooms), *Golden Eagle* (6 rooms), *Links* (13 rooms), *North Beach* (13 rooms), *Parkstone* (32 rooms), *Queen's* (39 rooms), *St Nicholas* (16 rooms), *St Ninians'* (17 rooms), *Towans* (57 rooms), *Earlston* (12 rooms), and many others.

Sports – Golf, bowls, tennis, bathing-lake, sea-bathing and boating.

Population – 13,450.

Four miles south of Troon is the ancient burgh of Prestwick famous first as a golfing centre, and later for its great Airport Terminal. There are three first-class golf courses available to visitors, and all have full catering facilities. The town has, in recent years, become a popular holiday resort. Although without architectural pretensions, it has an interesting ecclesiastical history. In the centre of the older part is the 'Mercat Cross' – one of few to be found in the south-west. Many legendary tales are told in connection with **Kingcase Well**, midway between Prestwick and Ayr. It is supposed to mark the spot where Robert Bruce built a lazar house and where he is said to have been cured of leprosy.

Prestwick Cross

Prestwick Airport–Prestwick, Scotland's international airport, has been completely modernized and can now handle all types of aircraft. The impressive new Terminal Buildings, costing £2 million, were opened by Her Majesty the Queen Mother in September 1964.

The airport concourse, a vast L-shaped hall with a gallery on three sides, contains a variety of shops, a bank, a Post Office, a restaurant and bar. The roof of the crossblock overlooking the apron is used as a spectators' terrace. This all-weather area is heated, and provided with canopies, screen walls and shelters. Facilities include a cafeteria and bar.

Prestwick has an unrivalled record as a fog-free airport for aircraft operating the Trans-Continental and Trans-Atlantic services. Frequently it has been the only open airport in Britain, thanks to Ayrshire's unique climate, and more than once it has been the only clear airport in the whole of Western Europe.

Two miles inland is the picturesque Church of St Quivox, of thirteenth-century date and still in regular use. An avenue leads past the church and manse to the **Dairy Research Institute and School** and adjoining the **West of Scotland Agricultural College** in Auchincruive House. Crosbie Church, between Monkton and Troon, and Monkton Church, about a mile north of Prestwick, have also historic associations. **Ladykirk**, about 2 miles north-east of Prestwick, was one of the pre-Reformation religious houses. Only a tower remains.

For Ayr, *see* p. 241.

The Ayrshire Coast

Ayr

Bathing – Safe bathing on a wide sandy beach. Chalets on foreshore.

Bowls – Greens at Northfield, Craigie Park, Seafield, Forehill and Crooksmoss, Whitletts.

Distances – Burns's Cottage 2½ m; Alloway Kirk 2¾ m; Ardrossan 19 m; Dumfries 59 m; Edinburgh 72 m; Glasgow 33 m; Kilmarnock 12 m; London 390 m; Stranraer 51 m.

Early Closing Day – Wednesday.

Hotels – *Station, County, Eldon House, Ayr-shire and Galloway, Berkeley, Marine Court*, etc. *Butlin's Holiday Camp. Youth Hostel.*

Parks – Belleisle, Craigie.

Population – 48,000.

Sports – Golf (3 municipal courses), tennis, bowls, bathing, boating, sea-fishing. Race meetings in April, May, June, July and September (flat), and in January, March, April, May, October, November, December (jumping).

Ayr is a busy and attractive town which owes something at least of its prosperity to its connection with Robert Burns. The town stands on the banks of the Ayr at the point where that river enters the Firth of Clyde, so that it can also offer the attractions of a seaside resort. The sandy beach is bordered by a wide expanse of turf, with a dance pavilion, amusements, etc. At the north end of the beach is the **Harbour** and swimming pool, and near the south end are two golf courses. Overlooking the beach are the County Buildings, but the town is dominated by the **Town Steeple**, a very fine piece of work which is perhaps best appreciated from a viewpoint at the far end of the **New Bridge**, by which the main road crosses the river. From this bridge also is a good view of the **Auld Brig** immortalised by Burns in his poem *The Brigs of Ayr*. Its antiquity is undoubted, and it still stands a champion of the soundness of thirteenth-century workmanship. The New Bridge against which Burns imagined it inveighing was a predecessor of the present New Bridge.

From the Steeple, **High Street** leads up to the Station, passing on the way the former *Tam o' Shanter Inn*, now a museum, though still with its thatched roof and primitive fittings, and boasting on its front a large picture showing Tam, mounted on his 'grey meare Meg', setting off for Alloway and the exciting incidents related by Burns. Just outside the station yard is a Burns statue by G A Lawson, and the road to the south at this point leads in about two miles to Burns' Birthplace and Alloway (*see next page*).

With Burns, Ayr honours Wallace: there is a Wallace Tower (reconstructed on the site of a tower in which he was confined) just below the *Tam o' Shanter* in High Street; on Barnweil Hill, about 6 miles north-east of the town, a prominent monument commemorates the patriot, while closer at hand in the same direction is the cairn at **Auchincruive** to the joint

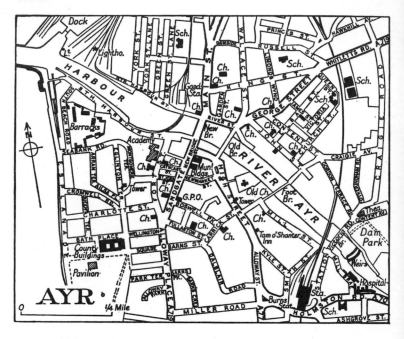

memory of Burns and Wallace. The Auchincruive estate now belongs to the West of Scotland Agricultural College. On this side of the town also is Ayr's very popular Racecourse.

Ayr's **Parish Kirk** is entered by a narrow way a little below the Wallace Tower in High Street: in the lych-gate are some of the heavy iron grave-covers which were common in the days of the body-snatchers. The grave-yard will interest epitaph hunters; the Martyrs' Tomb is near the river on the east side of the church—its inscription concluding:

> 'Boots, thumbkins, gibbets were in fashion then,
> Lord, let us never see such days again.'

The building was erected in 1654 and still retains its original canopied pulpit and three galleries.

Ayr is said to have been the site of a Roman station, but there is little evidence as to this. William the Lion, who built a castle at the mouth of the River Ayr, granted the town a charter in 1202, raising it to the dignity of a Royal Burgh. It was here that Wallace first openly organized resistance against the English forces, and the town was the scene of one of his notable exploits, 'the burning of the Barns of Ayr'. A parliament convened by Robert the Bruce for the purpose of settling the succession to the Scottish throne met here, and it was from the port of Ayr that Edward Bruce embarked in 1315 with a small army for the purpose of invading Ireland. In 1652 the English Commonwealth built the fort of Ayr, of which traces remain on the height to the west of the harbour. The ancient church of St John, founded in the twelfth century, which stood here, was converted into an armoury. By way of compensation, the Protector gave a donation of 2,000 merks to assist in building the Church already referred to.

Excursions from Ayr include walks beside the river and to the Wallace and Burns memorials mentioned above, and visits by rail or road to various spots associated with Burns, pre-eminent being that to—

Burns' Birthplace

Admission charge to Cottage and Museum. Catalogues. Open every weekday and on Sundays in summer, 2–7. July–August Sundays from 10. Free car park.

The 'Auld Clay Biggin' built by Burns's father stands beside the road to Alloway, about 2½ miles south of Ayr steeple. On the way from Ayr one passes various points associated with the wild ride of Tam o' Shanter. About a mile from the steeple, the Alloway road crosses the Slaphouse Burn about 200 yards east of—

'the ford
Whare in the snaw the chapman smoor'd,'

and a short distance beyond the ford in the garden of a wayside cottage may be found the—

'meikle stane
Whare drunken Charlie brak's neck-bane.'

A little farther on an ash-tree surrounded by a paling marks—

'the cairn
Whare hunters fand the murder'd bairn.'

Burns' Birthplace is a low thatched cottage abutting on to the pavement and with little external suggestion of its value and importance in the world of literature. The inner rooms contain various articles of simple furniture, and there is a 'set-in' bed similar to that in which Burns was born on January 25, 1759.

Adjoining the birthplace is a museum of manuscripts, letters and other relics of the poet, and the gardens are pleasantly laid out.

Robert Burns was born at Alloway, January 25, 1759, and died at Dumfries (p. 179), July 21, 1796. The first seven years of his life were spent here; in 1766 the family moved to Mount Oliphant, 2 miles from Alloway. His father was a peasant farmer who gave his son the best available education, and this education inclined to the literary side. His youth was spent working on the farm, with a brief interlude at Irvine (p. 235), where he tried his fortunes as a flax-dresser. When William Burns died in 1784 Robert and his brother took on the farm at Mossgiel (p. 247) and shouldered the maintenance of the widow and several younger children. It was, however, an unfortunate venture, and Robert's interest in the farm was lessened by his affair with Jean Armour—an affair which so incensed the Armour family that Burns thought it best to seek his fortunes abroad. Meanwhile, Jean Armour and he parted with some show

View over Ayr and the river

of recrimination, and Burns turned to 'Highland Mary'–Mary Campbell, dairymaid at Montgomery Castle near Mossgiel–who, however, died shortly afterwards. Burns decided to go to Jamaica, and had indeed composed his farewell song ('The Gloomy Night is Gathering Fast') when the success of his first book of poems introduced him to literary circles in Edinburgh, and brought in a sum of money that was welcome, if small, and sufficed to banish ideas of emigration.

After a tour of the Border, he returned to Mossgiel, this time to be received with open arms by the Armours–a welcome not without embarrassment, one imagines, for by now the correspondence with Clarinda (Mrs Maclehose) was flourishing. However, in 1788 he rented the farm of Ellisland (p. 182) near Dumfries and married his Jean. Farming was no more prosperous at Ellisland than at Mossgiel, and ere long he applied for the post of excise officer, which brought him in an additional £50 per annum. Once again, too, farming was subjugated to other interests, and in 1791 he sold the farm, moved to a small house in Dumfries, and turned from poems to political squibs which, as the work of an excise officer, were looked at askance by some of his strictly loyal and carefully-spoken superiors. Then came that almost quixotic period when, notwithstanding his poverty and that of his family, he refused to accept payment for the grand series of songs he contributed to Thomson's *Collection;* refused, too, an annuity of £50 offered in return for poetical articles for the *Morning Chronicle.* Scotland has been much blamed for the poverty of his final days, but the blame can hardly go undivided.

Following the main road southward from Burns' Birthplace for a quarter mile, one comes on the right to the old **Church of Alloway**, where Tam o'Shanter–

> 'saw an unco sight!
> Warlocks and witches in a dance . . .'

244

and from the winnock-bunker in the east wall 'Auld Nick'–

> 'Screwed the pipes and gart them skirl
> Till roof and rafters a' did dirl.'

Another side of the poet's genius is displayed in the inscription on his father's tombstone–

> 'O ye whose cheek the tear of pity stains.'

Across the road from the Church is the **Burns' Monument** (*admission, fee; open weekdays all day, Sundays in summer*, 2–7)–a Grecian temple copied from the monument of Lysicrates at Athens. It contains various relics, including Jean Armour's wedding ring, and two Bibles said to have been exchanged between Burns and Highland Mary. Many admirers of Burns will consider that a more fitting memorial than the Grecian temple is the summer-house in the garden containing Thom's clever sculptures, representing Tam o' Shanter and Souter Johnie. The gardens are pretty and give nice views of the Auld Brig o' Doon, and the riverside grounds of the adjoining Burns Monument Hotel are also open for a small fee.

The farm of **Mount Oliphant**, to which the Burns family removed in 1766, is on rising ground about 2 miles east of the Auld Brig. It was here that Burns composed his first song, 'My Handsome Nell'.

Burns' Birthplace, Alloway

Ayr to Maybole and Girvan

The road crossing the New Brig o' Doon climbs to give good views eastward and in about 5 miles reaches –

Maybole (*King's Arms*, *Carrick*), a sleepy old town with a reputation for the manufacture of footwear and agricultural implements, and of interest to Burns students as the place where the poet's father and mother first met.

From Maybole our road to Turnberry is across the hills, passing the ruins of –

Crossraguel Abbey on the left a few miles out. The ruins (*weekdays 10–7 in summer, 10–4 in winter. Sundays 2–7 or 4; admission, fee*) comprise nave and chancel of the Abbey Church, the chapter house, south of the chancel, remains of the cloisters, dovecot, and the gatehouse at the south-west, still imposing.

Kirkoswald is a neat village notable as the burial-place of Burns' Tam o' Shanter. (The gravestone is at the west end of the Church, Tam's real name being Grahame.) In the centre of the village is Souter Johnie's Cottage, preserved as nearly as possible as it was in Burns' day.

Kirkoswald is not far from the coast, along which a road has come from Ayr by way of **Dunure**, where is a ruined cliff castle. It was in the black vault of this grim keep that the fourth Earl of Cassillis, anxious to enrich himself at the expense of the Church, in 1570 'roasted in sope' a commendator (= lay abbot) of the neighbouring Abbey of Crossraguel in an attempt to secure a share of the ecclesiastical revenue. The dignitary, however, remained obdurate, and, escaping, appealed to the Privy Council, with but little satisfaction. The Kennedys of Dunure are now represented by the Marquis of Ailsa, who has given his former seat, Culzean Castle, the next notable building passed, to the National Trust for Scotland.

Culzean Castle (*policies and castle open 10–dusk, fee*) was built as a residence towards the end of the eighteenth century and contains a National Guest Flat placed at the disposal of General Eisenhower after the Second World War.

Turnberry of today is manifestly Turnberry Hotel (120 rooms) and a hamlet. The famous resort hotel surmounts the scene of its two 18-hole golf courses – the championship Ailsa and the newer Arran, on which non-resident visitors may play. On the neighbouring 'Bogle's Brae' was kindled the mysterious beacon fire which summoned Bruce and his followers from Arran: an incident familiar to readers of Scott's *Lord of the Isles*.

Girvan

Distances–Ayr 21 m; Dumfries 65 m;
Edinburgh 93 m; Glasgow 54 m; London
397 m; Maybole 12 m; Newton Stewart
30 m; Stranraer 30 m; Turnberry 5 m.
Golf–18-hole course.

Hotels–*King's Arms* (34 rooms), *Hamilton
Arms* (12 rooms), *Ailsa Arms* (12 rooms),
Royal (7 rooms), *Cranford* (8 rooms),
Marcliff (5 rooms).
Population–7,400.

Girvan, 5 miles south of Turnberry, is a small seaport and holiday resort. There is good bathing, golf and fishing, tennis courts and bowling greens, indoor pool and trips to the lonely rock of **Ailsa Craig**, 10 miles out at sea, are popular, although the rock is uninhabited except for the keepers of its lighthouse and the myriads of seabirds.

Ten miles north-east of Ayr by road is **Mauchline** (*Poosie Nansie's Inn, Loudoun Arms*), 'the Mecca of Burns pilgrims'. Most of the buildings associated with the poems have gone, but Poosie Nansie's hostelry remains. The churchyard was the scene of 'The Holy Fair', and here are the graves of Daddy Auld, Mary Morison, Holy Willie and many others mentioned by Burns. Close by the churchyard and the ruins of Mauchline Castle is the house where Gavin Hamilton lived and where Burns and Jean Armour were married. Also close at hand is the small house in which they lived until the house at Ellisland was ready.

Chief interest of the neighbourhood centres in the farm of **Mossgiel**, where Burns lived for seven years. It is 1½ miles north-west of Mauchline, on the Tarbolton road. Burns and his brother, Gilbert, rented this farm for four years from the time of their father's death, in 1784, and here were written *The Cottar's Saturday Night* and many other of his best poems. Here is the field where he ploughed up the daisy and turned up the mouse's nest– simple events which his muse has immortalised. The house has been rebuilt. Some way farther along the Tarbolton road is a turning leading to the farmstead of **Lochlea**, which was Burns's home from his seventeenth to his twenty-fourth year, his father having moved here from Mount Oliphant. It was at Lochlea that the elder Burns died.

At **Tarbolton** Burns became a freemason. Here he founded his first debating society–the Bachelor's Club–in an old house (National Trust: museum). At Coilsfield House (now Montgomerie Castle) near by, 'Highland Mary' was a dairymaid. Still pointed out is the spot near the old thorn tree, at the junction of the Fail with the River Ayr near the main road 2½ miles west of Mauchline, where Burns and Mary last met 'to live one day of parting love'. (Mary, it will be remembered, went to visit relatives in Argyllshire, and fell sick and died at Greenock, on her return journey.)

YOUR HELP IS REQUESTED

A GREAT part of the success of this series is due, as we gratefully acknowledge, to the enthusiastic co-operation of readers. Changes take place, both in town and country, with such rapidity that it is difficult, even for the most alert and painstaking staff, to keep pace with them all, and the correspondents who so kindly take the trouble to inform us of alterations that come under their notice in using the books, render a real service not only to us but to their fellow-readers. We confidently appeal for further help of this kind.

THE EDITOR

WARD LOCK LIMITED
116, BAKER STREET,
LONDON, W.1

Index

Abbotsford, 57
Abercorn Church, 174
Aberlady, 37
Abington, 87
Ailsa Craig, 247
Airdrie, 215
Allermuir, 170
Annan, 179
Antonine Wall, 215
Ardmore Point, 229
Ardrossan, 233, 235
  Castle, 233
Ashiestiel, 65
Auchincruive, 241
Auld Brig, Ayr, 241
Auldgirth, 183
Ayr, 241–245
Ayton, 29

Baldoon Castle, 193
Balerno, 171
Ballantrae, 195
Balmaclellan, 196
Barnton, 168
Barnweill, 237
Barscobe Castle, 197
Bass Rock, 35
Bathgate, 215
Beith, 234
Bellshill, 215
Bemersyde, 52
Berwick-upon-Tweed, 27
Biggar, 68, 87
Binns, The, 174
Black Dwarf's Cottage, 67
Blackford, 155
Blackford Hill, 155
Blackness Castle, 174
Blantyre, 218
  Priory, 218
Bonaly Tower, 171
Bonnyrigg, 175
Bore Stone, The, 154
Borgue, 191

Boroughmuirhead, 153
Borthwick, 63
Bortincross Castle, 233
Bothwell, 216, 217
Bothwell Brig, 219
Bothwell Castle, 216
Bowling, 228
Braes of Gleniffer, 228
Braid Hills Golf Course, 155
Braids, The, 154
Branxholm Tower, 71
Bridge of Weir, 228
Broughton House, Kirkcudbright, 190
Broxburn, 215
Bruntsfield, 153–4
Bruntsfield House, 153
Bruntsfield Links, 153
Burnmouth, 29
Burns's Birthplace, 243
Burns's House, Dumfries, 180
Burns Monument, Ayr, 245
Burns, Robert, 243

Cadzow Castle, 220
Caerketton, 170
Caerlaverock Castle, 179
Cairnryan, 195
Cairntable, 225
Caiystane, The, 155
Cambusland, 222
Carberry Hill, 38
Cardoness Castle, 191
Carfin, 223
Carham, 42
Carleton Castle, 195
Carlops, 171
Carluke, 178
Caroline Park, Granton, 165
Carronbridge, 183
Carsphairn, 197
Carter Bar, 47
Cartland Crags, The, 224
Castle of Avondale, 221
Castle, Berwick, 27

INDEX

Castle Douglas, 188
Castle Kennedy, 194
Castle of Park, 193
Castle of Qua, 224
Castlemilk, 222
Cat Castle, 221
Cessford, 44
Chatelherault, 220
Chirnside, 45
Church of Alloway, The Old, 244
Church Hill, Bruntsfield, 154
City Hospital, The Braids, 154
Cloch Lighthouse, 231
Clyde, The, 216, 226
Clydebank, 228
Coatbridge, 215
Cockburnspath, 29, 30
Cockpen, 63
Cockpen Church, 175
Coldingham, 30
Coldingham Priory, 30
Coldstream, 41
Colinton, 166, 170
Corstorphine, 168, 169, 215
Craig House, The Braids, 154
Craigcrook Castle, 166
Craigendoran Pier, 229
Craigenputtock, 181
Craigentinny Marbles, 159
Craigiehall, 172
Craiglockhart, 170
Craigmillar, 157
    Castle, 157
Craignethan Castle, 178, 224
Cramond, 166, 167
Crawford, 87
Crawfordjohn, 177, 185
Creetown, 191
Crichton Castle, 63
Criffel, 186
Crookston Castle, 228
Cross Church, 66
Crossford, 224
Crossmichael, 196
Crossraguel Abbey, 246
Culzean Castle, 246
Cumnock, 185

Dairy Research Institute, 239
Dalbeattie, 187
Dalhousie Castle, 175
Dalkeith, 175
    House, 175
Dalmellington, 185, 197

Dalmey Church, 172
Dalmeny House, 172
Dalry, 197, 234
Dalswinton, 182
Dalveen Pass, 183
Darnick, 62
Dawyck House Gardens, 68
Dechmont Hill, 222
Deil's Causey, 221
Denholm, 72
Devil's Beef Tub, 84, 87
Dirleton, 36
Dr Guthrie's School, 174
Douglasdale, 177, 225
Douglas Water, The, 225
Drumclog, 221, 237
Drummore, 194
Dryburgh, 51, 55
    Abbey, 51
Dryhope Tower, 77
Dumbarton, 228
Dumfries, 81, 179
Dunbar, 30
Dunbar Castle, 31
Dundonald Castle, 235
Dundrennan Abbey, 189
Dunfermline, 174
Dunglass Castle, 228
Duns, 45
    Castle, 45
Dunure, 246
Durisdeer, 183

Earlston, 60
East Linton, 32
Ecclefechan, 79
Edinburgh, 91–151, 215
    Abbey Court House, 124
    Academy, 152
    Acheson House, 122
    Adam House, 138
    Albert Memorial, 146
    Archers' Hall, 142
    Arthur's Seat, 132
    Assembly Hall, 100
    Assembly Rooms and Music
        Hall, 145
    Bailie Macmorran's House, 109
    Bakehouse Close, 122
    B.B.C. 149
    Bells Wynd, 117
    Bible Land, 121
    Blackfriars Wynd, 118
    Broughton, 150

Edinburgh (contd.)
Burns Monument, 133
Calton Hill, 133
Candlemaker Row, 139
Canongate, 120
Canongate Kirk, 121
Canongate Tolbooth, 121
Canonmills, 150
Castle, 103
Castle Esplanade, 101
Castle Hill, 107
Castle Terrace, 128
Central Public Library, 139
Chalmers Hospital, 143
Chambers Street, 138
Church of the Sacred Heart, 143
City Chambers, 116
City Museum, 122
City Police, 113
Cockburn Street, 117
College of Art, 142
College Wynd, 131
Comely Bank, 150
Convent of St Catherine of
    Siena, 143
County Buildings, 111
Covenanters' Prison, 140
Cowgate, 130
Cross, The, 115
Darien House, 143
Dean Bridge, 147
Dean Cemetary, 152
Dental School, 138
Duddingston, 131
Duke of Wellington Statue, 96
Dunsapie Loch, 131
East Princes Street Gardens, 97
Empire Theatre, 143
Fettes College, 150
Fire Station, 142
Fountain Close, 119
Free St Columba's Church, 109
Freemasons' Hall, 145
General Post Office, 96
George IV Bridge, 139
George Heriot's School, 142
George Square, 140
George Street, 145
Gladstone's Land, 109
Gladstone Statue, 146
Grassmarket, 130
Greyfriars, 139
Haymarket Station, 146
Heart, 111

Edinburgh (contd.)
Heriot Row, 147
Heriot-Watt University, 138
Highland Tolbooth-St John's
    Church, 107
Holyroodhouse, 124
Holyrood Park, 131
Horse Wynd, 131
Huntly House, 121
Inverleith Park, 150
Jeffrey Street, 120
John Knox's Grave, 114
John Knox's House, 119
King's Stables Road, 130
Lawnmarket, 108
Lady Stair's Close, 109
Lady Stair's House, 109
Magdalen Chapel, 130
Martyr's Monument, 140
Meadows, The, 140
Melville College, 147
Melville Drive, 142
Middle Meadow Walk, 140
Milne's Court, 109
Milton House, 122
Moray House, 121
Moray Place, 147
Moubray House, 120
Mound, The, 98, 100
Muschat's Cairn, 131
Museum of Childhood, 119
National Gallery, 98
National Gallery of Modern Art,
    150
National Library of Scotland,
    139
National Monument, 133
National Museum of Antiquities
    of Scotland, 149
Nelson Monument, 133
New Calton Burying Ground,
    133
New College, 100
New Observatory, 133
New Register House, 96
North Bridge, 136
Old Calton Burying Ground, 135
Old Tolbooth, 111
Outlook Tower, 107
Parliament House, 115
Parliament Square, 114
Pleasance, 137
Princes Street, 95
Queensberry House, 122

INDEX

Edinburgh (contd.)
Queen Street, 149
Ramsay Lodge, 100
Regent Bridge, 135
Roman Catholic Cathedral of
St Mary, 150
Royal Bank, 144
Royal Botanic Garden, 150
Royal Circus, 149
Royal Company of Archers, 142
Royal High School, 133
Royal Infirmary, 142
Royal Lyceum Theatre, 129
Royal (Dick) School, 142
Royal Scottish Academy, 98
Royal Scottish Museum, 138
Royal Society of Edinburgh, 145
Royal Stables, 124
St Andrew Square, 144
St Andrew's & St George's
Church, 145
St Andrew's House, 134
St Anthony's Chapel, 131
St Cecilia's Hall, 118
St. Cuthbert's Church, 100, 128
St George's West Church, 146
St Giles' Cathedral, 113
St John's Cross, 121
St John's Episcopal Church, 99
St Leonard's Hill, 132
St Margaret's Loch, 131
St Margaret's Well, 131
St Mary's Episcopal Cathedral,
146
St Patrick's Roman Catholic
Church, 118, 119
St Stephen's Church, 152
Salisbury Crags, 132
Samson's Ribs, 131
Scottish Central Library, 110
Scottish National Portrait
Gallery, 149
Scottish Regalia, 106
Scottish United Services
Museum, 106
Scott's House, 145
Scott Monument, 97
Sheriff Court, 111
Shoemakers' Land, 121
Signet Library, 115
Society of Solicitors, 115
South Bridge, 136
Stockbridge, 150
Surgeons' Hall, 143

Edinburgh (contd.)
Trinity College Church, 120
Tron Church, 117
Tweeddale Court, 119
University, 137
Usher Hall, 128
Vennel, 142
Water Gate, 122
Waterloo Place, 135
Waverley Station, 96
Wells o' Wearie, 132
West Bow, 108
West Kirk, 100, 128
West Princes Street Gardens, 99
Western General Hospital, 150
Whinny Hill, 131
Whitefoord House, 122
York Place, 149
Ednam, 44
Eglinton Castle, 234
Eildon Hills, 59
Elderslie, 228
Ellisland, 182
Elvanfoot, 183
Enterkin Pass, 183
Erskine Bridge, 228
Esk Valley, 174
Eskdale, 70
Ettrick Church, 78
Ettrick Forest, 77
Evandale, 84, 87
Eyemouth, 29

Fairlie, 232
Castle, 232
Fairmilehead, 154
Farland Head, 233
Fast Castle, 30
Ferniehirst Castle, 49
Fisherrow, 38, 160
Floors Castle, 42
Forth Bridges, 172, 173
Forth and Clyde Canal, 215

Galashiels, 47, 62
Galloway Hydro-Electric Scheme, 196
Garliestown, 193
Gatehouse of Fleet, 191
George Watson's College, 154
Gifford, 39
Gilbertfield, 222
Girvan, 192, 195, 247
Glasgow, 199–214
Anniesland Cross, 211

Glasgow (contd.)
  Argyle Street, 203
  Art Gallery and Museum, 207
  Auld Brig of Cathcart, 214
  Baillies' Institution Library, 210
  Bank of Scotland, 202
  Bearsden, 211
  Bellahouston Park, 213
  Bible Training Institute, 210
  Birkenshaw, 213
  Blythswood Square, 210
  Botanic Gardens, 209
  Bothwell Street, 210
  Broomielaw, 212
  Carmunnock, 214
  Cathcart, 214
  Cathedral, 203
  Cathkin Braes Park, 214
  Cathkin Hills, 214
  Charing Cross, 210
  Church College, 211
  Citizens' Theatre, 214
  Crossmyloof, 213
  Dawsholm Park, 211
  Dental Hospital, 210
  Ear, Nose & Throat Hospital,
    210
  Eglinton Toll, 212
  George Square, 202
  Glasgow Academy, 212
  Glasgow Bridge, 212
  Glasgow Green, 203
  Gorbals Church, 212
  Haggs Castle, 213
  Hampden Park, 214
  High School, 210
  Hillhead, 212
  Hunterian Museum, 209
  Hutcheson's Hospital, 202
  Jew's Sepulchre, 205
  Kelvinside Academy, 211
  Kelvingrove Park, 208
  King George V Bridge, 212
  King's Park, 214
  King's Theatre, 210
  Langside, 213
  Lansdowne Church, 212
  Linn Park, 214
  Mains Castle, 214
  Martyrs' Monument, 214
  Maryhill, 211
  Maxwell Park, 213
  McLellan Galleries, 210
  Merchants' House, 202

Glasgow (contd.)
  Milngavie, 211
  Mitchell Library, 209
  Mosspark, 213
  Municipal Buildings, 202
  Museum of Transport, 212
  Necropolis, 205
  Old Glasgow Museum, 203
  Park Church, 211
  Pavilion Theatre of Varieties, 210
  Pollok Grounds, 213
  Pollokshaws, 213
  Pollokshields, 213
  Post Office, Head Office, 202
  Provand's Lordship, 206
  Queen Mary's Seat, 214
  Queen's Park, 213
  Queen's Park Recreation
    Ground, 214
  Reservoirs, 211
  Roman Wall, 211
  Rouken Glen Park, 213
  Royal Exchange, 202
  Royal Mental Hospital, 211
  Royal Scottish Automobile Club,
    211
  St Aloysius' Church & College,
    210
  St Matthew's Church, 210
  St Vincent Street Church, 210
  Saltmarket, 203
  Sauchiehall Street, 209, 210
  School of Art, 210
  Scottish College of Commerce,
    211
  Speirs Bridge, 213
  Strathbungo, 213
  Strathclyde University, 207
  Thornliebank, 213
  Trongate, 203
  University, 208
  Victoria Road, 213
  West End, 209
  Whiteinch, 209
  Y.M.C.A., 210
Glen App, 195
Glenarn Castle, 195
Glencorse Reservoir, 171
Glenluce, 193
Glen Trool, 192
Gordon, 60
Gourock, 230
Govan, 226
Grange, The, Blackford, 156

INDEX

Granton, 165
    Castle, 165
    Harbour, 165
Grantshouse, 29
· Great Cumbrae, 233
Greenlaw, 60
Greenock, 229
Gretna Green, 79
Grey Mare's Tail (Moffat), 78, 83
Grey Mare's Tail (Thornhill), 183
Gullane, 37

Habbie's Howe, 68
Haddington, 32, 33
Hailes Castle, 32
Hailes House, 170
Halidon Hill, 45
Hallside, 222
Hamilton, 216, 219
Hamilton House, 37
Hart Fell, 83
Hawick, 69, 71, 72
Hawthornden, 63, 175
Hermitage of Braid, 155
Hermitage Castle, 69
Hillend Public Park, 154
Hillend Ski Centre, 154
Hillhouse, 235
Hirsel, The, 41
Hoddam Castle, 80
Hopetoun House, 172, 174
Hopetoun Monument, 37
Horndean, 40
Howgate, 176

Inchgarvie, 172
Inch House, 174
Inchkeith, 165
Innerleithen, 65
Inveresk, 160
Inverkip, 231
Irongray, 181
Irvine, 235

Jedburgh, 47, 72
    Abbey, 48
Jerviswood, 225
Jock's Lodge, 159
Johnstone, 234
Joppa, 38, 159
Juniper Green, 170

Kelso, 40, 42
    Abbey, 42
Kempock Stone, 231

Kenmure Castle, 196
Kilbarchan, 234
Kilbirnie, 234
Kilmacoln, 228
Kilmarnock, 185, 236
Kilspindle, 37
Kilwinning, 234, 235
Kingcase Well, 238
Kingsknowe, 170
King's Buildings, Blackford, 156
King's Theatre, Bruntsfield, 153
Kippford, 187
Kirk Yetholm, 44
Kirkcudbright, 190
Kirkfieldbank, 224
Kirkmadrine, 194
Kirkmaiden Old Church, 194
Kirkoswald, 246
Knock Castle, 232

Lady Isle, 237
Ladykirk, Kelso, 40
Ladykirk, Prestwick, 239
Lamberton, 29
Lanark, 178, 223
Langholm, 70
Largs, 232
Lasswade, 63, 175
Lauder, 45, 60
Lauriston Castle, 166
Leadburn, 68
Leaderfoot, 51
Leadhills, 184
Lee Castle, 224
Lennoxlove, 39
Lincluden College, 181
Lindean, 75
Linton, 44
Little France, 174
Loanhead, 175
Loch Dee, 192
Loch Doon, 197
Lochlea, 247
Loch of the Lowes, 78
Lochmaben, 81
Loch Muck, 197
Loch Ryan, 194
Loch Skeen, 78, 83
Loch Trool, 192
Lochryan Hall, 195
Lochwinnoch, 234
Lockerbie 80, 81
Logan Gardens, Port Logan, 194
Longniddry, 37

Loretto, Chapel of, 160
Loudoun, 237
Lyne, 84

Machars Promontory, 193
Manor, 67
Mary Queen of Scots House, 49
Mauchline, 247
Mausoleum, The, Hamilton, 220
Maxwelltown, 181
Maybole, 246
Mellerstain House, 60
Melrose, 47, 52
   Abbey, 55
Mennock Pass, The, 184
Mercat Cross, Preston, 37, 38
Merchiston Castle, 154
Merrick, 192
Milliken Park, 234
Millport, 233
Minchmoor, 65
Minnigaff, 192
Moat of Urr, The, 188
Moffat, 77, 81
Moffat Dale, 82
Moniaive, 182
Moniaive Valley, The, 181
Monkton, 237
Monreith House, 193
Morebattle, 44
Morningside Parish Church, 154
Morton Castle, 183
Mossgiel, 247
Mosspaul, 71
Motherwell, 223
Mount Oliphant Farm, 245
Muirfield, 36
Musselburgh, 38, 160

Napier Technical College, 154
Neidpath Castle, 67
Nethanfoot, 224
Netherhall, 232
Nether Liberton, 174
New Cumnock, 185
New Galloway, 192, 196
Newhaven, 164
New Lanark, 224
Newark, 77
Newbattle Abbey, 175
Newington, 156
Newington House, 157
Newstead, 55
Newton Stewart, 192

Norham, 40
North Berwick, 34, 35, 36
North Berwick Law, 36

Old Jedward, 50

Paisley, 224, 227, 234
   Abbey, 227
Parton, 196
Paxton, 40
Peebles, 47, 66
Penicuik, 68, 176
Penicuik House, 176
Pentlands, The, 166, 170, 171
Pinkie House, 160
Pinwherry Castle, 192
Polton, 63, 175
Polwarth, 45
Port Glasgow, 229
Port of Leith, 161–3
Port Logan, 194
Port Mary, 189
Port William, 193
Portankill, 194
Portobello, 38, 159
Portpatrick, 194
Preston, 37
Preston Mill, 32
Prestonpans, 37
Prestwick, 238
   Airport, 239
Princess Margaret Rose Orthopaedic
   Hospital, The Braids, 154

Qua, Castle of, 224
Quarter, 221
Queensberry, 82

Raehills Glen, 82
Ranfury Castle, 228
Ravelston House, 169
Renfrew, 226
Reston, 29
Restalrig, 159
Riccarton, 237
Ringsdale Castle, 221
Robert Burns, 243
Rockcliffe, 187
Roslin, 63, 174, 175
   Castle, 176
Roslin (or Rosslyn) Chapel, 175
Rosyth Naval Base, 174
Roxburgh, 44
Royal Blind Asylum, Newington, 157

INDEX

Royal Edinburgh Hospital (Psychiatry), The Braids, 154
Royal Observatory, Blackford Hill, 155
Rutherglen, 221
Ruthwell, 179

St Abb's Head, 30
St Boswells Green, 50
St Bride's Parish Church, Bothwell, 217
St Kentigern's, 224
St Margaret's Convent, Bruntsfield, 153
St Mary's Kirk, Yarrowford, 77
St Mary's Loch, 77, 83
St Medan's Chapel, 194
St Ninian's Cave, 193
Saltcoats, 233, 234
Salt Pans, The, 160
Sandhead, 194
Sanquhar, 183
Scald Law, 171
Sciennes Hill House, 156
Scotsdyke, 69
Scottish National Memorial to David Livingstone, 218
Scottish National Zoological Park, The, 168
Scottish Youth Hostels Association, 153
Seamill, 233
Selkirk, 74
Seton Chapel, 37
Siccar Point, 30
Silverknowes, 167
Sir Walter Scott, 58
Skelmorlie, 232
Skelmorlie Aisle, 232
Skelmorlie Castle, 232
South Queensferry, 172
Soutra, 61
Spittal, 29
Stanwix, 69
Stevenston, 234
Stobo, 84
Stonehouse, 221
Stoneykirk, 194
Stow, 61
Stranraer, 194
Strathaven, 221
Swanston, 155
Sweetheart Abbey, 186
Synagogue, Jewish, Newington, 156

Talla Reservoir, 84
Tantallon, 34
  Castle, 34
Tarbolton, 247
Teviothead, 71
Thirlestane Castle, 61
Thistle Foundation Settlement, 157
Thornhill, 183
Threave Castle, 188
Threave House, 188
Tibbers Castle, 183
Tibbie Shiel's', 77
Tinto, 87, 178, 225
Tolbooth, The, Kirkcudbright, 190
Tollcross, Bruntsfield, 153
Tongland, 191
Torthorwald, 81
Tranent, 33
Traprain Law, 32
Traquair House, 65
Trimontium, 59
Troon, 237
Turnberry, 246
Tushielaw, 78
Tweeddale, 65
Tweedmouth, 29
Tweedsmuir, 84
Twizel Castle, 40
Tynecastle, 170

Upper Clyde, The, 216
Upper Liberton, 174
Upsettlington, 40
Usher Institute of Public Health, 153

Walkerburn, 65
Wallace's Cave, 224
Wanlockhead, 184
Wark Castle, 42
Well of St Triduana, 159
Wemyss Bay, 232
West Kilbride, 233
West Linton, 171
West of Scotland Agricultural College, 239
Whitburn, 215
White Coomb, 83
Whitelark, 34
Whithorn, 193
Wigtown, 193
Wishaw, 223

Yarrowford, 77
Yester Castle, 39